IN THE TRENCHES AT CORINTH

Quinton Howitt

Acknowledgments

*I would like to say a special thanks to
Colleen, Derek, Dott, Ockert and Tim,
for all your help.*

About the Author

Quinton Howitt served as the Academic Dean, and as a Professor of Theology, for The Vineyard Biblical Institute until 2012. Prior to this, he spent several years assisting in the establishment of the South African Theological Seminary (SATS). His Masters (M.Th) and Doctorate (D.Th) degrees were in the fields of Systematic, Biblical and Practical Theology. Quinton also specialized in the field of Industrial Psychology prior to his ministry studies. He is presently professor of theology and education at the Vineyard Institute. He is married to Trish and has two daughters, Hayley and Robyn. They currently reside in Johannesburg, South Africa.

Cover design by Zelda Pringle

ISBN-13: 978-1499589412
ISBN-10: 1499589417

Contents

Preface

I have been attracted to this particular Epistle for a long time. My interest began in 1996 when I was asked to write a course on this epistle for the South African Theological Seminary. It was actually one of the first courses ever written for the seminary. Over the years, I have reworked that course numerous times, from what it started out as, viz. an outcomes based distance learning course, to what it is now, a textbook for studious church members and students alike.[1]

I think Paul's First Epistle to the Corinthians is brilliant. It presents us with a vivid picture of the on-going battle between the evil rule of this present age and the Spirit of God breaking in from the future. This battle manifests itself in, and impacts upon, humanity in the practicalities of daily community and individual living. In fact, it is because of this that I decided to entitle this book, "In the Trenches at Corinth". I can almost imagine Paul climbing down into the dingy sinfulness of the city in order to pull Christians, who were ensnared with wrong values and priorities, back out into the light.

---

[1] The nature of the target audience brings me to a disclaimer. This book is not written for the advanced scholar, and as such, does not contain in-depth explanations offering multiple scholarly opinions on particularly, the controversial passages within the epistle. Make no mistake though, the book was born out of significant research over more than a decade, and I have tried as best possible, wherever difficult passages arise, to represent the most accepted thinking by the foremost scholars.

That said, I welcome you to the ancient world where people and churches began the process of announcing (and wrestling with) the message of Jesus Christ.

It is my hope that this textbook will take you on an exciting journey through Paul's First Epistle to the Corinthians. This epistle majors on knowledge and life application. For the bulk of those at Corinth, pagan religion and Greek ideologies about "knowledge", represented by concepts and theories detrimental to true holistic life, ruled the roost. One could believe, or believe in, all sorts of things without ever seeing any behavioural life change. However, for Paul the Hebrew, the "knowledge" he brought to them was very different. This was a "knowledge", which if ingested correctly, would so alter their lives that Paul said that it would cause them to "die to self."[2]

Of course, the "knowledge" to which I am referring is the gospel. This gospel carried relational implications for them in terms of their relationship with God and their relationship with other people.[3] These relationships were stretched to their breaking point as the people faced the daily challenges of life as Christians.

Time and again, you will get a chance to read how God's inspired apostle advises on how to live the Christian life in a diabolical world. You will find it highly appropriate for today. In fact, to demonstrate this, at the end of each chapter, I have included a section entitled, "For reflection." Therein you will find just a few examples of how a particular section of Paul's teaching applies to contemporary Christianity. Whatever you do, make sure not to skip these sections.

Furthermore, probably the most important part of this book is the section entitled, "Why did Paul write this Letter?" Here, I briefly touch on certain key beliefs and theologies that were rife within the city, and thus, in its people. Of course, if they were in the people, and some of those people were in the church, it meant

---

[2]"For to me, to live is Christ and to die is gain." (Phillipians 1:21 NIV)
[3]Morphew, D. *The Spiritual Spider Web, a Study of Ancient and Contemporary Gnosticism*, p. 23.

that Paul had his hands full dealing with dangerous heresies which had been enmeshed within the gospel.

If you can come away with the ability to articulate clearly the following in this book, you are well on your way to avoiding a multitude of pitfalls bound to turn up in your Christian walk:

- describe the cultural and historical background of Corinth;
- explain the reason why Paul wrote the First Epistle to the Corinthians as well as its underlying structure;
- differentiate between the wisdom of the world and the true wisdom of God;
- review Paul's understanding of the nature of leadership and the church;
- explain how the base of Christian conduct is love and not knowledge;
- illustrate how the local church should handle sin and matters of sensitivity, with specific emphasis on immorality and litigation;
- identify Paul's guiding principles for marriage and related matters;
- describe Paul's views on gender roles and equality;
- discuss the nature of the Lord's Supper and the correct and incorrect ways of celebrating it;
- explain the nature of spiritual gifts and their correct use within the local church;
- examine the validity of the bodily resurrection of the dead;
- highlight the valuable lessons we can learn about taking up collections within the local church.

All that is left for me to say is, "gear yourself up for a complete overhaul! Join me as we journey together through the fascinating world of the Corinthians." Let me leave you with this thought;

"… if we can understand the nature of these problems [covered in this epistle] and the nature of Paul's divinely inspired instruction in response to them, then we will gain great insights into numerous

debates that threaten to divide today's church and keep it from having the world-transforming impact God intends it to have."
Craig Blomberg[4]

Quinton Howitt, April 2014

---

[4]Blomberg, C. *1 Corinthians – NIV Application Commentary*, p. 1.

Background Information

It is fundamentally important for anyone seeking to understand this epistle, or for that matter, any text, to begin by asking the question, "what/how would the recipients have interpreted/understood the text?"

Obviously, we can never answer this question fully, especially when dealing with a text that was written approximately two thousand years ago. However, due to the number/quality of ancient sources and a multitude of archaeological findings at Corinth, we can establish quite a detailed picture of the city and its people, which will take us some way down the road to answering the question.

Therefore, before we begin with our study of the First Epistle to the Corinthians, read through the section that follows highlighting important detail about Paul travels and the city of Corinth.

I will begin by drawing your attention to certain chapters within the book of Acts that trace Paul's second missionary journey, where amongst other things, he planted the church at Corinth. Note that it was while he was on his third missionary journey, and residing at Ephesus, that he actually wrote the First Epistle to the Corinthians.

Following this, I will cover some of the history, geography, demographics and culture of Corinth in Paul's day.

Without further ado, please consider the map (Paul's Second Missionary Journey),[5] together with the text from the book of Acts that follows.

---

[5]Map by Gordon Smith http://www.ccel.org/bible/phillips/JBPhillips. htm Available at Christian Classics Ethereal Library: http://www.ccel.org/ bible/phillips/CN092MAPS1.htm

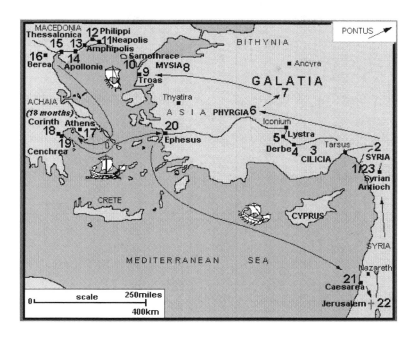

Paul's Second Missionary Journey

I will utilize portions of the text from Acts 15:40–18:23 (NRSV) in reconstructing Paul's movements immediately before and after his planting of the church at Corinth.

> *Following a sharp disagreement with Barnabas about taking John Mark with them on their journey, Paul and Barnabas decided to split up. Barnabas and John Mark sailed to Cyprus while Paul chose Silas and travelled from Syrian Antioch [1] to Syria [2] and Cilicia [3], strengthening the churches.*
>
> *[From there, they] went on also to Derbe [4] and to Lystra [5], where there was a disciple named Timothy, the son of a Jewish woman who was a believer; but his father was a Greek. He was well spoken of by the believers in Lystra and Iconium. Paul wanted Timothy to accompany him; and he took him and had him*

circumcised because of the Jews who were in those places, for they all knew that his father was a Greek. As they went from town to town, they delivered to them for observance the decisions that had been reached by the apostles and elders who were in Jerusalem [attending the council meeting]. So the churches were strengthened in the faith and increased in numbers daily.

They [Paul, Silas and Timothy] went through the region of Phrygia [6] and Galatia [7], having been forbidden by the Holy Spirit to speak the word in Asia. When they had come opposite Mysia [8], they attempted to go into Bithynia, but the Spirit of Jesus did not allow them; so, passing by Mysia, they went down to Troas [9]. During the night Paul had a vision: there stood a man of Macedonia pleading with him and saying, "Come over to Macedonia and help us." When he had seen the vision, we immediately tried to cross over to Macedonia, being convinced that God had called us to proclaim the good news to them.

[Therefore] we set sail from Troas and took a straight course to [the island of] Samothrace [10], the following day to Neapolis [11], and from there to Philippi [12], which is a leading city of the district of Macedonia and a Roman colony.

It was while they were in Philippi that they met up with Lydia who readily responded to Paul's message. [Paul, Silas, Timothy and occasionally Luke, would bring the Gospel to Lydia from Thyatira]. Furthermore, on one occasion when Paul and Silas were going to the place of prayer, they had a run-in with the slave girl who had a spirit of divination. She made a great deal of money for her owners through fortune-telling. However, once Paul had driven the spirit out of her, she was of no use to her owners. They turned their anger against Paul and Silas, having them severely flogged, and thrown into prison. Paul and Silas were ultimately freed from the prison by an angel. The jailer was so taken by the events that both he and his household were saved.

[Following this] After Paul and Silas had passed through Amphipolis [13] and Apollonia [14], they came to Thessalonica [15], where there was a synagogue of the Jews.

Paul and Silas preached the gospel with great effect in Thessalonica. Many people turned to the Lord, but Paul and Silas also caused a great uproar within the city infuriating many Jews. Both Paul and Silas were in great danger.

That very night the believers sent Paul and Silas off to Beroea [16]; and when they arrived, they went to the Jewish synagogue. These Jews were more receptive than those in Thessalonica, for they welcomed the message very eagerly and examined the scriptures every day to see whether these things were so. Many of them therefore believed, including not a few Greek women and men of high standing. But when the Jews of Thessalonica learned that the word of God had been proclaimed by Paul in Beroea as well, they came there too, to stir up and incite the crowds. Then the believers immediately sent Paul away to the coast, but Silas and Timothy remained behind. Those who conducted Paul brought him as far as Athens [17]; and after receiving instructions to have Silas and Timothy [still in Beroea] join him as soon as possible, they left him.

While Paul was waiting for them in Athens, he was deeply distressed to see that the city was full of idols. So he argued in the synagogue with the Jews and the devout persons, and also in the marketplace every day with those who happened to be there. Also some Epicurean and Stoic philosophers debated with him … After this Paul left Athens and went to Corinth [18]. There he found a Jew named Aquila, a native of Pontus, who had recently come from Italy with his wife Priscilla, because Claudius had ordered all Jews to leave Rome. Paul went to see them, and, because he was of the same trade, he stayed with them, and they worked together—by trade they were tentmakers. Every Sabbath he would argue in the synagogue and would try to convince Jews and Greeks.

When Silas and Timothy arrived from Macedonia, Paul was occupied with proclaiming the word, testifying to the Jews that the Messiah was Jesus. When they opposed and reviled him, in protest he shook the dust from his clothes and said to them, "Your blood be on your own heads! I am innocent. From now on I will go to the Gentiles." Then he left the synagogue and went to the house of a man named Titius Justus, a worshiper of God; his house was next door to the synagogue. Crispus, the official of the synagogue, became a believer in the Lord, together with all his household; and many of the Corinthians who heard Paul became believers and were baptized. One night the Lord said to Paul in a vision, "Do not be afraid, but speak and do not be silent; for I am with you, and no one will lay a hand on you to harm you, for there are many in this city who are my people." He stayed there a year and six months, teaching the word of God among them.

But when Gallio was proconsul of Achaia, the Jews made a united attack on Paul and brought him before the tribunal. They said, "This man is persuading people to worship God in ways that are contrary to the law." Just as Paul was about to speak, Gallio said to the Jews, "If it were a matter of crime or serious villainy, I would be justified in accepting the complaint of you Jews; but since it is a matter of questions about words and names and your own law, see to it yourselves; I do not wish to be a judge of these matters." And he dismissed them from the tribunal. Then all of them seized Sosthenes, the official of the synagogue, and beat him in front of the tribunal. But Gallio paid no attention to any of these things.

After staying there for a considerable time, Paul said farewell to the believers and sailed for Syria, accompanied by Priscilla and Aquila. At Cenchreae [19] he had his hair cut, for he was under a vow. When they reached Ephesus [20], he left them there, but first he himself went into the synagogue and had a discussion with the Jews. When they asked him to stay longer, he declined; but on taking leave of them, he said, "I will return to you, if God wills." [He did return to visit them on his third missionary journey.] Then he set sail from Ephesus. When he had landed at Caesarea [21], he went up to Jerusalem [22] and greeted the church, and then went down to Antioch [23]. After spending some time there he departed [on his third missionary journey]. (Acts 15:40–18:23)

Paul's Second Missionary Journey
The City of Corinth

"History is who we are and why we are the way we are."
David McCullough

From the quote, we may infer that by looking at the history of Corinth, we will know its people and what makes them tick. This will undoubtedly also aid us in framing the context in which Paul devised his letters.

There is obviously a great deal of history to which one can turn when considering an entire city, and I would encourage you to research this in greater depth, should you desire to specialize in understanding this book of the Bible. "But for the purposes of Paul's book and the level of person for which it was written, the following appropriately categorised is more than enough to aid in understanding various problems in Paul's epistle."

To begin with, in the mid-2nd century BC relationships between Rome, Corinth, and the Achaean league were damaged significantly. Issues surrounding "freedom" together with a financial crisis led to a war between the Achaeans and Sparta, the latter being one of Rome's allies. The Romans, under General Lucius Mummius, ultimately defeated the Achaeans and destroyed Corinth following a siege in 146 BC. When he entered the city, Mummius put all of the men to the sword and sold the women and children into slavery. He then torched the city.

Julius Caesar re-founded the city in 44 BC for a number of reasons:

- at the time, Rome was no longer at war and this meant that there was a large number of veterans and freedmen, together with tradesmen, resulting in an overpopulated Rome. Caesar needed somewhere for his people;

- Corinth was an ideal location for entrepreneurial enterprise because it was on the main shipping trade route, (I will return to this shortly); and

- the area was rich with raw materials such as marl, clay, sandstone and limestone, not to mention the almost limitless supply of fresh water from the Peirene Springs.

At the time of its inception, Corinth went by the name "Colonia Laus Julia Corinthiensis (colony of Corinth in Honor of Julius)."[6] Corinth went on to become the seat of government for Southern Greece or Achaia – it became the official capital of the Province of Achaia in 27 BC.

The Geography

I mentioned previously that Corinth was strategic for business. This is because it sat along the coast that divided the major Eastern and Western trade centres from one another. Furthermore, it was also ideally placed for trade between Asia, to the north, and Africa, to the south. It must be said though that the East West trade was by far the most lucrative. An additional reason for the prolific trade was the Diolkos, upon which I will elaborate shortly.

You will note from the map below that there are two harbors close to Corinth. Cenchreae, which was approximately 6 kilometers east of Corinth, received all of the trade coming in from Asia and Ephesus across the Aegean Sea via the Saronic Gulf. Lechaeum, on the

---

[6]Wolfgang, S. *Der erste Brief an die Korinther,* pp. 25–29.

other hand, was approximately 2 kilometers north west of Corinth and serviced the Corinthian Gulf on the way to Italy and beyond.

Lechaeum & Cenchreae Harbours and
Southern Cape of the Peloponnese[7]

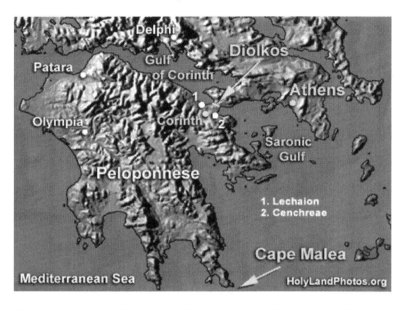

The mountain to the south of Corinth, the "Accrocorinth", was a strategic location for worship. The Aphrodite temple rested on top and was supposedly the home of Aphrodite (to the Romans, her name was Venus), the goddess of love. The ruins in the foreground are those of the Temple of Apollo.

---

[7]Image courtesy of www.HolyLandPhotos.org

Accrocorinth[8]

There is evidence to suggest that cult prostitution was entertained in this and other temples. Cult prostitution implied acts of sex between worshippers and cult prostitutes. This practise apparently stimulated the gods to make love, which in turn brought various blessings on the worshippers. Some scholars suggest that there were perhaps 1000 cult prostitutes providing a service atop the Accrocorinth.

In addition to the Accrocorinth's temple role, the mount, together with the Peloponnese mountain range (further south), formed a natural barrier of defence against would be attackers.

The Isthmus, a short (±9 kilometer) stretch of land separating the Saronic and Corinthian Gulfs, played a vital role in the commercial success at Corinth. Cargo carried on large ships was unloaded and transported across this strip from ship to ship along a paved trackway called the Diolkos. Smaller boats were actually rolled across. This was instead of taking the treacherous 6 day trip around the

---

[8]Image courtesy of <u>www.HolyLandPhotos.org</u>

Southern Cape of the Peloponnese known as Cape Maleae. It was so treacherous that sailors had coined the phrase, "when you double Maleae, forget your home."[9] It was actually while Paul was on his way to Crete and while rounding this point that he experienced a severe storm with winds that blew his vessel all the way to Malta (see Acts 27). It is very likely that a hefty toll was required of any ship owners wishing to use the Diolkos.

The Isthmus[10]

[9]Thiselton, A. C. *The First Epistle to the Corinthians: A Commentary on the Greek text,* pp. 1–2.
[10]Courtesy of Google Earth.

Diolkos in 1960

Δίολκος - περίπου 1960   Προσωπικό Αρχείο Φοίβου Βερδελή

Modern Day Corinth Canal[11]

Modern Day Corinth Canal[12]

---

[11]Courtesy of Google Earth.
[12]Image courtesy of <u>www.HolyLandPhotos.org</u>

The Demographics

Corinth was a cosmopolitan city owing to its strategic location being a seaport and major trade route.

Corinth was the third largest city after Alexandria and Rome. It is estimated that it had a population of some 250,000 people.

The city consisted mainly of Jews, Greeks, Romans and Asians. According to Wiseman, following 44 BC, a large number of immigrants from the East, which included Jews and Syrians, joined Caesar's veterans and artisans, slaves and various labouring classes.[13]

Thiselton lists three helpful aspects that assist in our understanding Paul's first epistle:

- "the city community and city culture of Corinth were formed after a Roman model, not a Greek one, even if many immigrants came from Achaea, Macedonia, and the East to constitute an equally cosmopolitan superstructure;

- the city community and the city culture felt themselves to be prosperous and self-sufficient, even if there were many 'have nots', who were socially vulnerable or dependent on others;

- the core community and core tradition of the city culture were those of trade, business, and entrepreneurial pragmatism in the pursuit of success, even if some paid a heavy price for business failures or for the lack of the right contacts or the right opportunities."[14]

The Authorities

Gallio was the proconsul of Achaia at the time Paul visited. He carried far more influence than usually ascribed to a proconsul. He was also the son of Marcus Seneca, a master of rhetoric. Gallio's brother was Lucius Seneca, philosopher and teacher to a young Nero, future

---

[13]Wiseman, J. *"Corinth and Rome, I: 228 B.C. to A.D. 267,"* p. 497.
[14]Thiselton. A. C. *The First Epistle*, pp. 3–4.

emperor and tyrant. (Nero was the Emperor who caused the death of a many Christians in the AD 60s.)

The Culture

While Corinth was first and foremost a Roman city, the Greek influences upon the city would have been inescapable. This could be seen in the nature of the religions and cults at Corinth. "Greek temples were rededicated to the same Greek deities in the Roman period, notably at Corinth, to Poseidon, Aphrodite, Apollo, Demeter, Kore, and Asclepios."[15]

All in all, there were an estimated 26 separate shrines/temples to different gods located in the city. These temples and shrines were the foundation for a number of sinful practices dominating the city, as well as the cause of a number of problems about which Paul wrote to the Corithian church. For instance, attending one of these temples to worship involved communal feasting, and this did not just mean having a friendly meal together. These feasts often included participation in a variety of sexually immoral practices as well (see my comments on the Accrocorinth previously). In fact, the city was so renowned for its sexual immorality that people who lived in or frequented the place coined the phrase *Korinthiozomai* ("to act the Corinth" – meaning to commit acts of sexual immorality).

I mentioned Asclepius[16] above: he was the god of healing. A common practice at Corinth was to form terracotta models/replicas of a person's diseased body part/s (hands, feet, arms, eyes and genitalia), and then to offer them to Asclepius as part of a healing ritual.

The city celebrated the Isthmian Games every second year in honour of the god of the sea, Poseidon. These games most likely constituted one of 4 great pan-Hellenistic festivals and would have generated a considerable income for the city. Common sports included boxing, running, javelin, and wrestling, but other activities

---

[15]Ibid., p. 6.
[16]Ascelpius (Greek), Ascelpios (Latin).

such as reading poetry and musical competitions were common. "The remains of the Games held in AD 49 shortly before Paul's arrival in Corinth (if he arrived in spring of AD 50 – see below) and the huge crowds which came to Corinth during the Games, which took place while Paul was ministering in Corinth (AD 51), would have been a significant part of the world of the Corinth that Paul knew [see 1 Cor. 9:24–27 – Paul's reference to athletes]."[17]

The study of philosophy and emphasis on intellectualism, amongst certain other sciences and arts, was very prevalent, often attracting the "wandering philosophers," also known as "Sophists" (Sophos or Sophia meaning "wisdom"). These men earned their living by engaging in rhetoric, entertaining crowds with their theories. In Western societies, one might visit the theatre or the movies for entertainment. In a city like Corinth, entertainment would have been a night out listening to these speakers. You will notice as we work through the epistle that this particular interest turned out to be quite a negative influence within the church at Corinth.

There were two forms of rhetoric at the time. The first was "classic rhetoric," which originated with Aristotle. Two important characteristics of classical rhetoric were the communication of truth and persuasion, based thereon. However, the second form of rhetoric had as its goal to win approval for self, and not necessarily for the case you were presenting,[18] even if it was at the expense of truth. It was this "pragmatic criterion of becoming a winner in the marketplace, sometimes with a sacrifice of personal integrity, that made its impact on Corinthian rhetoric. Declamation increasingly became the major opportunity for oratorical displays. … In the classroom the competition might be over theory. But in declamations … the contrast was … between rival performers. The drive for adulation, we learn from Seneca the Elder, often overcame the more basic goals

---

[17]Ibid., p. 10.
[18]Pogoloff, S. M. *Logos and Sophia: The Rhetorical Situation of 1 Corinthians,* p. 175.

of rhetoric."[19] Seneca observes that too many times the aim was "to win approval for yourself rather than for the case."[20] Quintilian laments that rhetoricians, like athletes or singers, were "greeted with a storm of ready-made applause ... shouts of unseemly enthusiasm ... The result is vanity and empty self-sufficiency ... intoxicated by the wild enthusiasm of their fellow-pupils."[21] The casualty is truth; the focus is "the speaker," as in the case of the twenty-first century chat-show host or participant in the mass media. It is of little surprise that party groups following their chosen leaders in the form of personality cults spring up (cf. 1:10–12, below).[22]

---

[19]Ibid.

[20]Seneca the Elder: *Declamations, Volume II, Controversiae*, Books 7–10. 9.1.

[21]Quintilian. *Institutio Oratoria*. 2.2.9–12.

[22]Pogoloff, S. M. *Logos and Sophia: The Rhetorical Situation of 1 Corinthians*, pp. 129–172 and 173–196 in Thiselton, A. C. *The First Epistle to the Corinthians: A Commentary on the Greek text*, pp. 14–15).

Paul's Second Missionary Journey
The Blue Print

This section will focus on the book's lay out – the "bigger" picture. Have you heard of the old adage, "you cannot see the wood for the trees?" i.e. you get so caught up in small details that you fail to understand the bigger picture? The danger of having insufficient knowledge of the big picture is misinterpreting or misunderstanding the smaller details. This section is very important. It will determine your mastery of this First Epistle to the Corinthians.

1 Corinthians and Paul's overall communication with Corinth

The epistle contains two letters addressed to the Corinthians. However, there is evidence from the letters themselves to suggest that Paul wrote four or more letters to them. Consider the following.

- Evidence of a letter predating 1 Corinthians is suggested in 1 Corinthians 5:9, where Paul states, "I wrote to you in my letter not to associate with sexually immoral persons …" This letter is often referred to as "the warning letter."

- Following on from this letter would be our 1 Corinthians.

- Next, there is what is referred to by some as "the severe letter" or "letter of tears." Paul makes mention of this in 2 Corinthians 2:3–4, "And I wrote as I did, so that when I came,

I might not suffer pain from those who should have made me rejoice; for I am confident about all of you, that my joy would be the joy of all of you. For I wrote you out of much distress and anguish of heart and with many tears, not to cause you pain, but to let you know the abundant love that I have for you." and again in 2 Corinthians 7.8 "For even if I made you sorry with *my letter*, I do not regret it (though I did regret it, for I see that I grieved you with *that letter*, though only briefly)."

- Paul's references to the contents of this letter do not match our 1 Corinthians. Therefore, this "severe letter" or "letter of tears" may have been written between 1 and 2 Corinthians. If this was the case, then 2 Corinthians would be his next letter. However, there are certain features within 2 Corinthians that lead some to believe that 2 Corinthians is not just one letter. For instance, there is an abrupt change of tone in Paul's writing from being previously harmonious to reproving in 2 Corinthians 10–13. This might suggest that chapter's 10–13 form part of the "letter of tears." There are others who disagree with this theory saying that the "letter of tears" no-longer exists.

Paul's Second Missionary Journey
The Occasion

History suggests four clear occasions to which Paul responded:

1. The first was evident in (1 Corinthians 1.11) a report that originated out of Chloe's household, "For it has been reported to me by Chloe's people" (amongst others, Fortunatus, Stephanas and Achaicus).[23]

2. Secondly, there is evidence that the Christian group wrote Paul a letter, since in (7:1) it states, "Now concerning the matters about which you wrote."

3. Thirdly, some of the members of the church wanted Apollos to pay them a visit, but he had been unwilling to go (16:12). Therefore, Paul was going to make an effort to visit them (16:5).

4. Finally, good news had come through Fortunatus, Stephanas and Achaicus (16:17–18), which would have added to the

---

[23]It was the custom at that time for families to be identified through the father's name, whether he was alive or not. This is similar to most Western first-world families today who use the father's surname. The mention of Chloe's name would have been out of the ordinary. However, one of the theories why she was mentioned is that "Chloe's people" might have been business associates acting on behalf of this successful Asian woman, travelling between Ephesus and Corinth. Fee. G. D. The *First Epistle to the Corinthians*, p. 54.

details of Chloe's report.

There is more to be said about the occasion for this epistle theologically, but before I address this, we must establish which parts of Paul's response answer either the report or the letter. This is important because it will better assist us in interpreting and understanding what Paul was trying to convey. How do we do this? Here, one must become a detective and meticulously search through the text for clues. Thankfully, this task has been conducted by J. C. Hurd.

A brief synopsis of Hurd's findings includes:

- Paul's tone of response varies between events of which the Corinthians seem to have been none the wiser (they had not expressed any concern about an issue to Paul), and those about which they had asked questions. For instance, Paul's response to the former was forceful, indignant and even aggressive. To the latter, his responses seemed kinder and considerably more reasoned.

- Paul seems to contrast issues more sharply when he has to call attention to something previously unnoticed, whereas he goes to much greater lengths to present both sides, and all sides of a question, which has been raised.

- In the case where Paul initiates the issue, more importance is placed in the past and the present as this is reported; whereas when questions have been raised, the future and future policy receives primary attention.

- It is likely that the numerous quotations from Corinth, which Paul cites, came from the letter (6:12–13; 7:1; 8:1, 4–6; 10:23; 11:2).

- Much discussion has centred around the words "Now about" (7:1, 25; 8:1; 12:1; 16:1; and 16:12) as a sign that he was commenting on their letter. However, caution must be exercised in linking the two haphazardly.

In spite of Hurd's outstanding work, there is some confusion regarding the placement of 11:2–16 and 15:1–58. Insufficient evidence is available to establish whether Paul's response was occasioned by the report or the letter. As is the case with most other scholars, we will deal with both sections in the letter.

I have used a table to illustrate some of the foremost scholar's allocations of portions of the Epistle to either the report or the letter.

Hurd	Barrett	Fee
Oral Report	**Oral Report**	**Oral Report**
1:10–4:21 [Splits]	1:10–6:20	1:10–6:20
5:1–8, 13a [Incestuous man]		
11:17–34 [Lord's Supper]		
Letter	**Letter**	**Letter**
7:1–24 [The Married]	7:1–16:24	7:1–16:24
7:25–38 [Unmarried]		
8:1–11:1 [Food/Idols]		
12:1–14:40 [Spiritual Gifts]		
16:1–4 [The Collection]		
Uncertainty Letter		
5:9–13a [Immorality]		
11.2–16 [Propriety in Worship]		
15:1–58 [Resurrection]		
16:12 [Apollos]		

I would like to return to the reason why Paul wrote the letter, but this time from a theological perspective.

There were at least 3 significant theological aberrations, and all of them stem from the Corinthian's take on "what it means to be spiritual."

The first aberration ties spirituality together with **wisdom (Sophia),**

knowledge (gnosis) and ecstatic experiences. The biblical scholar, Gordon Fee, states:

> Although one cannot be sure, their understanding of being *pneumatikos* [spiritual] is most likely related to their experience of Spirit inspiration,[24] especially their overemphasis on the gift of tongues[25] (see especially the introduction to chaps. 12–14) ... If, as suggested in 13:1, "speaking the tongues of angels" reflects their own understanding of this gift, then one can begin to appreciate how they made it the basic criterion for their understanding of spirituality. *Glossolalia* [tongues] was for them the evidence that they had already assumed the spiritual existence of the angels. This in turn is probably related to their interest in *sophia* and *gnosis* (wisdom and knowledge), two words that occur primarily in the context of specific behavioral aberrations (chaps. 1–4 and 8–10 respectively). Both of these "gifts" have become their special possession by means of the Spirit. They are spiritually endowed, hence they have special wisdom and superior knowledge. It is probably no accident that the statement "if anyone thinks that he/she is ..." (3:18; 8:1; 14:37) is found in each of the three major sections of the letter (chaps. 1–4; 8–10; 12–14) and reflects these three crucial Corinthian terms ("wisdom," "knowledge,"

---

[24]Many of the Christians in the church had come out of paganism and in that belief system, one had to construct your own spirituality since the gods could not do it for you. Remember, they served gods made of wood, iron etc. Thus, the spirituality of the person was closely tied with that person's apparent higher/superior levels of knowledge and wisdom, together with their outwardly visible ecstatic experiences. This was in total contrast with having Christ as Lord. (More will be said about this topic later on in the book.)

[25]"Tongues" was chosen to demonstrate spirituality because it most closely mimicked their belief of engaging in ecstatic experiences (see previous footnote).

and "spiritual"). [26]

Closely tied to this false understanding of spirituality, and still linking with "what it means to be spiritual," is their second aberration, **dualism**. The Corinthian's pagan background brought with it a form of Hellenistic dualism and this led them to believe that even though they were still living bodily lives, they were now angels (spiritual ones).[27]

Very briefly, dualism suggests that the universe is the result of two equal but opposite forces, one good, the other evil, one light, and the other darkness. These two forces remain in continual conflict with one another. Furthermore, dualism employs the idea that the universe consists of two different substances, viz. matter/body and spirit/mind. The former is considered evil while the latter good. As such, the spiritual realm is far superior to the physical element of our reality. The objective is one day to escape this physical reality and return to the superior spiritual planes. This belief system plays havoc with morality in two distinct ways: because the belief identifies matter/body as evil, the "spiritually superior," incline themselves towards either denying the body its pleasures, like sex for example, or feeding them in wild abandonment – of course, this is being done in an effort to demonstrate their spirituality. The former approach is called asceticism (which is often associated with Stoicism and Monasticism) while the latter, libertarianism (associated with Epicureanism). An example of asceticism would be the practice of celibacy, and an example of libertarianism is sexual immorality.

Some examples of dualism in 1 Corinthians include the boastful man involved in incest in chapter 5:1–13 and the fact that the church's apparent approval of it. This would be a case of libertinism. Notice the complete lack of morality that accompanies it.

Then there is the situation in chapter 6:12–20, where many are

---

[26]Fee. G. D. The *First Epistle to the Corinthians*, p. 11.
[27]Three texts point to the way things were in their pagan days (6:9–11; 8:7; 12:1–3).

boasting about their regular visits to prostitutes. To these, the body was temporal and insignificant, thus it was acceptable to "do with it what you like." This is another case of libertinism and moral collapse. Thirdly, there were the splits between the "strong" and "weak" about the ethics of eating meat sacrificed to idols in temples or/ and the market place. Here was a case of clashes between libertines and the ascetics in the name of "being the most spiritual." Lastly, in chapter 15 Paul tackles the disbelief on the matter of Jesus, and then all Christians, undergoing a "bodily" resurrection. For the dualist, this idea was abhorrent, since at death, the deepest desire was to shed the weak and worthless body.

In response to this thinking, as you read ahead, you will notice that Paul had in mind to instruct them "to think of themselves, corporately, individually and cosmically, in a more thoroughly Jewish fashion, in terms of the great Jewish stories of God, Israel and the world."[28]

The third aberration is **overrealized eschatology and it links with "what it means to be spiritual**." Fee suggests that

> they had a considerably "overrealized" eschatological view of their present existence … This would follow directly from their view of being pneumatikoi (people of the Spirit, whose present existence it is to be understood in strictly spiritual terms). The Spirit belongs to the Eschaton, and they are already experiencing the Spirit in full measure. If tongues is understood as the "language of angels," then their experience of glossolalia is evidence for them that they have already arrived (already they speak the language of heaven) … They are now experiencing a kind of ultimate spirituality in which they live above the merely material existence of the present age.[29]

Perhaps a bit more explanation is required to clarify what is meant

---

[28]Wright, N. T. *The Resurrection of the Son of God. Christian Origins and the Question of God,* p. 280.
[29]Fee. G. D. *The First Epistle to the Corinthians,* p. 11.

by "overrealized eschatology".

Eschatology denotes the study of the end times. What many people do not realise is the vast influence eschatology has upon the New Testament. In fact, Christ initiated the end times through His incarnation. The Jewish people would have understood this idea of a "coming age" because they were familiar with the prophet's writings and quite literally were waiting for it to happen. According to Dunn:

> Hebraic thought typically conceived of time as a succession of ages. History was understood as an onward movement or progression, with beginning (creation) and end (final judgment), rather than a repeating cycle [unless of course we think of 'cycle' as going back to paradise in the Garden of Eden]. It was divided into two (or more?) ages, the one to succeed the other in accordance with the predetermined plan of God. The straight line, in others words, was divided between the present age and the age to come (as depicted in the diagram below).[30]

Older Eschatological Schema

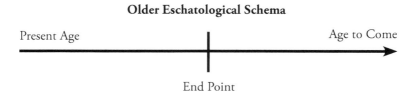

In their minds, when this new age came, some dramatic changes were expected. For instance, they expected the temple to be cleansed or rebuilt (many of the Jews disapproved of the existing temple, which Herod built in an attempt to win their favour). Secondly,

---

[30]Diagram and citation taken from Dunn. J. D. G. *The Theology of Paul the Apostle*, pp. 462–464.

God would return to His temple like He did following Solomon's building of his temple (see 1 Kings 8 and specifically verses 10–13). Thirdly, God would forgive Israel for her sins, free her of her oppressors and bring her out of exile (even though Israel had returned from the Babylonian exile, many still believed that Israel was in a form of exile). Fourthly, Israel would once again have her own land and every family would sit under their own vine (Isaiah 36.16), i.e. the good life would be back to stay. The dawning of the "new age" would bring righteousness, health, peace and joy. Very importantly, there is evidence to suggest that all of the above would happen through God's agent called "Messiah".

As mentioned above, this would have been clear to the Jewish converts, but would the "Gentiles" in the church at Corinth have seen it this way? There are certain scholars who believe that they would not have, but I agree with Thiselton in that it is implausible to assume that people in the church at Corinth would have misunderstood Paul's eschatology after he spent 18 months doing ministry with them.[31]

Therefore, it is reasonable to believe that all would have been aware of this way of thinking and attributed Messiahship to Jesus. Thus, they saw Him as coming to usher in this new age and having done so; whether they all believed it exactly as told is another question. For them, the end had arrived, which meant that they could expect the blessings spoken of by the prophets: "peace" (Isaiah 2:4); "righteousness" (Isaiah 11:4–5); "a New Covenant" (Jeremiah 31:31–34) and "the fullness of the Holy Spirit" (Joel 2:28–30). The problem was that these blessings were only partially fulfilled. Allow me to explain.

Those who followed Jesus during his earthly ministry were continually watching him and expecting him to become a great king

---

[31] I still believe this applies even if one takes into account that there was growth or the addition of new believers after Paul's departure. Thiselton, A. *Realized Eschatology at Corinth*. New Testament Studies. Vol. 24 / Issue 04, pp. 510–26.

and conquer all of their enemies. In fact, at one point, the people became desperate for this to happen so they tried to force him to become king (John 6:15). However, what happened next served as a devastating blow to them. He died! All their hopes and dreams were dashed. Of course, they did not realise that God had another plan up his sleeve.

Three days later, the impossible happened. Jesus was resurrected. This would have raised their expectancy of a new king's arrival again. No such luck – another devastating blow! Jesus ascends into heaven after spending 40 days with his disciples, this time to be with His Father. He then sends the Holy Spirit ten days later to take His place. It is at this point that errors in terms of eschatology began to surface. This "new age" had come, but not altogether. What Jesus' followers (Corinthians included) did not initially understand was that the consummation of this partial inauguration would only occur at the Lord's return, i.e. the Second Coming. Oscar Cullmann explained this concept through the example of D-day and V-day in World War 2. On D-Day, the Allies defeated the Germans. However, although the battle had been won, small skirmishes continued to take place for another ten months in certain areas before the Nazis surrendered completely.[32] Thus, the Corinthians lived in uncomfortable, yet exciting times, as do we. There was and is a tension between the "already" and the "not yet."

Of course, the Apostles did not always remain blind to this. We read in Acts 3 that they had realized the end of the end had not yet dawned.

The following diagram[33] should help clarify the view Christians should adopt with respect to eschatology.

---

[32]Cullmann, O. *Christ and Time*, p. 84.
[33]Adapted from Venter. A. *Doing Healing*, p. 53.

Christian framework for the "end times"

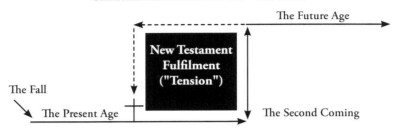

Both the Corinthians and we fall within the coloured block between the cross and the Second Coming. The Kingdom of God has broken into our "present age" from the future age. Think of the dawning of a new day. We see the light long before we see the sun. Likewise, we see symptoms of what Christ has done, but we have yet to see him in all His glory. What does this partial fulfilment of the future age look like? To get a glimpse, all you need do is examine the gospels. We read how Jesus healed people, but not all were healed (this still happens today); He cast out demons, but not every single one in existence; He showed His glory on the Mount of Transfiguration, but it was not there for all to behold all the time. If we look at this paradox from Paul's perspective, we see him saying things like:

- Christ has freed us from all condemnation, but we still have to stand before the judgment seat of God (Romans 8:1; 2 Corinthians 5:10), albeit for very different reasons;

- redemption is something that all believers already possess, but at the same time, they are still waiting for it, that is "the redemption of the body" (Romans 8:23; Ephesians 1:14; 4:30);

- freedom is something experienced by every Christian, but not in totality, because the rest of God's "creation itself will be set free from its bondage to decay and will obtain the freedom of the glory of the children of God." (Romans

6:18, 22; 8:21); and

- Christians are already heirs of the kingdom of God, but then on numerous other occasions, he suggest that the inheritance of the kingdom of God is still unsettled (Galatians 4:6–7; Ephesians 1:14).

Essentially, this "already/not-yet" aspect of life in the Kingdom forces us (and resulted in certain problems Paul had to address at Corinth) to adopt any one of three beliefs. We can live as if nothing has happened, i.e. saved, but life does not change, that the gifts of the Spirit are not for today. (This is the route many conservative evangelical churches have taken.) Secondly, we can believe that the Kingdom of God has arrived in all its glory and live believing and expecting that all of God's blessings are available to you right now – we only need to realise it and take hold of it by faith. There is no place for sin, sickness, pain, suffering, etc. (Many Faith Movement churches would be inclined to follow this route.)[34] Thirdly, we can live knowing that we are between times, i.e. expecting glimpses of the future, but realising that they will remain "glimpses" for now.

Unfortunately, the Corinthians were more than likely caught up in the second scenario more often than not. They behaved as if "the age to come was already consummated, as if the saints had already taken over the kingdom (Daniel 7:18). For them there [was] no 'not yet' to qualify the 'already' of realized eschatology.[35] Because of this, Wendland and Wolff add that they [Corinthians] transpose the gospel into a mixture of wisdom-gnosis and Spirit-centered enthusiasm."[36]

Consider Paul's sarcasm in 1 Cor. 4:8 as an example of this error. He says to them, "<u>Already</u> you have all you want! <u>Already</u> you have

---

[34]This theology often justifies the "still present" sicknesses and hardships endured by believers as resulting from a "lack of faith".
[35]Barrett, C. K. *The First Epistle*, p. 109.
[36]Wendland, *Die Briefe an die Korinther,* p. 40; Wolff, *Der erste Brief,* p. 86 in Thiselton. A. C. *The First Epistle*, p. 358.

become rich! Quite apart from us you have become kings! If only it were so …" Of course they had not really become any of these things – they were in error. Tongues, as mentioned by Fee earlier, would be another. (Then there was the case of the women in chapter 11 who sought to live out their overrealized state by going against the culture of head coverings. There will be a detailed discussion on this later in the book.)

This brings us to the close of this section dealing with why Paul wrote the letter. However, you need to keep these three aberrations in mind while working through the book because at least one of them, if not more, contributes to each problem Paul writes about.

Questions and Thoughts for Reflection

You will notice that most chapters will include a section entitled "For reflection." It is important for you to consider each of them as they test your knowledge of a portion of text, apply the text to contemporary issues, and get you to introspect on some of Paul's important teaching points.

1. Reading wider than the book, chapter or verse you are studying is an important hermeneutical principle. To establish this principle, read through Paul's Second Missionary Journey again and then try to identify, in as many ways as possible, how it helps you to better interpret and understand Paul's dealings with the Corinthians.

2. Discuss the benefit of having a cursory knowledge of the history, geography and demographics of the city of Corinth.

3. Many people build their theology on top of a lifetime of reading the Bible with a magnifying glass, i.e. studying the minute meanings/nuances of individual texts/words, or by listening to pastors who do it for them. Do we do this in daily life/practice? Think about how you approach an article in a newspaper, for example! Do you go and pinpoint one sentence or word in the

article to understand what the author is saying, or do you read the bulk of the article and then come back to try and understand the specifics?

3.1 Discuss why we do this (why do you do this, assuming you do?) and the results thereof; and

3.2 Discuss the benefits of knowing/understanding details such as *authorship, date of writing, structure and the "occasioning"* of a book of the Bible. Furthermore, try to develop a list of the types of books one would utilise to find such information, and where you could locate/purchase them. It would be particularly helpful if you could draw up a list of "reputable" websites that might help with providing such information as well.

4. Discuss the nature/essence of the Gospel of Jesus Christ

5. While you have only begun your study of 1 Corinthians, discuss how you think the predominant culture within the city would have positively and negatively impacted Paul's mission to fulfil the "Great Commission" in Matthew 28:18–20 ("make disciples by baptizing them and teaching them to obey everything that I have commanded you," i.e. making followers of Jesus. A clue: think about the nature/elements of the gospel Paul proclaimed and consider how they would fit in with the cultural paradigms).

6. Relating to question 6. Identify and discuss the positive and negative aspects within your culture that most impact your fulfilling the "Great Commission". Go into this in as much depth as possible.

Chapter One
Greetings All!

I hope you have formed a reasonably good idea of the "big picture" and occasion for the letter, because from here on out, we launch ourselves into the details or symptoms of their aberrations.

The salutation – Chapter 1:1–9

If you have ever written a letter to a friend before, you will know that the manner in which you begin your letter plays are large part in setting the tone for the rest of it. This said, when I read Paul's opening to the Corinthians, I am struck by his deep sense of love and concern for them, and even though many of his words to follow are harsh and caused upset, it is clear to me that his intention was to help them follow Jesus.

Chapter 1:1–9 represents a conventional opening to a Greco-Roman letter. It takes the form of an address and greeting (1:1–3) followed by thanksgiving (1:4–9). Paul's choice of words is important to the rest of his letter.

As we move through this short introduction, I will highlight some of the words Paul uses as, among other things, these words point to the underlying concerns about the church.

The first words are located in verse 1 – "called to be an apostle." Here Paul's concern is first to stress that he has been specifically commissioned by none other than God to carry out an apostolic ministry and secondly, to emphasize that a call to apostleship entails being a witness to Christ, in terms of doctrine, and the living out of Christ's death and resurrection in practice.

Verse 2 has the words "Church of God," "sanctified in Christ Jesus" and "their Lord and ours." Paul uses "church of God" to remind the Corinthians that the church is God's, not that of any one particular leader, and thus, they should not tamper with its unity. He uses "sanctified in Christ Jesus," i.e. set apart for God to remind the Corinthians of their overarching purpose in the Christian life. "Their Lord and ours" brings attention to the unity that all believers share in Jesus Christ. This being a vital point they had woefully misunderstood.

Verse 4 onwards contains the following words of interest – "grace," "enriched," "knowledge", "eagerly awaiting" and "day of the Lord". In using the word "grace," Paul reminds the Corinthians that what they received was a gift. Of course, they were not behaving like this at all. The church was plagued by issues of competitive "status seeking" and "rights." The second word "enriched" seems a strange one to use since Paul later uses it sarcastically to highlight the misguided views held by many of the Corinthians (4:8). Nevertheless, they must understand that they only have what they have through Christ, and this includes "knowledge."[37] Last, "eagerly awaiting" brings into focus the issue of eschatology (by this I mean "the already/not yet"), which they had misunderstood. "Already" they have been "enriched", and yet he says that they are "still eagerly awaiting" the "day of the Lord" (the return of Christ) which still lies up ahead.

---

[37]Note that Paul uses the word 'Christ' five times in his thanksgiving (4–9).

Questions and Thoughts for Reflection

1. These first 9 verses share some very important facts about the
    Christian, and I am assuming you are one. Firstly, YOU are
    sanctified, that is, "set apart" or "made holy," and this by the
    sacrifice of Jesus Christ. In some mysteriously beautiful way,
    His sacrifice enables you to belong to God. What we have here
    is Paul, and not only he, but many parts of scripture, suggesting
    that you are incredibly valuable. But, this is a far cry from what
    the devil or secular society would have you believe. Do you
    realize your inherent value, and I am not talking about value as-
    cribed to something you can do, but value in the sense of "who
    you are" in Christ (remember, the sacrifice was made for you
    the way you are)? Spend some time meditating on the mean-
    ing of 2 Corinthians 5:17, "So if anyone is in Christ, there is a
    new creation: everything old has passed away; see, everything
    has become new!" as it applies to you as well as its implications.

2. YOU are sanctified for a purpose; you must "bear the character
    of the God who has thus set [you] apart. Thus holiness forms
    part of God's intention in saving [you] (cf. 1 Thessalonians 4:3;
    5:23). Paul's concept of holiness regularly entails observable be-
    havior. That will be particularly the case in this letter, which
    is addressed to a community whose "spirituality" and "higher
    wisdom" have been largely divorced from ethical consequences
    …"[38] Keeping in mind the bit that says that "God loves you just
    the way you are," I now want you to meditate on God's purpose
    for your life, which is the second bit, "but He refuses to leave
    you that way", viz. He wants you to be transformed into the
    image and likeness of His Son (Romans 8:29). What does this
    actually mean? How is one supposed to achieve this? Where
    does the Bible fit into this? Do you agree that one's holiness
    should be observable? That one's spirituality should be intrinsi-

---

[38]Fee. G. D. The *First Epistle to the Corinthians*, p. 32.

cally tied to their ethics, their behavior? How do you measure up with these last 2 questions?

3. Every Christian is called into a community with boundaries that stretch to the ends of the earth. It is important to remember that you are part of the universal church of God throughout the earth. You are a peace of the puzzle in the awesome unfolding of the greater plan of God. The problem is that many societies today place more value on individualism – "me, myself and I." Would you say that your society espouses individualism or community? Scripture clearly suggests that Christianity is entrenched in the latter. What about yourself? If you are the former, what has driven you in that direction? How can you change this?

Chapter Two
Upsetting News from Corinth

This is the first of eight chapters in this book that will grapple with Paul's response to the news he heard from Chloe's household.

Choosing among Servants? – 1 Corinthians 1:10–17

"In the structure of the letter and in Paul's present argument this section fulfills a threefold purpose: firstly, *it introduces the body of the letter*; secondly, it states in a very specific way *the nature of the problem* that is first to be taken up and the source of Paul's information about it; thirdly, vv. 13–17 in particular offer *an initial apologetic*, which at the same time serves as a means of shifting the focus from the problem of 'splits over leaders' to the greater theological issue underlying its visible expression."[39]

The key word in this section is "splits" (*schismata*) and Paul hears that this is taking place in Corinth via members from Chloe's household. *Schismata* is used in Mark 1:19 to indicate the tear in a fishnet. Thus, it is more than just a division, but the ripping apart of something. This becomes very serious if that which is being ripped apart is the body of Christ. *Schismata* is also used metaphorically

---

[39]Ibid., p. 52.

46

to point to political divides, which is exactly what was going on at Corinth. The splits were the result of power struggles and not doctrinal matters. We know this because Paul condemns all of the sub-groups, even those who follow him. If these were splits because of doctrinal matters, condemning those who followed him would be tantamount to Paul saying his teachings were wrong, don't follow him. In the face of this tragedy, Paul pleads with them to take the same side (mend the tear), i.e. adopt the same mindset, which he later refers to as "the mind of Christ" (1 Cor. 2.16).

But what had caused these splits? There were personality favourites within the church, and it was going to take Paul almost 4 chapters to address it. You will recall my mentioning the high emphasis placed on intellectualism and the popularity of the sophists in the Corinthian culture at the time. People would listen to these sophists and then attach themselves as disciples to those they thought most intellectual and rhetorically eloquent. They would go around boasting about their teacher and even quarrel about which was the greatest. Thus, when we see Paul referring to people who side with him, Apollos, Peter or Christ, it is not too difficult to make a connection with where it originated – Corinthian culture.

Paul had arrived in Corinth with a teaching, which resulted in establishing a church. But, not long after that, Apollos also visited Corinth, making quite an impression. In terms of Peter (Cephas)[40], there is no certainty as to whether he ever visited Corinth, but he might have been followed as possibly the "senior Apostle." Lastly, there was the Christ group. This group probably saw themselves as the "super-spirituals" who weren't prepared to accept human ministers. They were the type of people who would be inclined to say, "well we have heard your opinions, but now let us tell you what Christ/Messiah is really saying." It is without doubt though that the biggest challenge was between Paul and Apollos, since Paul mentions the latter's name no less than seven times in the letter.

---

[40]Cephas was the Aramaic equivalent of Peter.

Apollos was a very eloquent speaker who was very learned in the scriptures and able to explain his teaching powerfully.[41] Quite naturally, his style was going to appeal to many given their backgrounds.

What made matters worse for Paul though is that some at Corinth questioned his authority (4:3, 18) because he did not behave like a high-class sophist. By this I mean:

- He possibly did not use the same rhetorical devices expected of the sophists in Corinth, which made him unimpressive;

- He had a sideline job; other philosophers usually made all of their money through speaking and debate;

- He did not want the Corinthians to support him financially. Exactly what they would have thought about this point is unsure, but we do know that it was an issue (9:1–18); and

- He did not treat them as "wise." In fact, he was treating them as "infants" (3:1–2).

As you can see, Paul had a challenge on his hands. Somehow, he needed to show the Christians that their attitude of boasting and quarrelling over leaders was completely incompatible with the cross. Thiselton explains this well:

"If Christ is 'split up,' so that each split claims to have a monopoly of Christ, how can anyone receive Christ in his wholeness and fullness (cf. 12:12)? Paul addresses an ironic question to what is supposedly 'his' (Pauline) group: 'Surely Paul was not crucified for you, was he? Are you putting a human leader

---

[41]Apollos came from Alexandria in Eygpt. He also went to Ephesus, where he met up with some of Paul's compatriots. Apollos had substantial knowledge of scripture as well as the ability to convey it (Acts 18:26–28). As a result, "Apollos had a following among some Corinthians. He had affected some Corinthians in the matter of wisdom, both in its rhetorical form and as esoteric content. These influences had managed to stir up the pot …" Ben Witherington, *Conflict and Community in Corinth: A Socio-Rhetorical Commentary on 1 and 2 Corinthians*, p. 96.

or patron in the place of Christ, and looking to him for your salvation through the cross?' The allusion of baptism reinforces the point by considering the question 'to whom was your allegiance made when you became Christians?'"[42]

Wright continues with comments concerning Paul's raising the issue of baptism in this light:

"Paul took baptism extremely seriously. It was the formal, outward sign, before God, one's family, and the wider community, and the whole church, that you were leaving your old identity behind and entering the new life of God's people in the Messiah. Baptism to the Christian was like crossing the Red Sea for Israel, at the time of the Exodus: it meant coming out of slavery into freedom – and responsibility (10:1–13). But the only name to be baptised into was the name of the Messiah. The person who did the baptizing was quite irrelevant. The relevant fact – and here we get to the heart of it, as we shall see from now on – was the clash between the good news, the gospel of Jesus, and the apparent power of human wisdom."[43]

Paul was about to force them into a position of having to choose between the wisdom of the world and the power of Jesus Christ. This is what Fee refers to in an earlier citation when he states, "the greater theological issue underlying its visible expression."

---

[42]Thiselton, A.C. *1 Corinthians: A Shorter Exegetical Commentary & Pastoral Commentary,* p. 41.

[43]The "wisdom" here referred to is that of the sophists (the instructors in the theory and practice of wisdom) who thought themselves big deals because of their own self-importance. Wright, N.T. *Paul for Everyone: 1 Corinthians,* p. 9.

Questions and Thoughts for Reflection

The Corinthian church sounds like a bit of mess, doesn't it? However, if you are honest with yourself, you will have to admit that nothing has changed. We still have splits over leaders. We still have splits because sinful aspects of our culture have crept into our churches. Consider the following:

1. For a start, I cannot help thinking of the history of Christian Denominations, e.g. Roman Catholic, Methodist, Baptist, Lutheran, Charismatic, Reformed, Pentecostal, Third Wave etc., and the impact this has had upon "Church Unity." I recall some interaction I had with a man after church one day. The man was aware that I taught theology and shook my hand saying, "I am a Calvinist, what are you?" I was speechless. The appropriate response should have been, "I am a Christian." I only thought later about how powerful such a reply would have been. The point is: our movements/denominations are similarly capable of diverting our true focus, thereby damaging attempts to bring unity to the body of Christ. The lack of unity in the Church today significantly compromises the effectiveness of the Christian witness – just imagine the evangelistic potential of a unified Church! "Not a few unbelievers, ancient and modern, have rejected the gospel because a religion as divisive as Christianity could scarcely reflect the truth."[44] Consider what Paul says in Ephesians 4.11–13. "The gifts he gave were that some would be apostles, some prophets, some evangelists, some pastors and teachers, to equip the saints for the work of ministry, for build-

---

[44]Blomberg, C. *1 Corinthians – NIV Application Commentary*. Available [Online] at http://books.google.co.za/books?id=GyWHbFph1SYC&pg=PT50&lpg=PT50&dq=Not+a+few+unbelievers,+ancient+and+modern&source=bl&ots=EqlAfHuN85&sig=tfsyfYTdOYScLZxPLfgj3B0nYHg&hl=en&sa=X&ei=rZ4SUK2UOoaJ0AXtp4CoBQ&sqi=2&ved=0CC4Q6AEwAA#v=onepage&q=Not%20a%20few%20unbelievers%2C%20ancient%20and%20modern&f=false

ing up the body of Christ, until all of us come to the *unity of the faith and of the knowledge of the Son of God,* to maturity, to the measure of the full stature of Christ." How could you make a difference in this area within your local town or suburb? One of my pastor friends has made a concerted effort to set up and nurture what has become a highly successful pastor's fraternity.

2. What about the Christian "celebrity phenomena?" People turn a pastor or teacher into a celebrity and in some extreme cases even call them the "Anointed of God." They hang on their every word and seldom check to see if what the speaker is saying is correct. I recall an incident where a highly acclaimed pastor used the parable of the sower to "bring in the tithe." I must have heard at least a thousand "Amens" from the audience in response to his message! His dynamic personality and fame distracted them from realizing that he had missed the point of the parable. Is this how Jesus intended it to be – one successful individual upfront while the rest of us sit in the pews? Before Jesus ascended, and subsequent to His ushering in the arrival of the Kingdom of God, he made a point of instructing His disciples to wait in Jerusalem for the power of the Holy Spirit. Ten days later, at Pentecost, the Spirit came, and it came upon ALL of them. Later, it fell on the Gentiles, to the absolute astonishment of the disciples. The point I am making is that the Holy Spirit did not show partiality. Each person was equipped to fulfil roles to achieve the Great Commission. That means that each person "gets to play" in the greater plans and purposes of God. What has been your position on this in the past? Consider your behaviour when answering the next 3 questions: Do you sit and wait for the pastor to do everything – preaching, teaching, ministry, evangelism etc.? Do you go to church to worship Jesus and fellowship with others or is your presence at church dependant on who is preaching that Sunday? Do you attend church services or conferences because some "great man

or woman" has come to town? If you answered "yes" to any of these questions, why do you do this? If you are one of the fortunate ones who answered "no," then how might you create a culture within your church in which everyone "gets to play?"

3. Discuss how Paul's understanding of the nature of water baptism compares with your local churches understanding and practice. What are some of the reasons why people refrain from being baptised in water shortly after their salvation?

Chapter Three
Alien Wisdom

I have entitled this chapter "Alien Wisdom" because, in comparison with conventional 'worldly wisdom', God's wisdom often seems almost alien.

This is a major section within the epistle. I have included summaries from time to time in the hope of separating the wood from the trees, because these first 4 chapters tend to tie people up in knots. Please study the following diagram before you read on.

Wisdom vs the Gospel	The Nature of Leadership and the Church	Paul's authority questioned
1:18–3:4	3:5–23	4:1–21
The gospel is not traditional wisdom	Leaders are servants	Paul's character and message
The irony of their boasting	Leaders must take care how they build the church	His dilemma (being a servant with authority)
The gospel and world thought	The church is the community in which the Spirit exists	Learning from Paul and Apollos
Knowledge through the gospel! How so?		His personal appeal
Having the Mind of Christ is proof of spirituality	Christ is the Head	
The Gospel seems crazy	The Field	Steward of the household
	The Builder	
"Low life's" of society	The Temple	Master – Servant relationship
The weak leader		Father – Child relationship

With this in mind, we come to the first major section of the Epistle, viz. chapters 1 through 4.

Here follows a glimpse of what is to come. The Epistle begins by addressing the issue of splits within the church (1:10–13) resulting from preferences of preaching/teaching styles and baptismal identity connected with Peter, Apollos and Paul (1:18–2:5). This part we have tackled already! We know there is confusion about the nature of wisdom, and that the splits are rooted in it, but how exactly are they related? Paul will address the link after a long explanation running through to the end of chapter 3. Chapter 4 takes on a more personal note because Paul turns to the issue of the Corinthian teachers, he being one of them. It appears from the letter that some of the Christians were judging him (4:3) because he did not want to pay them a visit (4:18). All the while, Paul is pleading with them to follow his example (4:14).

This is no ordinary gospel – 1 Corinthians 1:18–2:5

Thus far, Paul has argued at a superficial level saying, "I baptized few of my converts; therefore, you cannot say that you were baptized into my name; therefore, you ought not to say, I belong to Paul. By analogy, you ought not to say, I belong to Apollos, or I belong to Cephas; and no one group should be allowed to say, I belong to Christ."[45]

The Corinthians were enamoured with human wisdom to the detriment of rightly perceiving the true worth of the gospel. Paul has to put an end to this immediately. His modus of operandi is to

---

[45]Just to recap. This "Christ group" should not be thought of as those on the correct track. Moffatt suggests that they were "ultra-spiritual devotees or high-flying gnostics who made a mystical Christ, no human leader, the centre of religion." Moffatt, J. *The First Epistle of Paul to the Corinthians*, p. 10. Furthermore, Wendland suggests that they were "pneumatics who invoke for themselves special direct revelations from Christ, as against other groups." Wendland, D. *Die Briefe an Die Korinther*, p. 19.

take them back to the heart of the gospel, viz. the cross of Christ, beginning in verse 18. Verse 18 actually discloses the main point of this section. Paul offers "an absolute contrast between God and the word about the cross, on the one hand, and the wisdom of the world on the other."[46] His method of achieving this is to start with an Old Testament text, then to discuss God's motive (that no man will boast) behind introducing the gospel in the manner that He did (the cross), and lastly to reveal the outcome (they are Christians, thus they must have believed it). Having done this, he uses paradoxical observations from their society, the types of people who have joined the church, and his method of preaching, to impress upon them the truth that the gospel he preaches is not of this age. In other places, Paul contrasts the two with words like "flesh" and "spirit", "old man" and "new man", "this present evil age" and "the age to come."[47]

Here follows his brilliant methodology:

Paul launches with an Old Testament text, "For it is written, 'I will destroy the wisdom of the wise, and the discernment of the discerning I will thwart.'"[48] Then he elaborates on or clarifies the quote with "Where is the one who is wise? Where is the scribe? Where is the debater of this age? Has not God made foolish the wisdom of the world?"

But why has He made the wisdom of this world "foolish"? What is His motive (1:20)? Paul spells out a couple of reasons:

---

[46]Lampe. P. "Theological Wisdom," *Int* 44, p. 120. Barth states that this contrast "is clearly the secret nerve of this section." Barth. K. *The Resurrection of the Dead*, p. 18.

[47]"The crucifixion and resurrection of Jesus for Paul marked the 'turning of the ages,' whereby God decisively judged and condemned the present age and is in process of bringing it to an end. Those who still belong to it, therefore, are in process of 'perishing' with it. From this 'old-age' point of view the message of the cross is foolishness." Fee, G. D. 1987. *The First Epistle to the Corinthians*. The New International Commentary on the New Testament (69). Wm. B. Eerdmans Publishing Co.: Grand Rapids, MI

[48]The quotation is almost verbatim from Isaiah 29.14.

- To silence the arrogant and supposed wise men of this age. Who in their right mind would consider a cross and a crucified Messiah (King) as a path leading to wisdom? "Corinth was a city where public boasting and self-promotion had become an art form … [and] *public recognition was often more important than facts* … In such a culture [honour-shame] a person's sense of worth [was] based on *recognition by others* of one's accomplishments … [with this in mind, Christ's crucifixion and kingship were an oxymoron, irrespective of His character. Furthermore, it would hardly have been a good idea to associate oneself with such a person for your own reputation sakes.][49] However, it was precisely that shamed individual that God had proclaimed Lord and "Anointed One". Thus, God had turned the idea of "status"[50] on its head, which is precisely what was of great value to the Corinthians (and dare I say, most of the Western culture today?).

- To demonstrate that God alone could save humanity from its diabolical self.[51]

The outcome is to ensure that salvation is not through human means. It does not come through human status, honour, achievement, wealth or political power. Nor does it come through learning techniques to increase your wealth and power and status and honour, which is what most pagan philosophers, including Aristotle,

---

[49]Witherington, B. *Conflict and Community in Corinth*: *A Socio-Rhetorical Commentary on 1 and 2 Corinthians,* p. 8 in Thiselton. A. C. *The First Epistle*, p. 13. Italics Thiselton.

[50]This idea of turning things upside down is a common thread within the context of the Kingdom of God. For instance, consider Jesus statements about power in Matthew 20:20–28. In these texts, we see power within the Kingdom of God coming through humility, service and sacrifice, whereas worldly or carnal power comes through influence, money, control, fame/status.

[51]It is a plan that conveys the truth about God and humans, and it does deliver on the promises of Isaiah 61:1–2 and Lk 4:18–19.

promised to teach. So, the aim of pagan philosophy was to understand the world in order to gain control over it and so to become more successful, powerful, respected. Paul points out – you can't own salvation, or grasp it or dominate it. It belongs to God. You can only gratefully accept it by faith (1:21).

Below follows a depiction of the environment into which the gospel began filtering.

Firstly, there were the Jews who possessed the revelations of God through scripture. However, they wanted signs and wonders (John 2.18) to verify that Jesus was the Messiah. They were looking for a king who would conquer the Romans and set them free. Their history taught them of a mighty God, who delivered the Israelites out of Egypt and then promptly wiped out the forces of Pharaoh in the Red Sea. With this mindset in place, "We might assume from this that God could not be believed unless He could produce His credentials, in this case in the form of identifiable and verifiable acts?"[52]

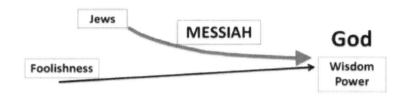

Then there were the Gentiles (everyone other than the Jews. In this case, specifically the Greeks and Romans). They did not have the wisdom of scripture. Therefore, they pursued techniques, knowl-

---

[52]Of course they were correct to a point, but the conquering/delivering was taking place in an entirely different manner. "For the resurrection of Christ constitutes the sign that the cosmic turning point has arrived and casts essential light on the Christological and cosmic significance of Jesus of Nazareth." Pannenberg, W. *Systematic Theology*, Vol. 2: pp. 343–379.

edge, and behaviour which would bring "success in politics, the courtroom, philosophy, or in everyday affairs of trade, love, or the household; what would bring 'mastery' of life and especially the approval or admiration of patrons, masters, and their own peer group."[53]

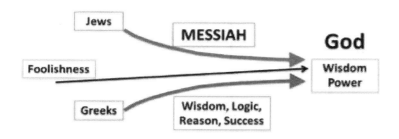

Thus, in essence, the irony here is that the "nature of the gospel" Paul presented was diametrically opposed to both party's expectations and yet there were many of them who had become believers and were in the church. This is the first of three paradoxes?

The cross was abhorrent to both parties. However, little did either party realize that the power of God became operational, effectual, and actualized through this event. As stated in (1:25), God's foolishness and weakness nullified worldly wisdom and strength.

---

[53]Pogoloff. S. *Logos and Sophia: The Rhetorical Situation of 1 Corinthians*, pp. 108–172.

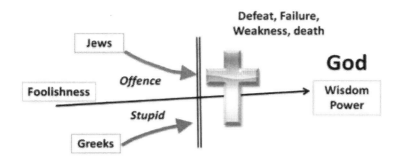

Paul's next paradox is much more personal (1:26–31). He turns to the members of the church, the very ones causing all the trouble. Allow me to paraphrase what I believe he was trying to point out to them.

"My beloved Corinthians, just imagine this scenario. There is a group called 'The Way' wishing to totally overturn the current understanding/expectations of the nature and coming of the Kingdom of God. They are aware of the type of Messiah the Jews are expecting – a conqueror who can deliver them from Roman oppression. They are also aware of what will draw the attention of the Gentiles: more security, happiness, acknowledgment, status, prosperity, success and control. Thus, knowing their target market, they choose 'you'; people who cannot even deliver themselves out of difficulty, let alone the nation of Israel; people who, for the most part, are not wise, powerful, or of noble birth! In fact, people who could even be considered despised, foolish and weak! I would say that 'The Way' would have to be teetering on the brink of insanity to launch their world takeover bid with people like yourselves!"

Thus, the second paradox focuses on God's choice of people (the nobodies) to launch His plan to save humanity.

As a result, Paul's message of the cross challenged any thoughts they had that the "gospel" was a form of "human wisdom" spread by the powerful and successful, which they could boast about. Furthermore, it also clearly pointed out that salvation in Christ is not a human self-improvement scheme, but a radical rescue. Grace is not only the great unifier, but also the great leveller.[54]

Therefore, they as Christians should be THE most grateful and humble people on the face of the planet. The world did not think anything of them and yet God had given them THE greatest gift in the history of humankind. "Let the one who boasts, boast in the Lord" (1:31c), because He is the one who has accomplished this magnificent achievement.[55]

His last paradoxical reminder (2:1–5) concerns the style of his preaching in their company._

For a moment, let us pretend that you are a "green peace activist" with what you believe is a radical strategy for reducing carbon emissions in oil companies. Your main thesis is that if oil companies cut their production by 75%, they will more than halve their carbon emissions. Although this will mean a steep decline in their shareholder profits, they can rest assured that it will significantly improve the future health of the environment. Oh, and I forgot to mention that you also have no credentials or figures to substantiate your estimations. By some miracle, after several months of trying, you manage to set up an appointment with a leading oil company. Come the big day, you walk into their boardroom where you meet some of the most dynamic, astute business people on the planet all dressed to

---

[54]Witherington. B. *Conflict and Community in Corinth: A Socio-Rhetorical Commentary on 1 and 2 Corinthians,* pp. 23–24 and 118.

[55]The "key theological point covers two issues: 1) God's sovereign freedom to choose to love and to give himself regardless of human deserving or achievement and 2) the discontinuity evidenced between God and the world. God is no human construct, called in to legitimate human power interests, but the very reverse. His love for the nobodies and the nothings discounted as nonentities and as insignificant in the value system of the world puts the world to shame by its reversal of judgment." Thiselton, A. C. *The First Epistle to the Corinthians: A Commentary on the Greek text,* p. 178.

the hilt. The boardroom is equipped with every conceivable form of presentation enhancement technology. You, on the other hand, are casually dressed, have one page with some bullet points scribbled on it, and not even a power point presentation. You launch into your presentation strategy. For most of the presentation, you fumble your words, speak softly and look down at your notes. At the end of your presentation, the boardroom is filled with applause. There is unanimous agreement and the company commits to an unprecedented drop in oil production. Shareholders praise your plan around the world, even though they will lose billions in revenues.

WHAT? No worldly plan could deliver such a result. In fact, your strategy and style of presentation would make you a laughing stock. However, the power of God could make it happen if this was His plan. With this in mind, let us turn back to the plan of God to save humanity.

I have already given you an illustration of the insanity of the content of Paul's message in the "launching The Way" example, but with this "style of presentation" illustration above, I wish to reinforce it and drive home another point Paul was making. God used him, an unimpressive looking character, using an unimpressive style of presentation (according to their method of manipulative rhetoric) to convince folk enamoured with contradictory goals (sex, money, power) to pull off the impossible – their buy-in to the gospel. Quite obviously, God, through His wisdom, wanted their faith to rest in His power, not in a man's oratory abilities or skill. Why? Any other way would rob the cross of its force! It would draw attention to the man, and not God. Thus, in effect, Paul might as well have been saying:

'And' guess what people, you listened to what I said and took the amazing step of believing an apparently 'weak' man with an apparently 'crazy' message, at least by human standards that is! Therefore, the outcome of your salvation is not because you are wise, or that the message is full of wisdom, as you know it, or even that I delivered it to you in an eloquent fashion. No! The outcome of your salvation is because of the power of God. Therefore, if you want to boast, boast in His ingenious wisdom and infinite power to realize it.

Christians must be wary of seeking clever schemes, devices or methods to win people over. In Paul's case, clever words and manipulative rhetoric would have hindered the spread and true understanding of the gospel message. When a Christian replaces faith in the power of the gospel with clever tactics (trust in their own abilities and resources), it nullifies God's power and grace, which are the very things that enable people to enter the Kingdom of God.

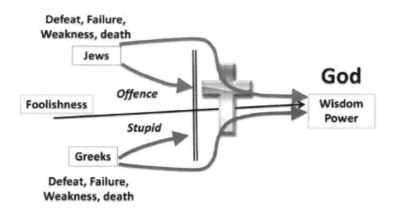

Salvation is only by the power of God through His grace! To what degree do you avoid sharing the gospels because you believe you are not sufficiently skilled or cut out for it?

Wisdom, nonetheless – 1 Corinthians 2:6–16

In this section, we have Paul elaborating on his previous comments, i.e. the gospel and its preaching are not a form of human wisdom.

Paul has spoken strongly against human wisdom previously, but changes back at this point by suggesting that the gospel is indeed a "form of wisdom", but a wisdom that is spoken among the mature.

Before reading further, it will be helpful to gain some under-standing of the way in which Paul uses the term "wisdom." Thus far, Paul has been insisting that the gospel owes nothing to human wisdom. It is almost as if he is saying that Christians should have nothing to do with wisdom, but this is not true because the gospel embodies the true wisdom of God.

"Paul is compelled to use the word 'wisdom' in four senses – two from a negative and two from a positive perspective. Firstly, wisdom is used in a bad sense when it refers to the skilled organization of human arguments used to convince hearers. Of course, this practice is not evil in itself. However, it takes on an evil persona when it becomes a substitution for authentic preaching thereby veiling the power of the Spirit by its demonstration of human persuasiveness [Something I alluded to at the end of the previous section.] Furthermore, it becomes more sinister when the truth, be it theological or ethical, is assessed by human standards rather than those of the Kingdom of God. To reasoning based on such standards, which asks ultimately what I wish to believe and to do, the cross is inevitably foolishness. This is the greatest error one can make and unfortunately, the error the Corinthian Christians were making. [It is also negative when it is used in order to point us away from God and towards admiration of the speak-er.] From a positive perspective, wisdom might mean God's wise plan of redeeming the world through a crucified Messiah, a plan which none but he could have prepared and man can only grasp if he is willing to surrender his natural man-centred values. Secondly, wisdom is also used to refer to the actual substance of salvation, itself given through the wise plan of sal-vation, i.e. wisdom is closely related to 'righteousness,' which is also the way in which God acts, and the gift which his act bestows upon man."[56]

Paul's next step is to develop a contrast between the "wisdom of this age" and "God's true wisdom."

Firstly, God's wisdom is "secret" ("mysterious," or too profound for human capacity to fathom).[57] Secondly, it was "hidden" before Christ's arrival.[58] Thirdly, those who have the Spirit can understand it. Finally, God's wisdom leads to "glory" i.e. it was always God's intention to redeem humankind through Jesus Christ. As regards its "mysteriousness", Paul mentions that the "rulers of this age" cannot grasp it. However, who are these "rulers of this age" mentioned in (2:6–8)? Are they demonic powers, political rulers, angels who have guard over the nations that could be both supernatural and political, or a combination of both? There are strong arguments for each one, but the most convincing is the last. I, like many others, believe that there is an unseen world far more sinister and powerful than we could imagine, and that this realm has a direct influence on what takes place at a "physical" or "earthly" level (Ephesians 6.12). So for example, Judas was not the only one behind the idea to betray Jesus. Satan was there spurring him on. In fact, it states that as Judas took the bread from Jesus, "Satan entered into Judas" (John 13:27).[59]

Alternatively, the human spirit can understand "human" wisdom because it falls within the capacity of the human's paradigm. Paul is showing them that he does not preach a traditional form of wisdom, but it is wisdom even though the rulers of this age would

---

[56]Barrett, C. K. *The First Epistle to the Corinthians*, pp. 67–68.

[57]The reason why the "rulers of the age" did not understand God's wisdom was because they did not have the Spirit of God.

[58]The message of the preaching of the cross was hidden until the time of the turning of the ages and even the demons were caught unawares. The fact is that if both the demons and humanity had known of God's wisdom, they would never have crucified Christ.

[59]For those interested in exploring the reality of evil in the world, read N.T. Wrights book entitled "Evil and the Justice of God."

not perceive it as such. Only the Spirit of God can unlock this form of wisdom.

In 2:10–11, Paul explains how one might acquire God's wisdom. The acquisition of God's wisdom is through "revelation." Some might argue saying, "but today we have thousands of Bibles in circulation in the Western world. Therefore, anybody can have access to God's wisdom. In one sense, they would be correct because the Bible is God's revelation through the Holy Spirit written down by authors. However, 2:12–14 points out that only the Spirit can bring understanding. One who does not have the Spirit does not have understanding. Think of it like this. When one looks at light under most circumstances, it appears white, but shine it through a prism, and you will see seven distinct colours with millions of shades between each of them. Imagine the Holy Spirit is that prism. Without him, we see, but we do not see clearly. We understand, but we do not understand fully.[60]

Paul ends this section with an astonishing statement: "but we have the mind of Christ" (2:16). By this he refers to one's mindset, mode of thinking, and character. Allo suggests that it is because Christ lives in those who have received the Spirit that their stance and outlook can be that of Christ. In this sense, they are truly "spiritual."

In 2:6–16 Paul has expounded the visionary results of the new world, which the Holy Spirit can reveal to Christians.

The wonder of what the Spirit can display passes all human experiences of sight and sound, and all human imagining (9). The truly 'spiritual' person … enjoys intimacy with God and assurance of salvation (12c). In one sense … Paul endorses the Corinthian catchphrase that people of the Spirit sift out everything, while no one else puts spiritual persons on trial or sifts them out (15)! However, for

---

[60]"My thoughts are not your thoughts, and my ways are not your ways," declares the LORD. "Just as the heavens are higher than the earth, so my ways are higher than your ways, and my thoughts are higher than your thoughts." (Isaiah. 55:8–9)

Paul, the test of whether people are truly 'of the Spirit' is whether the Spirit has formed within them the mind-set of Christ (2:16).[61]

Spiritual Babies – 1 Corinthians 3:1–4

In the preceding paragraph, Paul has elaborated on the theme of Christian wisdom: not only the contrast between it and the wisdom of the age, but also its positive content. Now he turns to the present situation. It is true that there is a Christian wisdom, which mature Christians can understand and discuss, but the Corinthian believers are not ready for this wisdom. This comment by Paul has infuriated them.

He mentions that he is unable to treat them as those who live a lifestyle determined by the Spirit of God. Instead, to his dismay, he has to treat them as fleshly. Barrett comments here that "fleshly people" are not those who go around habitually committing sensual sins. They are "those whose existence is determined not by God but by considerations internal to themselves, or internal at least to humanity as distinct from God … to call his readers 'fleshly' is to imply that they are completely outside the Christian way, and this would go too far. 'Mature' provides a better basis of comparison than 'spiritual'. Mature the Corinthians are not. They may be described as 'babes' in Christ."[62] Therefore, Paul cannot engage in a "spiritually mature" discussion with them, that being the word of the cross. The message is similar for both babes and the mature, but as Barrett puts it, "it is different in form rather than content, as meat and milk are both food, though differently constituted."[63]

To summarize, Paul has detailed discussion on the revelation of the Spirit and divine wisdom (1:10–3:3a) and then takes us from

---

[61]Allo, *Première Épitre.*
[62]Barrett, C. K. *The First Epistle*, p. 80. Consider also the statements: "He must increase, but I must decrease" (Jn 3:30) and "For to me, living is Christ and dying is gain" (Phil 1:21).
[63]Ibid. p.81.

when he introduced the issue of "splits" (1:10–12) to the rhetorical questions (3:3–4) that drive home the point. "If the Corinthian Christians divide over favourite teachers the way the worldly intellectuals do, they exhibit infantile wisdom rather than that given by God's Spirit."[64]

Questions and Thoughts for Reflection

1. I mentioned earlier that salvation does not come through human status, honour, achievement, wealth or political power. Nor does it come through learning techniques to increase your wealth, power, status and honour. Nor can we understand the world in order to gain control[65] over it and so become more successful, powerful, or respected. But, many at Corinth did believe that this was the way and many today are addicted to this mind-set as well. Of course, most will not call it "salvation". In Western secular society, it might rather go by names such as, "having arrived", or "health, wealth and happiness", or peace (*Nirvana),* "the good life", "the American Dream" (if you live in the USA) etc. However, what about you? Are you pursuing a lifestyle to attain, or for the sake of, attaining meaning, status, honour, wealth, control, success, power, self-actualization … ? It might help to analyse your behaviour/actions and fantasies (that is fantasies about anything) to arrive at an honest answer. This mind-set pursued in Corinth and secular society today comes from the devil. If one considers the implications of pursuing these "ideals", you will find "naval gazing" (life is revolves around ME); "illicit sex, perversion, promiscuity, idolatry, drug

---

[64]Keener, C. S. *1–2 Corinthians*, p. 40.

[65]I have noticed something interesting about the nature of "control": when we try to take control of our lives, we actually loose control – all of the anxieties flood in as our minds work frantically to keep up. However, when we relinquish control to God in faith, He gives us back a degree of control, but this time we are able to rest in His peace.

use, hatred, rivalry, jealousy, angry outbursts, selfish ambition, conflict, factions, envy, drunkenness, wild partying, and things like that" (Galatians 5:19–21). Think about it! Do you agree? Then, what about the values found within the Kingdom of God and the implications that accompany them? The list of values includes things like living with every fibre of your being in pursuit of "being transformed into the image and likeness of Jesus Christ"; fulfilling the Great Commission by baptising and teaching people to obey the commands of Jesus; forgiving others, because He forgave us; faith in God for our provisions; humility; thankfulness to God for His sacrifice and His creation; respect for all people, since they are made in the image of God and He instructed us to "love our neighbour"; pursuing a moral lifestyle because your body is the temple of the Holy Spirit; standing up for truth and justice; helping the poor, aged, sick/diseased, weak, orphans, drunkards, prostitutes, prisoners, and generally oppressed. Instead of "naval gazing", there is servant-hood and sacrifice (which represent an outward focussed lifestyle), climbing off the throne of your life and allowing its rightful owner (Jesus) to take His seat. In short, all of the above involves "Dying to yourself." As John the Apostle said, "He must increase, but I must decrease." (John 3:30) Paul actually draws up a contrast between good and bad fruits in Galatians 5:19–23 – (I refer to the bad fruit above). "By contrast, the fruit of the Spirit is love, joy, peace, patience, kindness, generosity, faithfulness, gentleness, and self-control."

2. I briefly touched on the possible meanings of the "rulers of the age" in this chapter. The text reads: "Yet among the mature we do speak wisdom, though it is not a wisdom of this age or of the *rulers of this age*, who are doomed to perish. But we speak God's wisdom, secret and hidden, which God decreed before the ages for our glory. None of the *rulers of this age* understood this; for if they had, they would not have crucified the Lord of glory"

(2:6–8). I also stated, "I, like many others, believe that there is an unseen world far more sinister and powerful than we could imagine, and that this realm has a direct influence on what takes place at a 'physical' or 'earthly' level' (Ephesians 6.12). What I have noticed is that Christians, and I am not referring to those who look for a demon behind every bush, might be aware that there is a battle between two kingdoms going on, but they don't live like it. Many are familiar with the profound scripture which states: "For our struggle is not against enemies of blood and flesh, but against the rulers, against the authorities, against the cosmic powers of this present darkness, against the spiritual forces of evil in the heavenly places" (Ephesians 6:12), but, I have to question whether they actually believe it. Remember, actions, that is, how we live, and not what we say, show us what we truly believe. How about you? What do your actions tell you about your beliefs in this area? How should one be acting knowing this war between kingdoms is on the go? If you are looking for answers, I suggest you read all 4 Gospels very carefully looking for symptoms of this on-going clash. Pay particular attention to what Jesus says and does in these circumstances. You could also read the Book of Acts, noting the Apostle's clashes with evil as they advance the church.

3. Consider God's strategic plan to infiltrate Corinth with His gospel, in light of Paul's comments in 1:18–2:5. Then juxtapose this with the possible strategies the so-called "knowledgeable" and "wise" would use. Taking this further. There are many other examples of God's using the young, small, weak, insecure, insignificant and generally disliked to action some of His most phenomenal displays of power. For example, Abraham, Moses, Gideon, David, Solomon, and the 12 disciples. Think about this stark contrast between the strategies of God vs. humanity. What differences would you imagine exist between God's motivating values and priorities and those of humanity? With

this in mind, if you are an employer, what criteria do you think God would advocate when it comes to you hiring employees? There are not many of us who do not, at some point, feel insecure or inadequate, excluded or abused. How does it make you feel to realise that God is more likely to use you than those who behave and live like superheroes?

4. Based on the previous question, what possible lessons might you learn from this fact, *"For my thoughts are not your thoughts, nor are your ways my ways, says the* LORD.*"* (Isaiah 55:8). Furthermore, what does this mean for us who are trying to do the will of the Lord? Clue: Consider this verse in Isaiah alongside Romans 12:1–2. Lastly, reflect on your local churches current plans, programmes, ministries, and activities. What do they say about the churches underlying/motivating values (the reasons why your church does what it does), priorities (what the church actually does in order of importance) and practices (how the church implements its values and priorities)?[66]

---

[66]A good way of identifying what is truly a priority is to consider where the most time is spent. Time is precious to everyone and it will not be wasted on anything that is not important.

Chapter Four
Christian Leader's Guide

Clearly, the situation within the Corinthian church was not ideal. There were splits within the church over who was the most "classy" leader. This is similar to our modern tendency to follow spiritual super-heroes, the renowned Christian leaders (famous or infamous) irrespective of their knowledge or quality of character. Christian conferences in many circles often centre on renowned Christians, not on community needs. Then, there was the crazy idea of the "cross," which did not gel with their concept of the gospel.

Therefore, in this section, Paul will have to re-educate them on the role of leadership. To complicate matters, while getting them to accept that leaders are servants, he has to elevate himself to convince them of his apostolic authority – not an easy task! Imagine addressing a pastoral leader's conference where your mandate is to drum into them that they are servants and then at the same time telling them that you are the chosen person God is using; that they must listen to you because you are their father, and they are your children.

The fact is that this battle between authority and servitude is very close to home for many of us. We live in a society where power and status are sought-after. People derive their sense of worth from and measure their success by it. Paul refutes status-based leadership by comparing it to servant-based leadership and team-based leadership. To accept Paul's idea of authority in servitude is paradoxical to the very core of our being. It is no wonder we hear of pastors falling because they hold onto the reigns too tightly.

Church politics is a very messy issue, and it has followed us all the way into the twenty-first century. In church politics, there are two issues at play: the role of the leaders and the role of the followers. In the Corinthian church, the trouble came from the community, with factions emphasising different leaders. One can well expect, especially from Paul's comments later in the letter, that there was a fair amount of gossiping circulating about the different leaders. Paul's teaching aims to set right these two groups; the leaders and the community. He sets the leaders in their proper place as team-servants, and he sets the community as disciples, rather than a campaign mob.

How does he win them over to his way of thinking? He uses three metaphors:
1. The field and colleague labourers (3:5–9),
2. The building and testing the builders' work (3:10–15),
3. The church as a representative of God's temple of the Holy Spirit (3:16–17).

He uses common imagery that they would have related to, to explain the principle of spiritual teamwork. Today, Paul might have used an illustration of different roles in a football team or the different roles employees take to provide efficient service to their customers. In so doing, he would move them through very natural and relatable roles, away from the idea of spiritual-superheroes.

Let us pick up on Paul's argument as he introduces their leaders.

God's farm and building – 1 Corinthians 3:5–9

In this section, Paul deals with one of the causes of their factions – "partiality towards leaders." As mentioned earlier, there were three leaders caught in these factions, Paul, Apollos and Cephas (Peter).

Paul explicitly states that they are servants. The term used for servants – *diakonoi,* meant "table waiter." The word indicated the lowly character of the services rendered by the waiter and makes a mockery of the thought of exalting the leaders. By this, Paul implies, "Who of you would put your servant (waiter) on a pedestal? Well, why do you do it with us? We are mere instruments through whom God does His work." Paul then illustrates his point by introducing the first metaphor of a field. The objects/characters within this metaphor include the Field (Church), Cultivator (Apollos), Planter (Paul), and Owner (God). Why do you suppose Paul used this metaphor of himself as being a planter and Apollos being a cultivator (see above)?

Let me illustrate the point Paul is trying to make for those of you not living in an agrarian society. You are looking for a job and like the idea of working at a five star hotel. You meet three people when you walk into the lobby: the janitor, the door attendant and the owner of the hotel. Can you imagine presenting the janitor or the door attendant with your resume and asking them for a job? Talk about crazy! They are the hired hands. They have no authority to deal with your request. The owner is the one with all the decision-making power so you would look to him for a job! Paul's point here is that he and Apollos have unimportant jobs when compared with God. The people must realise that it is God who is important, not the leaders.[67] Quite a few of our leaders today could take a tip from Paul here. Far too many think they are the "hotel owner."

His metaphor of the planter and waterer is essentially emphasising unity of purpose, although each person's labour might be different (just like the janitor and the door attendant strive to make the guests' stay an enjoyable one). The one would not be able to function without the other (a plant without water and water without a plant equals nothing). This is a very different perspective from

---

[67]"I first cast the word into the ground … Apollos added his own part. But the whole was of God". Chrysostom, *Hom. 1 Corinthians.* 8:5.

being rivals. Actually, they are one in purpose but with different functions. The point is not what role or task is the most important, or even that everyone has different roles, but the accomplishment of God's will through unity.

In 3:8b Paul adds another interesting dimension to the argument. He mentions that their common purpose is rooted in God. They labour under Him, and He is the one who will ultimately determine their wage. In effect, this means that Paul and Apollos owe it to God to do their best. It is God, and not the community, who will judge their efforts and value them.

To use an example,

the ineffective, shallow, prayerless minister may perhaps never see the "reward" of men and women coming to faith and growing to maturity, however hard his or her labor, and however long his or her hours. On the other hand, an authentic ministry may bring "rewards" of which only God and the minister know [and sometimes the latter might not know] … The reward for those who are bodily resurrected in the same manner as Christ (15:44–49) might be to discover that work done in their earthly existence has in some manner remained a condition of some established effect in the new world order of "what abides" as the fruit of the Spirit or as the work of God's kingdom (13:8–13).[68]

Thus, to recap, Paul is saying that the congregation must realise that leaders are servants, that they have unity of purpose, and that their purpose is rooted in God.

The foundation and the building – 1 Corinthians 3:10–15

Although there is a sudden change of metaphor, this section continues to deal with the issue of the Church and its leaders. This portion of Scripture has often been misinterpreted. We will look at some of these errors as the argument unfolds.

---

[68]Thiselton, A. C. *The First Epistle*, p. 304.

You will recall from the previous section that Paul explained that the church is "God's field." However, in this section, the church becomes "God's building." The particulars of the two metaphors remain the same. In 3:5–9, the particulars were planter, waterer, field and owner. In 3:10–15, the planter equates to the one who lays a foundation – Paul. The waterer equates to the one who builds upon the foundation – Apollos – and the field equates to the building – the Church. The owner still refers to God. The foundation is Jesus Christ.

Paul changes the metaphor to make a new point. The first metaphor pointed out that the leaders in the church were not to be exalted, because they are servants. Each servant had a job to do, but both had the same purpose and everyone belonged to God. However, what is Paul's point under this section?

His emphasis on being "rewarded for one's labours" (3:8b) is connected with a solemn warning as to "how one builds the church." Therefore, his emphasis is on the quality of the materials used.[69] In short, he says that they should make use of imperishable materials (durable – 3:12–13) because on that final day, each person's work will be tested and his or her reward determined accordingly.[70]

It is like having two manufacturing teams at a John Deere Combine Harvester factory. Team A is lazy and careless with their assembly of the combine harvesters while Team B is scrupulous in

---

[69]There is consensus that two, and not six separate categories of material are in view here: non-flammable (gold, silver, costly stones) and flammable (wood, hay, straw). The point is that the non-flammable elements will withstand the eschatological "fire" and produce authentic lasting results.

[70]A sub-point to this section is that the church, being a "community", can be tied in with the "building" concept. What the leaders must realize is that they are not on their own mission to create "their" church. For example, I have heard pastors say, while chatting amongst each other, "how is your church doing", or "my church/my people are this or that …" This language is wrong! Rather, the "Church" is to be understood as a corporate structure – a community belonging to God. I believe that it is Jesus who should be identified as the senior pastor!

their efforts. A few months down the line, the John Deere factory comes to a gathering of all the major crop producers in the land. At the meeting, statistical evidence demonstrating the effectiveness of John Deere's machinery reveals that there are significant discrepancies in harvesting machines' productivity. After some research, it is discovered that machines coming out of Team A's work shops were actually unproductive due to much repair "down time," whereas machines from Team B's work shops are proving highly productive. Team A and B's work has been revealed and each will face the appropriate consequences. As they say, the proof of the pudding is in the eating!

Fee suggests that 3:10–11 forms a chiasmus:[71]

    (A) Paul has laid a foundation (3:10a)
    (B) Others are building on it (3:10b)
    (B) They should take great care how they do so (3:10c)
    (A) The foundation is Christ (3:11a)[72]

Therefore, we have two themes here. Theme (A) is about the foundation on which they build, and theme (B) has to do with the quality of their workmanship. Let us apply these thoughts.

Whatever we do as Christians, we must do for the glory of Jesus Christ. There is no way that we, in this life, can be certain that what we have built will stand the test, and there is certainly no place to pass judgment on how others are building. What we build will either stand or fall on Judgment Day. One thing you can be certain of is that if you build for self-gain, you have done so in vain.

Interestingly, 1 Corinthians 3:15 has led to a significant false doctrine, viz. The Roman Catholic doctrine of Purgatory?[73] The

---

[71]"Chiasmus" refers to the inversion in a second phrase or clause of the order of words in the first. A typical chiasmus takes the form of A B B A, where the letters correspond to grammar, words, or meaning.

[72]Fee, G. D. *First Epistle*, p. 137.

[73]It is "for those who, departing this life in God's grace, are, not entirely free from venial [sins], or have not fully paid the satisfaction due to their transgressions." Available [Online] at http://www.newadvent.org/

Catholic Church's understanding is that being saved "as through fire" happens in a place or condition of temporal punishment called Purgatory, an event that takes place after death but before Judgment Day. However, "This cannot be a reference to purgatory since Paul is referring to what happens on the judgment day … after the return of Christ … He is not referring to what happens to a person after death and before the final judgment … 'As through fire' is a metaphor for escaping … by the skin of one's teeth."[74]

The real issue in this portion of text is, "leaders, you are responsible for building the church on the foundation of Jesus Christ."

God's Temple – 1 Corinthians 3:16–17

This section is crucial in Paul's efforts to rectify the Corinthians' misunderstanding of the nature of the church and its leaders.

The "you" Paul refers to in 3:16–17 is plural, indicating that the community of believers (not the individual, in this case) in Corinth is God's Temple. They, corporately, are His people.[75]

The previous metaphor suggested that the church is God's building, but the nature of this "building" is not brick and mortar. It is people, and they constitute God's Temple in which the Holy Spirit abides. The Spirit in relation to the Temple (church) is like atoms in relation to a building – atoms occupy every part of the building, the bricks, the steel, the wood, and the air, etc. Alternatively, it is like the effect of white paint mixed into colour. If you take a batch of black paint and pour white into it, the white will pervade all the black and change its colour to grey. The fact is that the Spirit dwells within every facet of the church, i.e. its people.

Because the church is God's Temple, they had better realize that their problematic views about leadership manifesting itself in splits,

cathen/12575a.htm
[74]Witherington, B. *Conflict and Community,* p. 134.
[75]Turn to 1 Corinthians 6:19. In this particular case, the "you" is singular and refers to the individual believer as the Temple of God.

quarrelling, and jealousy are banishing the Spirit of God from the church, thereby destroying what belongs to God. Beware those who damage the church, because it will invite God's judgment upon them! Scripture states, "It is a dreadful thing to fall into the hands of the living God" (Hebrews 10:31 NIV).

Be a Fool – 1 Corinthians 3:18–23

Paul has been referring to Apollos, Cephas and himself, wisdom and folly, this age, and boasting intermittently since 1:18. The following portion of scripture splits into two sub-sections (3:18–20 and 3:21–23). Both subsections begin with "Let no one," and lead to a preliminary conclusion on these matters.

His argument against their behaviour demonstrates two issues:

- They must guard against deception from what they classify as "wisdom." How were the Corinthians deceiving themselves? What were they thinking? They thought that they were already mature or holistically spiritual, which also meant that they might not see any need for ministry. With this attitude, they were closing the door to all that God could provide them for the task of ministry. Paul states that they must become "fools" to become "wise." To become a fool means to become foolish in the sense that God is foolish, i.e. to take on the values and principles of the Kingdom of God, which in most instances are opposed to the world's way of thinking and behaving. This does not mean that God or His people are foolish. People of the world only perceive them as being foolish.

- He explains why they must not boast in their leaders. He states, "Don't you see, you say 'I belong to Paul,' or 'I belong to Apollos' when you should actually be saying 'Paul belongs to us, and we all belong to Christ.' Stop exalting men because you prove your foolishness and immaturity before God when you do this! We are a community. We are inextricably linked and belong to each other in Christ."

Finally, in 3:23, he reminds the believers that they have great possessions, but only because they belong to Christ. Therefore, they must stop acting as though they are their own masters when they actually belong to Christ.

Questions and Thoughts for Reflection

This portion of text running from 3:5–3:23 is rich with problems still rife within the church today. I find it a tragedy that we cannot learn the lessons we need to and then move on to more important tasks within the Kingdom of God. Consider again some of the major lessons with which this section presents us.

1. I mentioned earlier that in church politics, two significant potential problem areas include the role of the leaders and the role of the followers. On the one hand, leaders can take on an inflated view of themselves and cause serious damage to the church. On the other hand, and this is the problem Paul was facing at Corinth, followers can exalt certain leaders and ministries and demean others, resulting in untold pain and even church splits.

    1.1 Can you think of cases where this has happened in your society? Is it perhaps happening in your church presently? What would Paul say to your congregation members to bring proper perspective to the situation?

    1.2 Which of the problems, viz. the exaltation of, or the demeaning of leaders, do you believe causes the most damage to the church today and why do you believe this?

2. We need to remember that THE CHURCH BELONGS TO GOD!!! Paul even believed that the church is the future bride of Christ. In 2 Corinthians 11.2, he states, "I feel a divine jealousy for you, for I promised you in marriage to one husband,

to present you as a chaste virgin to Christ." Paul sees himself as their (the Corinthian Church) father who has betrothed them to Christ. Betrothal to the Jew represented the first stage of marriage and this happened when the bride was very young. It was taken far more seriously in their culture than in the western culture. In fact, if the betrothed were to have sex with another person, the law interpreted it as adultery, not fornication. This image of the Corinthian churches betrothal to Christ suggests firstly that Paul is charged with the responsibility of safeguarding the future bride (see Deuteronomy 22:13–21) and secondly, that this marriage will be consummated when Christ returns.

2.1 Considering the immense responsibility Paul places upon church leadership, do you think that pastors (in general) lead their local churches appropriately? Explain your thoughts and opinions.

2.2 Discuss the nature of the difference between a pastor/ leader who holds to this verse as opposed to one who has more of an 'ownership' mentality.

3. Paul states that anyone who works for the church (I am not talking about only those who are employed by the church) must take care/ do their very best, because it will be evaluated on the Day of Judgment. Paul talks about their work as surviving that day and moving through to the other side, or being completely consumed by fire. The profound thought here is that we actually have the privilege of being able to use our gifts, talents and love to achieve things that have eternal use/ influence/ benefit. Consider the following.

3.1 Do you work/minister in the church with this mindset, or are you more focused on the here and now? Use your values, priorities[76] and practices as a type of barometer in responding to this question. What about other people you know?

---

[76]You will know your priorities by what you give your time to.

3.2 If your mindset has been more focused on the hear and now, how might the quality or nature of your work for the church change, knowing its potential eternal impact and consequences?

4. Paul states, "The one who plants and the one who waters have a common purpose, and each will receive wages according to the labor of each. For we are God's servants, working together … (3:8–9)." His metaphors of the field, building and temple all point towards the churches communal nature. Another metaphor that could be used to describe the church is that of an orchestra. Few things in life are as beautiful as the sounds produced by a high-class orchestra playing in unison. But, the problem is that most Christians who come from a Western background bring their individualistic mindset into the church, and church cannot work like that. Have you ever heard of an orchestra with musicians who want to play their piece of music and then in accordance with their tempo? I doubt it, because that would not be called an orchestra. Unfortunately, this is what we often encounter in the church – people who are on their own mission – and we still call it the "Church". In your opinion, what could a church do to encourage the formation of community as both a value and priority (*koinonia* of the Spirit – we exist for each other as true family)?

5. Paul mentions that the church is "God's temple." This means that it is, amongst other things, holy and to be treated as precious (remember here that we are talking about the church being the community of believers and not a building). One interesting aspect of temples in ancient times was that they were supposed to reflect the nature of the god who dwelt within. My question is, does your church represent Jesus to the people in your neighbourhood? If you believe that it does, how so? If not, what should change or be added?

Chapter Five
The Servant Apostle

Paul has come to the end of his argument regarding the Corinthians faulty understanding about the gospel, the church and its leaders. However, he has not yet dealt with their accusations against him personally: some at Corinth had openly opposed Paul's teachings and his authority as an Apostle.

It was going to be decidedly difficult for Paul to win them to his side because he faced a dilemma. On the one hand, he had been arguing in favour of their leaders being mere servants, but on the other hand, he had to remind them of his authority. If they did not take him seriously, they would not take his gospel seriously either, and that was a non-negotiable.

This portion of scripture (4:1–21) consists of three subsections. Let us reason through Paul's method of dealing with this delicate issue.

Quit Judging Me – 1 Corinthians 4:1–5

Paul launches his argument by bringing them back to the model of leaders being servants; they must continue to regard Apollos and him as servants. However, there is a shift in metaphors from farming to maintaining a household. This time, stewards carry the responsibility to reveal His divine "mysteries." He uses this new metaphor to indicate to them how foolish it would be for them to judge him. It is true that he and Apollos belong to the Corinthians, but they must understand that they are not first-and-foremost accountable to the Corinthians.

Let us unravel this thought process. Verse 1 has these words, "As those entrusted." These words translate as *oikonomai*, which refers to a person who supervises a large estate. It is a responsible position with charge over others. However, this person is subject to and reports to the master. In relation to the master, he is a servant, but in relation to other servants, he is a master. The main characteristic expected of one of these *oikonomai* was faithfulness (trustworthiness). In 4:3, Paul alludes to the people as being partial to human judgement, while he rejected it.[77] The leaders are indeed servants of the people, but the people were not their masters. Therefore, the people had no right to judge him. Only the master (God) could, and who better to do the job?

Take my example of the hotel again. Let us suppose this time that Paul is the hotel manager and the Christians at Corinth are represented by the door attendant and janitor. Try to imagine a scenario where the janitor or door attendant conducts the hotel manager's performance appraisal, instead of the board of executives or the owner? This just does not happen.

There is an additional lesson in this for us. Paul's attitude is, "leave the past in the past." Entrust the deeds of the past to God; He alone knows their value as well as the secret desires of a person's heart. We should rather focus our efforts on the present, march forward not judging matters before the time (4:5), and always remember that our works are not in vain (15:58).

---

[77]"Not judging" others here refers to making premature judgments or final decisions. It is important to understand that Paul is not saying that nothing should be judged before the appointed time. Rather, he is stating that all judgment in the sense of using *discernment* or *discrimination* is acceptable provided that its fallible and provisional nature before the last judgment is fully recognized. Thiselton, A. *The First Epistle*, p.342.

Learn from your Servants – 1 Corinthians 4:6–13

There are two themes in this portion, their pride, which had made them "puffed up," [(4:6–8 and 10), also see 18, 19; 5:2; 8:1; 13:4)] and Paul's apparent weakness (4:9, 11–13). This section focuses on drawing a contrast between the two. Firstly, in 4:7, Paul poses certain rhetorical questions intended to bring them back to reality. A likely response to them might read: "How can people who have no native endowment other than that which they received from God, be boastful about anything – all they have has been given to them?" Following this, Paul draws up a stark contrast to demonstrate their erroneous assumptions and the true nature of apostleship.

Christians at Corinth (4:8, 10)	The Apostle (4:9–13)
Already you have all you want	For I think that God has exhibited us apostles as last of all, as though sentenced to death
Already you have become rich	We have become a spectacle to the world, to angels and to mortals
Quite apart from us you have become kings	We are fools for the sake of Christ
You are wise in Christ	We are weak
You are strong	We [are held] in disrepute
You are held in honour	We are hungry and thirsty
	We are poorly clothed, beaten and homeless
	We grow weary from the work of our own hands
	When reviled, we bless; when persecuted, we endure; when slandered, we speak kindly
	We have become like the rubbish of the world, the dregs of all things

This must have had quite an impact on the Corinthians' perception of what an apostle ought to be. One can assume that Paul's observation about the way they were behaving was their idea of a model apostle – to them, the apostle was the "head honcho," "the man of God," "God's anointed," and why not? This is how success and status appear in many of our societies. His descriptions of the character traits of a true apostle were the very ideas that they scorned. It is no wonder that they opposed him.

It is worth emphasizing the issue of being "puffed up" a little further, because what underlies it is of great danger to us.

Verse 8 states, "Already you have all you want! Already you have become rich!" The people thought that they had made it, they had arrived, and they had it all! Paul certainly could not have been referring to "money," because although Corinth was rich, very few people in the church were rich, of noble birth or royal. No! These people had an arrogant and misguided view of their level of maturity and spirituality. The phrase "You have all you want" refers to one of the major problems the Corinthian Church suffered from, "*over-realised eschatology.*" I have already addressed this earlier on.

The phrase "you have all you want" translates from the Greek as "satiation." The people thought themselves completely filled by "spiritual" food, a feeling of self-satisfaction. This contrasts with the blessing Jesus pronounced, "Blessed are those who hunger and thirst for righteousness, for they will be filled" (Matthew 5:6). Ironically, the Corinthians were neither hungry nor thirsty. The other words "rich" and "king" denote that these people felt very secure and wanted for nothing spiritually. This is a dangerously deceptive place to be. If the entire Messianic blessing had come, Paul suggests that surely he would also be partaking in it with them. Instead, he feels just the opposite, and he knows that he is following the way of the cross. On the other hand, the Corinthians' approach was much like that of the Stoics, who would say, "I am rich" or "I am a king," which was the ultimate form of self-sufficiency. These churchgoers thought themselves above Paul. They saw him as weak and lacking eloquence, amongst other things. They could not possibly regard him as their leader.

A while back, we dealt with the section where Paul described the gospel as "foolish" and "weak" in the eyes of the world. Why? Well, the world did not possess God's Spirit and was blind to Him. He shows the Corinthians that the gospel only seems foolish and weak, and He only appears to be unimpressive. The way they are thinking is the way the world thinks, which stands in contrast to the way of the cross.

Follow me, Follow Christ – 1 Corinthians 4:14–21

The argument in these first four chapters began in 1 Corinthians 1:10, but is only now completed. At this point, Paul's discussion on leadership reaches its climax.

You will recall that earlier on I mentioned Paul's difficulty in bringing across a dilemma of thought, i.e. that he is both a servant and one who has authority. Thus far, he has spoken a lot about "servanthood" and the lowly position of an apostle. In this last section, he argues for the latter, namely his authority. The question is: how does he do it without undoing all he has done thus far? Firstly, he adopts a new metaphor (father/child) and secondly, he informs them of his intention to visit the church and deal with any outstanding matters. Let us deal with each in turn.

Paul makes use of the father/child relationship to bring to remembrance that he founded the church (3:6, 10). Therefore, because he is the father, he has a right to warn them if they are in error (3:14) or even to discipline them if they do not respond to his correction (3:18–21). Paul is careful not to take this metaphor of father and child too far. His use of the word "father" ("in Christ Jesus I became your father through the gospel" – 4.15) is used in the sense of his "begetting" them. To "beget" something means to become the father of that thing. Imagine that you are the heart surgeon who invented the procedure known as "Coronary Angioplasty."[78] This procedure has revolutionized heart surgery. If other surgeons want to use your technique, they will carefully have to study your theory of praxis; if they use it, you will have "begotten them" or become a father to them in the sense that you converted them over to your way of thinking and acting.

This is what Paul means. He has begotten them in Christ Jesus through the gospel.

The nature of his concern was that they were still living dangerously close to the world. His use of the metaphor took care of the cognitive side of trying to stop this. However, there were certain elements within the church that would require more action on his behalf. Some were making statements along the lines of, "forget Paul. You will never see his face again. He won't dare show up here again!" This brings us to "Paul's promised visit."

He cautions these people, intimating that their assumptions are incorrect. The only one who would prevent him from coming is the Lord. He says that his opponents might be full of fancy words, but do they have power? Paul does have power, divine power that comes from God.

Lastly, he asks the Corinthians to choose how they would prefer him to come to them, with a whip (rebuke) or in gentle love.

Note that the intention behind these stern words is not to break down their sense of worth. He warns them because he loves them. Like a father to the child, he is intimately concerned with their well-being. Remember, they lived in an honour/shame society. As a result, their need for status would have been greater than usual. Paul's motive would have been to give new meaning to the idea of "status," i.e. their status should come from identification with Christ in His suffering and cause. "Paul's concern is that the Corinthians'

---

[78]Coronary angioplasty is a procedure used to open narrow or blocked coronary (heart) arteries. The procedure restores blood flow to the heart muscle. Available [Online] at http://www.nhlbi.nih.gov/health/health-topics/topics/angioplasty/

lifestyle should reflect the having-died-with-Christ experience, which is demonstrated in the lifestyle of authentic apostleship. It is not simply 'do as I say,' but 'do as I do.'"[79]

Questions and Thoughts for Reflection

There are numerous issues dealt with in this portion of text. Here follow some examples.

1. Paul begins chapter 4 by stating, "Think of us in this way, as servants of Christ and stewards of God's mysteries." – this is the role of the pastor or leader. He mentions that the pastor/leader is a "servant of Christ." Note that he does not say "servant of the congregation." There is a huge difference between the two. What would you say are some of those differences? One thought would be that if the scenario were the latter, the pastor/leaders ministry would be determined or led by every whim and of the people. Imagine if Paul had allowed himself to be a "servant of the congregation" there at Corinth, considering all they were doing and saying about him? Words like "crushed", "disillusioned", "mortified" and "ministry abandonment" come to mind. There is no difference today! People can still be extremely harsh and will strive to get their way at virtually any cost.

2. Paul continues in verses 3–4 stating, "But with me it is a very small thing that I should be judged by you or by any human court. I do not even judge myself. I am not aware of anything against myself, but I am not thereby acquitted. It is the Lord who judges me." Pastors and leaders, it is important to see Paul's perspective here. He does not allow himself to be bothered by the judgments of others because he knows that his function is

---

[79]Martin, D. B. *Slavery as Salvation: The Metaphor of Slavery in Pauline Christianity*, pp. 122–23; cf. pp. 50–68 in Thiselton, A. *The First Epistle to Corinthians,* pp. 368, 371.

that of a steward to the church at Corinth. As such, he is accountable to God, not the people. It is God who will judge him for how he takes care of the congregation. I can guarantee you that if you adopt this mindset, the peace of Christ will come upon you and your fears of rejections and need for affirmation will melt away. On the other hand, if you are a member of the congregation, you need to refrain from judging your leader/s and rather pray for them. After all,, as Paul states, "Not many of you should become teachers, my brothers and sisters, for you know that we who teach will be judged with greater strictness" (James 3:1).

3. The Corinthians were "puffed up" about themselves and the leaders they followed. Paul counters though by asking, "What do you have that you did not receive? And if you received it, why do you boast as if it were not a gift?" (4:7) We so seldom implement this in our lives. Our talents and abilities are not self-created, they are a gift from God which we can develop with due diligence in most cases. We need to rise above this immature thinking and realize that all of us have a role/purpose within the kingdom of God. This is made clear in texts like 1 Cor. 12:13–27 and Romans 8:28. If we walk according to his purposes for us, we can be sure that he will supply whatever need he knows is necessary for us to accomplish it.

4. I mentioned earlier that the nature of the Kingdom of God is often paradoxical to the nature of our societies. In this particular text, we see a big difference between what is considered "successful" in secular society and the kingdom of God. In the West, and fast becoming the case with the East as well, there is the idea that success has close ties with achieving high levels of learning, wealth and fame. Because we as Christians live amidst this powerful mindset, we tend to believe this is how it should be with respect to our Christian walks as well. As a friend of mine likes to say, people coming to Christ are often

led to believe that their life as a Christian will be like floating to heaven on an inner spring mattress drinking Coca-Cola. Thus, if things are going badly in our jobs, church, or ministry, we automatically think we have failed or are outside of the will of God. But this assessment could be totally wrong. Consider what Paul mentioned he went through in 4:6–13 and 2 Corinthians 11:23–28 – and he was one of the great Apostles. From now on, be careful not to fall into this trap. You just might be involved in one of God's boot camps.

5. As a revision exercise, try to answer these questions in as much detail as possible:

   5.1 How does the Corinthians' view of wisdom relate to the problems in 1 Corinthians?

   5.2 What three arguments did Paul use to prove that the gospel was not just another manufactured philosophy?

   5.3 Explain the nature of God's wisdom and compare it with the wisdom of the world?

   5.4 Why were the Corinthians' attitudes towards their leaders wrong and what was Paul's solution?

Chapter Six
Incest

How could it be that a case of gross immorality such as incest could be taking place and condoned in the Christian church at Corinth? Could our churches also be allowing similar scandalous events to take place? How is it possible?

The Corinthians' troubles are very relatable to postmodernism. In postmodern culture, we dislike judgment as it provokes a sense of hypocrisy and superiority. Our failure to address sin often leads to immorality in the church. Paul was challenging a spiritual relativism in his day that is quite similar to ours. For them, a further question arose: "How do we engage the freedom of Christ?" Some were using liberty as an excuse for licence.

In 1 Corinthians 5 and 6, Paul takes on the very unpleasant task of dealing with some of the horrid symptoms caused by the problems raised in chapters 1–4. This chapter will demonstrate just how worldly and confused they were. Some of their behaviour was so blatantly wrong that it is hard to imagine how a church could condone it.

Three chapters in the epistle cover these issues. Each deals with a separate area of sin, viz. incest, lawsuits, and sexual immorality. I will introduce each of them using a court-case drama scene.

Let us imagine that you are sitting at the back of a courtroom. You are in the high court of God. He is sitting on His judgement seat with Jesus Christ to His right. To your left is Paul, the prosecutor. Sitting next to you are the informants from Chloe's household. On the opposite side of the courthouse stands the accused, the incestuous man. Behind him, sit a group of believers from the church at Corinth. They are the defence for the accused.

Drama in Court

- *A mighty angel announces:* Court now in session. Would the prosecution please state its case against the accused?

- *Paul:* Father, reports from Chloe's household state that there is sexual immorality among church members of a kind that does not occur even among pagans: A man has his father's wife.

- *Church:* But Paul, we do not feel that there is anything wrong with what he is doing.

- *Paul:* I cannot believe what I am hearing; you sit there all complacent while this is going on!!! Have you gone mad? His actions are appalling! He is guilty of a heinous sin. In the days of Moses, he would have received the death penalty (Lev. 20:11). You should pass judgement on him right here in the presence of God. Then, you should throw him out of the church, back into the domain of Satan.

- *Church:* Paul, what of our new-found freedom in Jesus Christ? This brother has displayed to those in Corinth that the law has no hold on us any longer.

- *Paul:* Have you forgotten that this is sin, and it is going to creep into the minds of the entire church like leaven in a batch of dough? Hurry up! Get rid of this sinner, before you are infected and thrown out with him. You are born again from on high. You should be living truthful and sincere lives now. Jesus did not die so that you could have a free license to sin. I have told you to stay away from sexually immoral people.

- *Church:* You mean we must stay away from all those who are greedy, swindlers or idolaters? Well, in that case we had better leave this world because they are everywhere.

- *Paul:* Actually, yes, stay away from any person who claims to be a Christian and is still a swindler, idolater, or immoral. In fact, you should not even dine with the likes of these. They are despicable! I am ashamed of you! Why did you not deal with this matter long ago? Leave the world to God's judgement. However, you must sort out problems that arise within the church.

This dialogue represents the gist of the situation.

Get that man out of there! – 1 Corinthians 5:1–5

In this section, Paul confronts two different problems: first, the immoral behaviour of the individual; and second, the corporate sin of the community in showing no concern for the individual or what he is doing.

It is worth considering just how severe a sin this was. Paul uses the word "sexual immorality," a term used for a variety of illicit sexual practices at the time. However, in this case, the incestuous relationship was even worse than other sexually immoral practices. In fact, it was so detestable that pagan societies would not tolerate it.[80]

Firstly, these two people were not just close friends that had tragically lapsed into a night of unbridled sexual passion. No, the phrase "has his father's wife" literally meant that they were involved in an ongoing sexual relationship. Secondly, Paul does not call the

---

[80]Apparently, a Roman jurist by the name of Gaius (c. AD 161) decreed that "It is illegal to marry a father's or mother's sister; neither can I marry her who has been quondam (formerly? at one time? ever?) my mother-in-law or stepmother." Muirhead. J. *The Institutes of Gaius and Rules of Ulpian*, pp. 24–25.

offence "adultery." This implies one of two things: either the offender's father had died or the father had divorced his wife. Another possible scenario could have been that the father and his son were living with her simultaneously, but this is highly unlikely.

An even bigger problem than the act itself was the issue of how the church could condone this man's actions. The answer is likely to come from what I raised earlier in chapter 3 – "over-realised eschatology."[81] Thus, they considered themselves free from the law and judgements of men. Secondly, their dualistic mindset led them to believe that their physical bodies were inferior and belonged to the passing age. Therefore, they had adopted the attitude of libertarianism, also mentioned in chapter 3.

If this were the attitude of the church, their reasoning would have been as follows. "Christ has set us free from the law, and we know that our bodies are fading away, therefore, let the brother continue as he is a testimony to the fact that we are really free."

A less extreme explanation for the church's actions comes from the meaning of the word "proud" (5:2). Some translations use words like "puffed up," "up", "inflated," i.e. with pride, self-importance, arrogance, complacency, or self-congratulation. It is possible that this first clause should also take the form of a question: "and can you really show complacency?"[82] All of these words carry the meaning of "to regard as natural." When Paul stated that they were "proud," he might have been referring to their general state of inflation about their freedom – this act is simply reinforcing their new preconceived ideas of what was natural for a Christian.

In 5:1, Paul mentions that the man is acting unbecomingly to his father's wife, but who was his "father's wife"? It is unlikely that the fathers "wife" was this man's biological mother. I find it beyond

---

[81]Some of the Corinthians saw themselves as people of the Spirit, whose present existence was strictly spiritual. They believed that Spirit belonged to the Eschaton, and they were already experiencing the Spirit in full measure. Thus, they were living as if the "age to come" had fully arrived.
[82]Thiselton, A. C. *The First Epistle*, p. 387.

the moral bounds of the Corinthian church to have allowed that to occur. Secondly, if it was his mother, why didn't Paul say, "mother"? A definitive clue to the nature of this person is found in Leviticus 18:7–8. "You shall not uncover the nakedness of your father, which is the nakedness of your mother; she is your mother, you shall not uncover her nakedness. You shall not uncover the nakedness of your father's wife; it is the nakedness of your father. Notice that a distinction is made between "mother" and "father's wife." The term "father's wife" commonly referred to somebody other than one's biological mother, for instance, a stepmother.

Next, I have to wonder whether this woman was part of the church at Corinth. In fact, chances are that she was not a Christian at all. How do we know this? In the first place, Paul does not mention her at all when he suggests the appropriate disciplinary action. Secondly, he only speaks of putting "the man" out of the fellowship.

Thus far, we have focused on the problems and their details, but what was the solution? "Put the man out of the fellowship" seems clear enough. However, the way Paul suggests they go about it and the words he uses are not clear at all.

To begin with, there is an apparent dilemma, which if genuine, suggests that the Bible contradicts itself. The dilemma is: "to judge or not to judge." The following three verses seem to oppose one other on this matter. Chapter 4:5 reads, "Therefore do not pronounce judgment before the time, before the Lord comes, who will bring to light the things now hidden in darkness and will disclose the purposes of the heart. Then each one will receive commendation from God" while 5:3 reads, "For though absent in body, I am present in spirit; and as if present I have already pronounced judgment". See also 5:12 – "For what have I to do with judging those outside? Is it not those who are inside that you are to judge?"

A quick look at the context will solve the dilemma though. The form of judgement referred to in Chapter 5 was an act carried out by the "community" of believers. Only offences causing potential destruction to the church were subject to this type of judgement, for example: idle believers who do not work but disrupt other believers' lives (2 Thessalonians 3:6; 14–15); divisive people (Romans. 6:17, Titus 3:10). In effect, Paul says that to prevent the church from splitting, this type of person should be "excommunicated." The word literally means to "put someone out of communion." The judgement mentioned by Paul in chapter 4 is of a "personal" nature, so we are not comparing apples with apples here. You will recall individual Christians within the church had been criticising Paul and very likely gossiping about him too. This kind of behaviour was in contradiction to the behaviour expected of those within the Kingdom of God.

What can we learn about church discipline from these passages? For one, consider the disciplinary model Jesus taught in Matthew 18:15–18. Firstly, there should be private conversation between the offended and offender. If this does not work, the matter goes before a group of impartial witnesses. If the offender still fails to take heed, the matter escalates to the level of official public confrontation.

With this in mind, Paul outlines the steps for excommunicating a person in 5:4. The words, "when you are assembled in the name of the Lord Jesus," suggest that they must pass judgement (excommunicate) when the entire church is gathered. This was a time when they all assembled to worship. It was at these times that the Spirit of the Lord presenced Himself and would legitimize the authority, decisions and actions of the gathered church. It is important to note that this was a "community" affair. This is the first of three important aspects dealing with the final act of excommunication.

Secondly, 5:5 mentions the words "hand this man over to Satan." These words have been at the centre of much debate over the centuries. There are a number of possible meanings. Some scholars believe that the words refer to an Aramaic idiom meaning, "Let them suffer with their evil devices" or "Let them stew in their own juice." Still others believe that it could mean that Satan can destroy the person's physical body. However, I, together with many scholars, believe it means to have the man put out of the sphere of the Spirit of God, which is God's church, i.e. Satan's sphere of influence. This might not sound harsh by today's standards because we have many churches in close proximity to each. An offender could easily go down the road and join another church. However, there was only one united church at Corinth making it impossible for the offender to continue worshipping in a gathering. Thus, it is unlikely that the man's physical body "being destroyed" is in view here, but rather the "'fleshly' stance of self-sufficiency of which Paul accuses primarily the community but surely also the man … If consigning to Satan means excluding him from the community, this spells the end of self-congratulation about their association with such a [person]; while for the offender himself sudden removal from a platform of adulation to total isolation from the community would have a sobering if not devastating effect."[83]

Thirdly, throughout this disciplinary procedure, Paul has two things in mind, "that the man might be saved on the last day" and the protection of the church's purity. Thus, Paul sees this action as being ultimately redemptive.

It is clear that Satan's power is real, although limited. Otherwise Paul would not have suggested handing the man over to him. In this case, we see Satan's power utilised for good – the ultimate redemption of this man.

There is one last comment I would like to make at this point; reserve the action of "excommunication" for individuals whose sin causes destruction in the church.

How does your church handle situations where one of the leaders has been caught in sin or where there is a member who is being destructive to the church? If you do not know, I encourage you to go and speak to your pastor about it. Chances are that he has not thought much about it either, let alone applied it.

The biggest problem with replicating the effect of Biblical disfellowshipping today lies with the element of ostracism originally

---

[83]Thiselton, A. C. *The First Epistle*, p. 396.

involved. The few churches that do excommunicate the defiantly immoral, usually watch those individuals go down the road, or move to a new town, and join another church that pays little or no attention to the reasons why they left their previous congregation.

Churches even hire pastoral staff dismissed from other ministries for unethical or illegal behaviour without conducting an investigation first. Becoming a church member or full-time worker at a new church should arouse the attention of that church. It is important to find out the reason/s for changing churches. It could well be that the person/s is running away from problems left unaddressed.

Sensitive but frank cooperation and networking between congregations becomes crucial if the original impact of "shunning" is to have any possibility of being reproduced in our transient world. We do this type of thing within business and among companies: can the church accept or tolerate bad leaders any less than a company would?

Virus Alert! – 1 Corinthians 5:6–8

Paul refers to the Jewish practice of purifying their homes and temples of all unleavened bread before the Passover feast (Exodus 12:15).[84] He uses this metaphor to show them the moral purity that

---

[84]One must recall that the theme of Passover was "deliverance", i.e. the commemoration of the Israelites deliverance out of Egypt. However, there was and still is a deliverance they enjoyed at that point in time which came through Jesus. This they were to celebrate and hope for in the future. "Leaven" is not quite the same as yeast. In ancient times, instead of yeast, a piece of dough was held over from one week's baking to the next [to achieve the same results as yeast]. By then it was fermenting, and so could cause fermentation in the new lot of dough, causing it to rise in the heat. This was a useful practice, but not hygienic, since dirt and disease could be passed on from week to week. Mitton. C. L. The *Gospel according to St. Mark*, p. 61. During Passover, Jews refrain from eating khametz, which is anything that contains barley, wheat, rye, oats, and spelt (a kind of wheat), and is cooked within 18 minutes after coming in contact with water. No

God expects from them, now that they are God's house and temple in Corinth. There are two reasons given in the illustration for putting the brother out of the community of believers. I have covered both, but to recap:

- If these believers did not remove the incestuous man, the effects of his behaviour would spread and influence the nature and identity of the whole community.[85]

- Paul exhorts the believers to "become what they are" thereby acting appropriately to the way God already considered them in Christ (Romans 6–8). God did not free the Corinthians so that they could sin. Rather, they must stop all forms of "malice" and "wickedness."

---

leavening is allowed. This signifies the fact that the Hebrews had no time to let their bread rise as they made a hurried escape from Egypt. Do you know what was just described? LEAVEN! Not yeast – yeast is a small microscopic plant and an important part of the substance, but it is the mixture – the mixture of sticky, pleasant smelling "stuff" that as a whole is the substance you add to knead into dough to make the dough rise. This is leaven. Yaweh said "no leaven is to be found in your houses", not "no YEAST"! We can't get the yeast out of our homes, but we certainly can get the mixture out (if we had it) which we don't really use these days – the small quantity of the starter material, the "chunk of leaven" … Continuing with the topic of yeast, the exact nature of yeast – where it comes from and what it is – has remained a mystery for thousands of years. It took, in fact, the invention of the microscope in the early 17th Century to finally allow scientists to see what single-celled yeast looked like and they soon realized that yeast cells multiplied in a sugar solution, but they did not realize in that era that the cells were actually alive. A 19th Century food chemist thought it was decomposition of the cells that caused fermentation, and refused to accept the theory that yeast was a living organism. Available online at http://www.therefinersfire.org/yeast_or_leaven.htm

[85]"In Jewish traditions, partly through an interpretative reading of Zeph 1:12, the purging of the house of all leaven was understood as a symbol of moral purification, with candles to look into corners. By metaphor, the church is to clean out what defiles its identity and purity." Thiselton. A. C. *The First Epistle*, p. 404.

Keep the church clean – 1 Corinthians 5:9–13

Paul clarifies an apparent misunderstanding that occurred when the church read his previous letter (5:9).[86] He points out that he did not suggest that they stop their associations with non-believers involved in sin – "In that case you would have to leave the world." Of course, this does not mean that they were free to associate in every instance with those of the world (6:12–20; 10:14–22). When dealing with those outside of the church, the objective must be their salvation.

However, what occurred within the domain of the church was an entirely different matter. The rule of thumb was thus strict discipline exercised within the church, but freedom of association with the outsider.

In 5:12–13, the matter of "judgment" comes to the fore. It is God's prerogative to judge those outside the church, presumably at the end of the age. However, it is part of church discipline to judge those within the church when issues arise. As mentioned earlier, this "judging" does not refer to individuals passing judgments on one another, but rather the community as a whole dealing with sin in their midst. A vital task of the community is to ensure ongoing purity within the church and therefore, excising corrupt members.

In summary, the Corinthians were failing to understand the dynamic balance between God's love and His holiness. They believed that because God loved them, He had set them free from the obligation to lead holy lives. This is a contradiction in terms. It is because God loves us that He calls us to holy living. A righteous lifestyle is not the entrance requirement for Heaven: holiness is the best way to live and the only way to be like Jesus. God's purpose is that we should be conformed to the image and likeness of Jesus.

Did you perhaps note the lack of reference to Satan as being the cause of this heinous sin? Paul did not believe that Satan was directly

---

[86]It was through the Latin commentator Ambrosiaster that the theory emerged that held that Paul wrote a letter prior to the 1 Corinthians we know today.

to blame. He also did not encourage the believers to correct the situation through "binding" or "defeating strongmen." Rather, he amended their thinking and called on them to respond by correcting their actions and life-styles. Notice how Paul positions Satan. He does not present him as the "lord of the earth" but, in a sense, as a servant of Almighty God. He gives the local church the authority to "hand the man over to Satan" and declares that the object of the exercise is the guilty party's salvation.

The way Paul deals with the issue of Church discipline arises from the underlying subtle, yet important distinction between the Church and the individual believers. Salvation is individualistic, but it is into the community of the church. Church discipline should correct the believer's doctrine and practice, as well as preserve the integrity and unity of the church community. It is not just for redemption sakes.[87]

Questions and Thoughts for Reflection

Consider the following personal and practical application at both the church and individual level.

1. The contemporary church often turns Paul's overall contrast between the association with non-Christian sinners and non-association with unrepentant Christian sinners on its head. We promote all kinds of separatism via Christian alternatives to secular institutions and activities. We can comfortably spend most of our lives in Christian schools, church meetings, Christian sporting leagues, church-based aerobics, in short, in fellowship groups for virtually any significant human activity, so that we need not interact in any intimate way at all with non-Christians! Indeed, most adults who convert to Christianity are so overwhelmed with new acquaintances that, within a few years, they have no atheist or agnostic friends to evangelise.

---

[87]Peppler, C.L. in Howitt. Q. J. *1 Corinthians*. Unpublished textbook for the South African Theological Seminary, p. 107.

In this regard: How many non-Christians do you know with whom you could have a meaningful conversation about Jesus Christ, the gospel and the Kingdom of God? If you cannot think of someone, there is something wrong! How can you adjust your lifestyle to gain more exposure to non-Christians?

2. Then, ours is an age where even church leaders commit sexual sin or defraud their congregations, at times with virtual impunity. Moreover, if a period of discipline and restoration is established, they may refuse to agree to their church's terms. In still other cases, such a period seems woefully inadequate to demonstrate a genuine and lasting change of heart and behaviour. Some Christian leaders even endorse a philosophy of restoring fallen leaders to a ministry as soon as possible in the name of grace and forgiveness! However, forgiveness and restoration to fellowship do not automatically carry with them the privilege of pastoring or leading a congregation. The criteria for overseers and deacons in 1 Timothy 3:1–13, including marital faithfulness and wholesome family life, are best understood as attributes that currently characterize one's life, and have done so over a long enough period of time that they may be assumed to be enduring character traits (note, especially 3:10). Consider the following questions in light of the above:

    2.1 How do you react to a Christian involved in on-going patterns of sin? Is your response or lack thereof determined by a Biblical model or your own fears of rejection or confrontation? I once read a book entitled, "When People are BIG and God is small" by Welch. Who would you rather offend, God or a person? Your head will say God, but what will your heart and actions dictate?

    2.2 Are you perhaps involved in on-going patterns of sin? Be careful, we are experts at trying to justify our actions or classify them into "grey areas" on the sin scale. If you are trapped in sin, stop right now and take action against it.

Confess your sin to a trustworthy other and ask them to help you get out of it. Do whatever it takes to free yourself, because until then, your relationship with God is in serious jeopardy. Note that there is no sin in your life that God does not already know about. Jesus states, "For nothing is hidden that will not be disclosed, nor is anything secret that will not become known and come to light." (Luke 8:17) There is also no temptation in existence that you cannot escape from. Consider Paul's words in (10:13 NIV). "No temptation has overtaken you except what is common to mankind. And God is faithful; he will not let you be tempted beyond what you can bear. But when you are tempted, he will also provide a way out so that you can endure it." God is waiting for you to come to your senses and, by a decision of your will, ask forgiveness and stop doing it!

Chapter Seven
Lawsuits

A large church hires a music teacher. Unbeknown to the church, this person happens to be homosexual. Sometime down the line, the church finds out about this and dismisses the person. After three years of legal proceedings, the court rules in favour of the teacher ordering the church to pay the equivalent of $10,000 for the dismissal. The implication of the judgment was that "a gay music teacher's right to equality and dignity should receive precedence over the churches right to religious freedom."[88] This event took place in South Africa and became quite a high-profile case. My questions are: generally speaking, what effect does an event such as this have upon the image of the church and what effect does this have upon the gay person's faith? In the specific case cited, there were negative implications all around!

Situations like this where our natural instinct would be to get revenge, confront us every day. However, obviously this is not how Jesus would behave. This section will shed light on the behaviour expected of a Christian who is done an injustice. It is also significant for those who offend or hurt others and serves to educate church leadership on the role it should adopt in these unpleasant situations.

Before I begin, please note that Paul will return to the issue of sexual immorality in 6:12 and Chapter 7. However, when ending

---

[88]The Citizen News Paper: Published 2008/08/20, p. 9.

off on the topic of the <u>incestuous man, he addressed the issue of</u> "<u>judgment</u>" (5:12), an area he wants firstly to clarify.

The second court case – more imagination required.

More Drama in Court

The characters in this court case include:

God (judge)

Paul (prosecutor)

Julius[89] (accuser)

Publius (accused)

Chloe's household (informant)

There is no defence

- *A mighty angel* stands up. "Order in the court. Would the prosecution, please present its case against the accused."

- *Paul:* May it please the court? Apparently, two brothers in the church are at loggerheads with one another. One is accusing the other of cheating. It has been most disappointing for me to find out that the church sat back and did not try to resolve this matter. Instead, they watched as one brother took the other brother to public court thereby making a mockery of themselves and the church in the presence of unbelievers – shame on you church of Corinth!

- *Church:* Objection! We are not professional judges with skill in passing judgements. Besides, we are a church, and we do not wish to concern ourselves with ungodly activities like stealing.

- *Paul:* Church, you are obviously not aware of the position you hold? One day you will judge the world and angels, yet now you cannot even judge such a simple matter. Moreover, Julius (accuser), do you not know that you have lost the

---

[89]Julius and Publius are fictious characters.

opportunity of winning a more important battle because you initiated this lawsuit against Publius (accused)?

- *Julius:* How can that be? I caught Publius trying to steal from me. He is not a righteous man and deserves punishment.

- *Paul:* Do you recall the non-retaliation ethic adopted by our Lord Jesus? Remember, you are not of this world any longer! Therefore, stop responding like those in the world. Rather be cheated and wronged than discredit the church. Lastly, I wish to address Publius. Publius, you are no longer the person you used to be. The Lord Jesus has redeemed you; stop this cheating immediately and reconcile yourself to Julius. Do not be foolish; God has said that anyone who does these and other despicable things will not inherit the Kingdom of God! You are treading on very dangerous ground!

Do not air your dirty laundry – 1 Corinthians 6:1–6

The specific sin Paul deals with involves the practice of suing fellow Christians in secular courts. He shows his disapproval of both parties involved in the lawsuit by firstly suggesting that Christians should be able to settle disputes within the church environment (6:1–6) and second, he infers that they should not be having disputes in the first place (6:7).

He uses strong words like "Dare, he," "Do you not know," "Are you not competent" and "I say this to shame you." Paul takes this line of argument because he believes that by their actions of going to a public court, they are insulting God and the church; one must remember the church is an eschatological congregation that should be living conditioned by the future, and the principles embodied in the Kingdom of God.

Paul begins his argument using their eschatological existence as a reason for the way in which he wants them to behave. The idea here is that a different mindset should result in a different lifestyle.

Chapter 6:1 makes a simple point. Cases that arise within the Christian community should stay in the Christian community. The word "dispute" (*pragma echon*) translated in context means "lawsuit." This term is of interest to us because it indicates that this civil dispute was most likely to do with property (*pragma*). In that situation, it is almost certain that the disputants were part of the upper class in the church since the poor could not afford property.

In addition, the words "ungodly" and "saints" serve to strike a contrast between those who are non-Christians (Roman courts) and Christians (saints). I do not believe that he writes this section to tackle the issue of pagan courts being unjust. He actually would have had special reason to show gratitude towards Gallio's impartiality in Acts (18:12–17). In certain respects, the Romans showed great tolerance for the customs and practices of those nations that had come under their government during the conquest. They allowed nations and groups to apply their laws and regulations in handling disputes between their people. The issue with the ungodly is that it is improper for them to be judging those within the Christian community because they do not posses the mind of Christ or the eschatological outlook on the Christian life.

Paul's next statement is quite astonishing. He comes to the Corinthians and suggests that the saints are to judge the world: they will assist in the final judgement. This idea ties in with (Daniel 7:22; Matthew 19:28 and Revelation 20:4). You will recall that Paul was using their eschatological existence as justification for the way they should act. Verse 2 is the first sign of his doing so. How are the saints to judge the world?

Logic would have us believe that Paul was saying to the Christians, "if you believe that you are going to participate in judging the great issues of this world, why do you feel unqualified to judge matters of little concern?" However, this still does not answer the meaning of "sitting as judges" over the world. Consider these alternative explanations. The most likely explanation is that the saints will not "judge" in the sense of demanding an account. It is more likely that "judging" spoken of here refers to a form of passive judgment like that of the Queen of Sheba, who condemned those who witnessed and listened to Jesus without believing (Matthew 12:42), i.e. Christians will judge the world of unbelievers because of their faith and obedience as a community of believers (the bride of Christ).

Consider my John Deere illustration again. Management has come to the realization that manufacturing team A is performing poorly, but they would have never known this unless team B had done an outstanding job. In a sense, we can say that team B have passively judged team A in that they have demonstrated the correct methods of assembling the combine harvesters.

With the same thought in mind, Paul also mentions that Christians "shall judge angels." Angels are by nature the highest class of created being that we are aware of. However, they too will stand in the court on the last day. The use of the word "angels" here likely refers to angels that have rebelled against God.[90] Nevertheless, as was the case with "judging the world," judgment should be understood as associated with the bride who bears the resurrected Christ's image and shares His destiny and likeness. It is more likely that judgment comes to the angels through the existence of the church (bride) on that great day than the actions of individual Christians.

The point of 6:4 is that a society consisting of potential judges in God's court demeans itself when it appears before even a Roman proconsul who, whatever his legal training, experience and natural virtue, stands outside the realm of the people of God.[91] Aside from

---

[90]See Matthew 25:41, "the fire prepared for the devil and his angels"; 2 Corinthians 11:15, "disguised as an angel of light and 2 Corinthians 12:7, "an angel of Satan" and Jude 6, "angels who did not keep their own position".

[91]"Secular judges are unqualified (of no account) because they judge by different standards. Would it not be out of character for people who had rejected the standards of the world to seek a judgement from a person who used those very standards they had just discarded? The church was an alternative community to the world – In, but not of the world – therefore it is the 'Elders' who should judge cases in the community of faith." Barrett.

the text, the criteria of the law used in the process of judging will also be very different. For example, certain countries accept same-sex marriages for various reasons, a major one of them being "freedom of rights." If one were to appear before such a judge for getting married to the same sex, the outcome would be very different from a judge applying the scriptural law.

This portion is actually quite ironic, given what we read in Chapters 1–4. You will recall that one of the main problems they suffered from was the belief that they were wise. In this section, Paul challenges them to demonstrate their wisdom by coming forward to help settle the disputes. "Surely there must be one wise enough among you," Paul asks?

Love your enemy – 1 Corinthians 6:7–8

"In fact, to have lawsuits at all with one another is already a defeat for you" (6:7). Because these lawsuits existed in the church, it proved that the Christians had abandoned the first principle Jesus taught regarding relationships between two fellow believers, viz. brotherly love. If each person, out of an attitude of love, displayed concern for the rights of another, these conflicts would never happen. This brings to mind what James said to the believers in the Jewish Diaspora.

> Those conflicts and disputes among you, where do they come from? Do they not come from your cravings that are at war within you? You want something and do not have it; so, you commit murder. And you covet something and cannot obtain it; so you engage in disputes and conflicts. You do not have, because you do not ask. You ask and do not receive, because you ask wrongly, in order to spend what you get on your pleasures (James 4:1–3).

Paul reminds the accuser that Jesus had taught that we are to love

The First Epistle, p. 137.

our enemies (Matthew 5:43–48). Paul himself wrote that we are not to repay anyone evil for evil (Romans 12:17). Rather, you should feed your enemy if he is hungry (Romans 12:20) with the intention of overcoming evil with good (Romans 12:21). Therefore, he says to the accused that by his action of suing, he has gone against the ways prescribed by Jesus. No matter whether he wins or loses the case, he has ultimately lost. Is Paul's expectation fair? It is no more "fair" than the divine grace which has eclipsed justice in Christ's giving himself and His "rights" up on the cross, indicating in turn God's surrender of His "right" to pronounce a negative judgment on humankind without transcending justice in costly, generous mercy.[92]

Behaving like an Alien – 1 Corinthians 6:9–11

Finally, he turns his attention to the man who had actually done the cheating by asking him a rhetorical question: "Do you not know that wrongdoers will not inherit the Kingdom of God?" (6:9) Paul shows the brother that by his cheating, he has acted in a spirit of dishonesty, greed and selfishness. These characteristics have no place in the Kingdom of God, but come from the world. Whether or not the believer gains some temporal advantage is immaterial, because he too has lost by moving away from the example set by Christ. It is unlikely that Paul is referring here to the standards set for salvation or entry into the Kingdom of God. Rather, these are vices repeated by Christians, which are alien to anything within the Kingdom of God.

The specific vices that Paul highlights as contrary to the nature of the kingdom include *fornicators, idolaters, adulterers, male prostitutes, sodomites, thieves, the greedy, drunkards, revilers,* and *robbers.* Most of these words clearly convey the nature of the sin in contradiction with the kingdom, but I want to briefly expound on two for clarity sakes, viz. 'sodomites' and 'male prostitutes'. The term used for 'sodomites' is *arsenokoitai, w*here *ársēn* refers to 'male' and

---

[92]Thiselton. A. C. *The First Epistle*, p. 437.

koites, 'sleep'. Within this Corinthian context, Paul is thus referring to "a man who lies in bed with another male, a homosexual."[93] Then, the term used for 'male prostitute', *malakoi, means* "effeminate or a person who allows himself to be sexually abused contrary to nature."[94] Nida and Louw have it as "the passive male partner in homosexual intercourse—'homosexual.'"[95]

In conclusion, the idea here is that if the person wishes to call him or herself a Christian, they must vigorously oppose anything that comes against the nature and character of the Kingdom of God. In Paul's mind, ultimately both the accused and the accuser have failed to act as saints washed, sanctified and justified in the name of the Lord Jesus Christ.

---

[93]Zodhiates, S. *The Complete Word Study Dictionary: New Testament* (electronic ed.). To better grasp Paul's meaning of *arsenokoitai* , reference should be made to what Paul finds offensive about same-sex intercourse in Romans 1:24–27." Gagnon, R.A.J. *The Bible and Homosexual Practice: An Overview of Some Issues.* Available [Online] at http://www.robgagnon.net/ZenitInterview.htm Robert Gagnon is the author of *The Bible and Homosexual Practice: Texts and Hermeneutics* (Abingdon, 2001). "What is clear from the connection between 1 Cor 6:9 and Romans 1:26–29 and their OT backgrounds is Paul's endorsement of the view that idolatry, i.e., placing human autonomy to construct one's values above covenant commitments to God, leads to a collapse of moral values in a kind of domino effect ... 1 Corinthians strongly affirms that *the body* and its practices occupies a place of paramount importance for those who are united with Christ." Thiselton. A. C. *The First Epistle*, p. 452.
[94]Ibid.
[95]Louw, J. P., & Nida, E. A. *Greek-English lexicon of the New Testament: Based on semantic domains.* Vol. 1, p. 771.

Questions and Thoughts for Reflection

How do we apply Paul's instructions to the way we live? Throughout this section, Paul defends his arguments by referring to the way Jesus had acted.

One of the biggest challenges we face in this regard is learning to view and react to our experiences from God's perspective. It is a perspective that, in most cases, goes against the grain of worldly behaviour. For instance, consider how difficult it is when wronged to first deal with our own attitudes towards people who have offended us through God's filter.

Instead of lashing out in an attempt to defend our best interests, we are to do good to the person who offends us. This type of behaviour is "worlds apart." Another challenge is to decide how to behave once you have reconciled such a matter with yourself. Being sufficiently sure of yourself to take righteous assertive action takes courage and is again, usually quite different from worldly approaches. So often, the natural reaction is the "back stab or gossip approach." Everybody but the offender gets to hear about the issue. If we would only listen to Jesus in the first place, we could prevent this.

Both steps mentioned above are extremely difficult to practice unless we adopt the mind of Christ.

1. Have you been harmed or caused harm? You now know Paul's thoughts and solutions to the matter. Try to solve the issue/s that have led to relational breakdown where possible! You are a child of God and should behave as one who is part of the Kingdom of God.

2. Jesus taught us in Matthew 18 how to deal with these awkward situations. How are you going to ensure that you apply this process in the future, because it is usually not in our nature to do so? We have to stand up and fight against the fears of rejection and confrontation. I suggest you apply the following rule of thumb. Whenever you speak about somebody, always speak as though s/he is standing next to you.

3.   1 Corinthians 6:9–11 touches on a very sensitive topic, that being sexual relations between the same sex. Go and read Romans 1:26–29, Leviticus 18:22; 20:13 and Gagnon's article entitled, *The Bible and Homosexual Practice: An Overview of Some Issues available [Online]* at http://www.robgagnon.net/ZenitInterview.htm in conjunction with this portion of text in Corinthians. What is your position on Homosexuality and Lesbianism? How do you feel about same sex marriage and gay preachers? How do you think the church should treat gay people?

Chapter Eight
Frequenting Prostitutes

Sex is God's plan for procreation and pleasure. However, humankind has turned it into something secretive, naughty, dark and dingy. "In today's society, intimacy means practically nothing more than having sex. Couples meet and immediately begin enjoying sexual intercourse, committing either to immoral hedonism or to the idea that sex will serve as the foundation for love. This goes a long way toward explaining why so many marriages, built on no stronger foundation than sexual thrills, end in divorce soon after the flames of passion have died down"[96] or become less of a priority.

In this portion of the book, we will examine the philosophies behind the Corinthian's relational behaviour contributing to their sexual immorality. We will also gauge from Paul what the true nature of sexual intercourse is and how this relates to us as Christians.

This is the last of three examples that deal with the issue of the body and its union with Christ. Since the section forms part of the previous two, I will make use of the court case example one final time.

---

[96]Phillips. R. D. Phillips. S. L. Holding Hands, *Holding Hearts: Recovering a Biblical View of Christian Dating*, p. 143.

Yet more Drama in Court

The characters I have chosen to fit the positions in the court case drama include:

God (the judge)
Paul (the prosecutor)
The sexual offenders (the accused)
Chloe's household (the witnesses)
Men in the church

- Once again, *a mighty angel* enters the courtroom. He stands at the bench banging his hammer saying, "Order in the court! Bailiff, would you please escort that rowdy man out of my courtroom before he upsets the judge? Thank you! I call on the prosecution to present their case against the accused.

- *Paul:* Your honour, witnesses from Chloe's people have informed me that a number of the church members in Corinth are committing sexual immorality. The evidence suggests that these men have been obtaining sexual favours from the temple prostitutes at the Aphrodite temple on the Accrocorinth.

- *Men in the Church*: Your honour, all of this is true. If this were a sin, we would be guilty. However, as we understand it, Christians are free from the duties of the law. Therefore, everything is permissible for us.

- *Paul:* You may be right that you are free from the chains of the law and that many things are permissible for you. However, not everything is beneficial. In fact, you can still do yourself a great deal of harm by allowing yourself to be mastered by anything; including this idea of 'freedom'.

- *Men in the Church:* In our eyes sex is simply a natural function of the body to be fulfilled when one feels the urge, and since we don't get much at home, the urge is strong. For example, the stomach goes together with food. Well, in the same light, sex goes hand in hand with the body.

- *Paul:* I can see that you have misunderstood the plan of God. God raised Jesus in His entirety, body and spirit. Have you forgotten the eternal destination of your bodies? Your bodies are valuable, created by God for good and purchased by the sacrifice of Jesus. You should realise that your bodies are the dwelling place of the Holy Spirit. You are a temple! Don't you remember what God said in Genesis 2:24 about becoming one with whomever you engage sexually? Now, if you are the temple of God, how can you take God's temple and unite it with another false temple? I feel sick to my stomach at the thought of this!

I will approach this section differently by taking you on an exploratory journey through the problem, after which we will examine Paul's response.

You will recall from the narrative at the beginning of this book that the Aphrodite temple, which was home to many prostitutes, was very popular in Corinth. Sexual activity in the city was so common that the word "*korinthiazō*," a phrase coined and used by most that knew what went on in Corinth, denoted the practice of prostitution. It is not difficult to imagine how sexual activity of this magnitude could find its way into the church.

To identify the root cause behind these acts, we must focus our attention on two useful clues given in 1 Corinthians 6.12 and 13. Paul mentions these strange sentences, "All things are lawful for me" and "Food is meant for the stomach and the stomach for food, and God will destroy both one and the other." The most sensible suggestion offered by commentators is that these were quotations made by those in the church at Corinth. They explain why men, and the church, practiced or condoned visiting with prostitutes.

The statement "All things are lawful for me" and "Food is meant for the stomach and the stomach for food, and God will destroy both one and the other" (6:12–13) came from a certain "libertine spirited" group in the church who suffered from eschatological indigestion and dualism. You will remember that these erroneous beliefs led in one of two directions, a life of asceticism, or a life of licentiousness. We are dealing here with the latter consequence. In Chapter 7 of the epistle, we will deal with some of the former, which played themselves out among the women.

With these attitudes buzzing about in the church, Paul had a very sensitive pastoral problem on his hands.

1 Corinthians 6:12–20 splits into sections based on Paul's response to two heretical beliefs adopted by the Corinthians:

- Libertinism (6:12); and
- Dualism (6:13–20).

The Stench of Dualistic Libertarianism – 1 Corinthians 6.12–20

We begin with the problem of libertarianism. "All things are lawful for me, but not all things are beneficial. All things are lawful for me, but I will not be dominated by anything" (6:12).

There were an unknown number of people within the church at Corinth who had come to Paul justifying their behaviour based upon their newfound freedom. Paul, on the other hand, proposes a different angle to their freedom. This idea relates to what will promote the identity of the church as a community, which stands for Jesus Christ. Paul's first qualification "but not all things are beneficial" addresses their misunderstanding as follows: he agrees that certain things are not expressly forbidden to Christians, but the results of these things should rule them out of a Christian's lifestyle.[97] According to Paul, Christians should live their lives in a spirit of

---

[97]"The traditional translation 'all things are lawful' [permissible] does not mean all things are sanctioned by the law, but denotes that which the law no longer prohibits, i.e. it is part of the Corinthian theology that Christian believers have been granted liberty from the law." Thiselton. A. C. *The First Epistle,* p. 463.

love, doing unto others what they would like done unto themselves (Luke 6:31). Additionally, Paul makes a second qualification: "but I will not be dominated by anything." By stating this, one could say, "All things are in my power, but I shall not be overpowered by anything." Paul knew that if people focused their attentions upon something so intently, that they would actually become a slave to that thing. Let us take freedom, for example. If you make it your life's goal to display your freedom as much as possible, you will become a slave in your efforts to demonstrate your freedom. Paul knew that as Christians, they were actually slaves of Christ (7:22, Romans 1:1). Therefore, how could these Christians enslave themselves to expressing freedom when they were already slaves of another? A slave does not have "rights."

As mentioned above, the next statement, "Food is meant for the stomach and the stomach for food, and God will destroy both one and the other" could be yet another popular saying among the Corinthians, stemming from dualism. Those suffering from a dose of libertarianism were bargaining on the fact that because food raised no moral issues (food laws preventing certain foods from being taken in had fallen away), that sexual acts were also morally irrelevant. On the one side, Paul agreed with the notion that food and the stomach would pass away, but not so for the future resurrected body. This still seems to confuse since the body and stomach are both material. Thiselton helps to clarify this:

> The particular uses of "stomach or belly" in first-century Greek literature helps us to understand their three-stage logic: (1) "belly" often means the digestive system rather than a location within the body, i.e. to say "food is for digestion" means that it soon passes through and is disposed of; (2) in this respect it stands as [an example] … for all things physical and transient; (3) hence, supposedly, on this line of reasoning, God is concerned only with those aspects of selfhood which will survive disintegration at death, i.e. what pertains to the spirit …

> Paul interposes a fundamental qualification, however, which interrupts the logic. The body is not to be equated with the digestive system, because physical life will be absorbed and transformed in the resurrection of the body in such a way that continuity as well as change characterizes the relation between the present body, i.e. present life in its totality, and the resurrection body, i.e. the transformation of the whole human self as part of the raised physical existence in Christ ... Hence the body is not for sexual immorality ... but for the Lord.[98]

Some in the church were using a natural law argument (sexual organs are for sex), just as Paul had often used natural law arguments to prove certain aspects of God's law, such as condemnation of homosexuality and rebellion (Romans 1). Paul had to counter this argument by a higher-order consideration. A modern application of their argument is "feel-good-ethics". It makes me feel good, so why can't I do it? One of the former Miss South Africa's sought to justify her divorce spiritually on this basis. She said that God wanted her to be happy, and her marriage was making her unhappy. Therefore, for her to divorce would be right. In both these situations, immediate gratification and natural expression are curbed by higher-order considerations, or as we more commonly refer to it, our moral faculties.

The relevance of this statement in Paul's argument against those in the church with this belief is that sexual intercourse is an act of the whole person, not just a "transient material thing." That the Father raised the Son from the dead, and did not simply cause his soul to persist through bodily dissolution, shows something of the dignity of the body. Bodily life enshrines permanent values. The resurrection forbids us to take the body lightly. Its destiny is not destruction, but resurrection. If God's original intention were that the body should simply dissolve away into nothing, why would He concern Himself with resurrecting the "body"? Why would Jesus

---

[98]Thiselton. A. C. The First Epistle, p. 463.

make a point of showing his disciples that he was not a ghost, but instead had numerous traits associated with a tangible body (Luke 24:39 and John 20:27). Paul will go into issues surrounding "body" and "resurrection" in detail in Chapter 15.

In 6:15–17, it becomes evident that the Corinthians had misunderstood the nature of sexual intercourse. However, it is important to bear in mind what the real issue is here. Paul is not dealing with just any extramarital sex, but rather sex with a prostitute who worships pagan gods. Please note that this should not detract from the sinful nature of extramarital sex. Many of the same arguments Paul uses to condemn sex with prostitutes can be used to show the sin of practising any form of extramarital sex.

Paul had recognised a horrible profanation of the body that contradicted its use in Christ. It was even worse if the prostitute involved so happened to practice this abominable behaviour in worship to a pagan god, because that would mean that there was a deity involved as well. If a Christian went and had sex with a temple prostitute, he was engaging in an act recognised as worship to a foreign deity. This is idolatry.

Paul says, "I cannot believe you can even think like this, you should know better." A Christian is one body (member), which when placed with all the other Christians forms part of the body of Christ. You all belong to Christ and should be available for service.

Thus far, he has established that those who have been "saved" at Corinth are all members of Christ's body. Furthermore, he refers to the parts that make up a human body, which all belong to Christ as well. Therefore, by implication, to play the harlot means to connect your spirit (there is a connection between your spirit and body) with Satan.[99] You should remember that when you have sex with

---

[99]The issue of becoming "united" with another frequently means to glue, to cement together by a method of bonding. Fee comments that "Paul is probably referring to the work of the Spirit, whereby through the 'one Spirit' the believer's 'spirit' has been joined indissolubly with Christ ..." Fee, G. D. *First Epistle*, p. 260.

someone, you become one body with him or her (Genesis 2:24). According to Hamilton,

> The verb "cling" often designates the maintenance of the covenant relationship (Deuteronomy 4:4; 10–20; 11:22; 13:5; and 30:20). Thus, to leave father and mother and cling to one's wife means to sever one's loyalty and commence another. Now covenantly joined with his wife, the man and his spouse become one flesh … A man by himself is not one flesh … and neither is a woman.[100]

Therefore, in light of all the above, it is impossible for a person one in spirit with the Lord to become one in body with someone in Satan's domain. Imagine that the body represents the human being at a place of decision. If you choose to join yourself to a harlot, you have made a wrong turn. You will have become fleshly, which in this instance means contaminated, that is, you have fallen away from God and are living as if humans were the most important being in the universe. If, on the other hand, you choose to turn in the Lord's direction, you will move into the realm of the Spirit, (living as if God is the most important being in the universe), not the flesh. However, you cannot go in both directions at the same time, i.e. you cannot have the mindset where you think that you belong to Jesus, but can use part of what you have given to Him (body) for ungodly purposes.

Here is a short illustration. If you take red paint and mix it with blue, you come out with a beautiful rich purple. Let us imagine that this purple represents your infused life with Christ. If you then take purple paint and mix it with yellow, it comes out brown. In the same sense, if you take your infused life with Christ and mix it with an idol-worshipping prostitute, you turn out differently from the way you should be.

In 6:18, Paul states that they must "Shun fornication,"

---

[100]Hamilton, V.P. *The Book of Genesis Chapters 1–17*, p. 181.

alternatively translated as "keep away from." The point he tries to make is, do not just avoid it, turn and run from it. I am reminded here of Joseph's reaction to Potiphar's wife when she made advances toward him (Genesis 39:12). Treat sexual sin like a deadly plague, because that is what it is. Verse 18, "Every sin that a person commits is outside the body; but the fornicator sins against the body itself" is difficult to comprehend. If you think of it, sins like gluttony, drunkenness, self-mutilation and suicide are also a form of destruction against the body. What could Paul have meant by this statement?

- Firstly, there are those who believe that (6:18a) is yet another quotation from the Corinthians. Those who believe this cite Paul's dependence on the Old Testament concern about prostitution (Proverbs 6:25–33). Whereas a thief only "forfeits his goods," a sexual offender "destroys himself" (Proverbs 6:32).[101]

- Secondly, others believe that "every sin … is committed outside the body" is a Corinthian slogan. Apparently, those at Corinth were insisting that the offender's personality is not affected.[102]

- Thirdly, the bulk of commentators see a qualitative difference in Paul's thinking, either in terms of (a) the destructiveness of this sin's effects; or (b) in terms of its intrinsic sinfulness; or (c) its damaging effects, specifically upon the self.

MacArthur writes, "No sin that a person commits has more built-in pitfalls, problems and destructiveness than sexual sin. It has broken more marriages, shattered more homes, caused more heartache and disease, and destroyed more lives than alcohol and drugs combined. It causes lying, stealing, cheating and killing, as well as bitterness, hatred, slander, gossip and unforgiveness."[103]

---

[101]Conzelmann. H. *1 Cointhians*, p. 112.
[102]Moule. C. F. D. *An Idiom Book of NT Greek*, pp. 196–197.
[103]MacArthur. J. *First Corinthians: NT Commentary*, p. 147.

Taking this last point further; a number of scholars have proposed that "whereas drunkenness, greed, and even suicide use means external to the body for the purpose of self-gratification or desire, only sexual acts are entirely and exclusively initiated by, and carried out by means of, the body."[104] Finally, it has been suggested the main point of this verse is that, since the Christian is now part of Christ, sexual immorality actually tears the body away from the body of Christ in both individual and corporate terms."[105] (Once again, consider my paint-mixing example.)

In 6:19–20, Paul rounds off his argument on sexual immorality. You might have noticed that 6:19 has some similarity with 3:16 in that both speak of the theology of the "Temple of God." However, you will recall that 3:16 refers to the community of believers as being the "Temple" whereas 6:19 refers to the individual believer as being the Temple. Paul explains here that Christians are full of the Spirit of God. They themselves are God's temples in the same way their churches are His temples. Therefore, "the body has been sanctified; let it fulfil its proper end, that of bringing glory to God whose temple it is."[106]

Then in 6:20, he returns to the position of their argument on freedom. They, together with many of us, make the mistake of thinking that Christ bought their freedom, when in fact Christ bought them.[107] Therefore, there has been a change of ownership from "slave to sin" to "slave of Christ."[108] The believer belongs to God (we are slaves). As a result,

> God accepts responsibility for clothing, housing, feeding, and generally caring for the slave who is the master's concern. For

---

[104]Meyer, H. A. W. *Critical and Exegetical Handbook to the Epistles to the Corinthians*. Vol. p. 185.
[105]Bailey. K. E. *Paul's Theological Foundation for Human Sexuality*, p. 37.
[106]Swete. H. B. *The Holy Spirit in the NT*, p. 181.
[107]Deissmann, A. D. *Light from the Ancient East*, pp. 319–332.
[108]Martin, D. B. *Slavery as Salvation: The Metaphor of Slavery in Pauline Christianity*, p.63.

a slave to have someone else to take responsibility for these things is a freedom. On the other side, the owner who has bought the slave with a price expects, and has a right (cf. 6:12) to expect allegiance, faithfulness, loyalty, obedience, and, on the basis of character and provision hitherto, also wholeheart-ed trust.[109]

I think you would agree that having God as your master is a pretty tremendous deal, since he knows exactly what you need. Therefore, do not use your body for sexual immorality, but rather, whatever you do, act in a manner that brings glory to God.

Before moving on to some discussion questions, I would like to touch on "extra-marital sex." In the writings of Paul, James and the Book of Hebrews, extramarital sex is contrary to the character of those who form part of the Kingdom of God.

Those who practice this are excluded (6:9; Ephesians 5:5). Idolatry and licentiousness are linked together in (6:9). The desert generation offers a warning (10:8, 11). Unnatural sex in the pagan world is an outworking of divine judgment (Romans 1:18ff.). The church must keep itself pure from such vices (5:1ff.). Individual sexual immorality ultimately pollutes the entire church (2 Corinthians 12:19ff.). Licentiousness is a work of the flesh; the Spirit opposes it. Marriage is a gift from God for protection against it (7:2). However, even though sexual immorality is sinful, there is forgiveness available (6:11).[110]

Questions and Thoughts for Reflection

This portion of text addresses some of the most prolific areas of sin within Christianity today, viz. sexual sin. I will raise a few issues on sexual sin below:

---

[109]Thiselton. A. C. *The First Epistle*, p. 477.

[110]Kittel, G., Friedrich, G., & Bromiley, G. W. *Theological dictionary of the NT*, p. 920.

1. Desensitisation against dodgy practices is rampant within society. Consider how many Christians, and even pastors and priests positions on issues like homosexuality, same-sex marriage, gay clergy, adultery and living together before marriage, have changed over the last 20 years. What steps would you imagine could be set in place to prevent this slow and subtle process of desensitization from taking place in your church and individual life?

2. Let's imagine that there is such a thing as a "desensitisation inquisition" for a moment. The following questions are posed to every Christian, including you – and you cannot hide! How would you fair?

    2.1 What are you reading? Are there books, magazines or files on your bookshelves or on your hard drives that you would prefer others not know of? The same applies to what you read or look at on the Internet.

    2.2 What movies do you watch on TV? Consider this – how much adultery did you watch last week? How many murders? How many did you watch with your children?

3. Taking point 2 a step further: besides prostitution, what other manifestations of libertinism can you see playing out in society today? Remember, libertinism has its roots in dualism, which degrades the body. This degradation can play itself out in bodily exploitation. What about pornography? Casual sex, or as some call it, "one night stands"?

4. Let us explore the practice of "extramarital sex." This is such a common practice that Christians have turned a blind eye and actually climbed on the bandwagon themselves. It has become a "grey area," or even a "white area." So, what are your beliefs about the practices of fornication or prostitution? Be honest with yourself? Are you perhaps involved in fornication (and I am not here thinking only of the "one night stands", but the

more subtle version where two people are involved in a long term sexual relationship)? Do you know somebody else who is committing this sin? What are you going to do about it? Do not be fooled. Most societies are shouting that this is perfectly in order, but life within the Kingdom of God only makes provision for sex within the safe confines of marriage. Remember what Paul said, "Do you not know that your body is a temple of the Holy Spirit"?

5. The last section in this Chapter speaks about forgiveness for this sin. However, there is no sense in even contemplating forgiveness if you are not prepared to repent. Remember that repentance involves turning your back on the practice. If you want to have sex, then follow God's provision for sex within marriage.

In closing, what would you say are some of the modern excuses people use to justify sin, and in particular, sexual sin?

Chapter Nine
Marriage

Family and Civilization

In Charles Swindoll's book, *The Quest for Character,* he notes that,

> sociologist and historian Carle Zimmerman, in his 1947 book *Family and Civilization,* recorded his keen observations as he compared the disintegration of various cultures with the parallel decline of family life in those cultures. Eight specific patterns of domestic behavior typified the downward spiral of each culture Zimmerman studied: marriage loses its sacredness and is frequently broken by divorce; traditional meaning of the marriage ceremony is lost; feminist movements abound; there is increased public disrespect for parents and authority in general; an acceleration of juvenile delinquency; promiscuity and rebellion occurs; there is refusal of people with traditional marriages to accept family responsibilities; a growing desire for, and acceptance of, adultery is evident; there is increasing interest in, and spread of, sexual perversions and sex-related crimes.[111]

Like many other sections within the Epistle to the Corinthians, this

---

[111]Levy. R. *Confident Living*, November 1987, p. 34.

portion is relevant for today. It deals with marriage, celibacy, divorce, and virgins.

Chapter 7 is fraught with difficult passages that cause much misinterpretation and application. We will address these problem texts and highlight some of the unfortunate misinterpretations later. For now, let us explore this Chapter from a wide angle.

What were the Corinthians on about? Crudely translated, Paul was likely hearing things like: "Stop having sex!" "Don't get married – your spirituality depends on it!"

Why would they say such things? Read carefully and you will see that this Chapter corrects the idea that refraining from sex equated to "greater spirituality" (an ascetic attitude). They were advocating chastity within marriage (7:1) and placing pressure on virgins to remain single (7:28), thinking marriage somehow sinful.

The keys to understanding this Chapter require an appreciation of the problems mentioned in 7:1 and 28. We will deal with the arguments in 7:1–24 first and those in 7:25–40 later.

The Problems

A number of the English Translations (CEV, GNT, LB, and NIV) interpret 7:1 as relating to marriage, i.e. "It is good for a man not to marry" (NIV). Then, 7:2 states that the reason why marriage might occur is to prevent immorality. Surely, this cannot be the motive to get married. It becomes even more confusing if you read on. Paul begins to discuss issues involving the married. The only manner of sorting this out is to accept that there is an error of translation within these versions. This phrase, "It is good for a man not to marry" is actually a translation of the Greek phrase, *haptesthai gynnaikos* which literally means, "To touch a woman." Proof of this is found in numerous manuscripts such as Aristotle, Plato, Josephus, Plutarch, Marcus Aurelius and the Septuagint (see Genesis 20:6 and Proverbs 6:29). Every case indicates that this phrase is a euphemism for "to have sexual intercourse." Today, we would use our own euphemism like "making love" or "sleeping together." The point is that nowhere in the ancient world does this phrase mean, "to get married."

The second problem has to do with who said these words. Surely, this statement could not have originated with Paul. This would have flown in the face of God's creation and command to "be fruitful and multiply" (Genesis 1:28). Furthermore, Paul clearly says that married couples must not deprive one another of sexual intercourse, except by mutual consent (7:5). Why would he say this if he had just said that it is good for a man not to have sexual intercourse with his wife? The only sensible answer is that he did not say this. He was quoting those who had mentioned the phrase within the community of the church.

You have to admit that it is a strange thing to say, no matter who said it. Therefore, why would they say it? The best explanation is their dualistic influence and desire for "spiritual elitism" (see Chapter 3). There were two manifestations of their eschatological error, libertarianism and asceticism. We discussed libertarianism earlier [people indulged themselves in immorality because they perceived the body as of no value, or evil, compared to the spirit (6:12–20)]. However, here is a case for ascetic behaviour. There were some in the Church, probably the women, who sought to realize their "spirituality" by depriving themselves of sexual intimacy, and if they could not achieve this within their marriage, they wanted to get a divorce.

Paul's advice – "remain as you are"

Paul turns to the specific subject on which the Corinthians had written to him, the first of which is marriage. In this passage, Paul makes every concession to their point of view. He agrees that celibacy is "good" and he points to some of its advantages. However, he regards marriage as normal. Celibacy requires a special gift from God, and Paul is aware of the stresses involved in living the Christian life in Corinth, what with its constant pressures from the low standards of pagan sexual morality, and what he calls "the present crisis" (7:26).

He prefers celibacy, but his support of that state is very moderate. He does not command a celibate life for all who can't sustain it, nor does he say that celibacy is morally superior to marriage. He regards marriage as the norm, but recognises that there are some to whom God has given a special gift to remain single.

It is interesting to note that throughout 7:1–40, the same advice of "remaining in the situation in which you find yourself" is given. For example: to the married, stay married and come together regularly (7:2–7); to the unmarried or widow, rather stay as you are, i.e. do not look for a marriage partner (7:8–9); believers who think they should get a divorce must not do so (7:10–11); to mixed believer/non-believer marriages, make every effort to stay married (7:12–16); to the virgins, try to remain single (7:25–38); and last, to the married women and widow: if you are married, you are bound until death; it is better for the widow to remain single (7:39–40).[112]

Like Jesus in Matthew 19, Paul offers the same test to determine the presence of the gift of singleness. The test is not "are you spiritual enough?" or "do you want to score brownie points with God?" The test is simply "are you able?" In other words, "are you tempted to lust after or desire sexually the opposite sex?" If yes, well then you most likely do not have the gift of celibacy. This understanding can help many singles struggling with guilt about a calling to singleness or not, although of course, nothing prevents them from praying for it if they wish.

Vows of celibacy have filtered down through history in, among other things, the Roman Catholic Church, but from time to time evangelical circles exalt singleness as well. Sometimes well-meaning, though usually fearful singles, try to assume a "gift" of celibacy as though to gain some form of "heightened spirituality" with God. However, Paul's advocacy of singleness in this Chapter is pragmatic. Indeed, today we often find that singles struggle more spiritually than their married counterparts do.

---

[112]Fee, G. D. *First Epistle*, p. 268.

Married folk – 1 Corinthians 7:2–7

The Corinthian women believed that they could "spiritualise" their lives through asceticism and this meant denying their partners their marital rights. This had resulted in a significant rise in sexual immorality, i.e. the men were seeking intimacy elsewhere (prostitutes).

Verse 2 is often misinterpreted. "To have a wife" is taken to mean, "to take a wife," to serve as a prophylactic against, in this case, prostitution. The problem with this reading is twofold. Firstly, at no time did "to have a wife" mean, "to take a wife" and also, the idea of a wife "taking for herself a husband" was out of the question in that culture. Secondly, as I have already mentioned, getting married for prophylactic motives is hardly "Christlike." A far more likely meaning of "to have a wife" comes from biblical Greek where the implication is either to "have sexually" (Exodus 2:1; Deuteronomy 28:30; Isaiah 13:16), or to be in an ongoing sexual relationship within the bounds of marriage.[113]

In 7:3–5, Paul offers the solution to their problem. He declares: "the wife does not have exclusive rights over her own body, but there is the husband (also to consider); similarly, the husband does not have exclusive rights over his body, but there is the wife (to consider)?[114] He affirms that married couples should remain sexually intimate. Each person in the marriage relationship has rights, and each owes it to the other to respect these rights. Paul stresses two things here: he places the sexes on an equal footing (he emphasised this in a male-dominated society) and the indispensability of sexual intercourse within marriage. Paul does not agree with a view of marriage that leaves the sexual act in the hands of the male, or sees sex as defiling. He also disagrees with abstention being a normal practice within marriage. His reference to the previous words being a concession and not a command related to abstaining for the sake of prayer.

---

[113]Fee, G. D. *First Epistle*, p. 278.
[114]Thiselton. A. C. *The First Epistle*, p. 505.

If you are married, do you agree with Paul's argument? Do you see the critical need for sexual fulfilment within marriage? Do you realise that you have a responsibility to meet the sexual needs of your partner? Do you often make excuses for not having sex? Do you try your best to satisfy your partner? Lastly, but *most* important, is sex between you and your spouse an act of giving or taking?

Singles

Let us move on to the singles. There are two errors concerning singleness: that singleness is a holier state than marriage, and that to be single is an unmitigated evil.

In 7:7, Paul shows his preference that "all men were as I am." The Chapter makes it clear that Paul is single. However, it is possible that he was married at some point in the past. Jewish men were expected to get married and have children.[115] Paul had had a vote on the Sanhedrin (Acts 26:10) of which membership would have required him to be married at that time. He realises that celibacy is a gift from God and that each person has different types of gifts manifesting in and through their lives. Thus, he makes it clear that both marriage and celibacy are gifts. It is important that no one try to live in a condition that does not complement their gifting.

Scripture suggests that for the person who is single and in the will of God, there is the possibility of higher fulfilment in his her relationship with God (Chapter 7).[116] Christ also taught that some people have the ability to remain single for the sake of God's Kingdom (Matthew 19:10–12). If a person does not have this gift or if circumstances impose singleness, one should ask in faith for the ability to live happily and productively in that God ordained state.

---

[115]No man may abstain from keeping the law "be fruitful and multiply", unless he already has children: according to the School of Shammai, two sons; according to the School of Hillel, a son and a daughter, "for it is written, Male and Female created he them" (Mishnah Yebamoth 6.6).
[116]That is, more exclusive and wholehearted relationship with the Lord and the potential of more unencumbered ministry for the Lord.

However, how is a person able to tell if he/she has the gift of celibacy? I have already answered this previously, but in this case we go a step further. This time, the person is trying to discern this while already involved in a relationship. Incidentally, this question raises yet another common misinterpretation, this time that marriage merely serves as a prophylactic (7:9). These misinterpretations have come from different translations of phrases in 7:9 in the Greek text, which are read to mean, "if they cannot exercise self-control" (RSV, NJB) and "to be aflame with passion" (NRSV); "burn with passion" (NIV); or "burn" (AV/KJV).

The problem with all of these translations is that they make marriage out to be some form of escape mechanism or protection against sin for those who cannot control their sex drives. If this were the case, one could easily jump to the conclusion that Paul identified two classes of Christian, those who were weak and had to get married, and those who were "holier" and could remain celibate. This sort of interpretation seriously misconstrues the context.

How should we understand 7:9? It is likely that his comments concern couples that are deeply in love with one another and who cannot think of anything else related to the Kingdom and the gospel because of unsatisfied desires. An alternative translation of this text would be "if they do not have power over their passions, i.e. to devote themselves to more fundamental Kingdom priorities ..."[117]

This idea of marriage being "second best" was probably a combination of confusion about Paul's teaching and the philosophy of dualism, which degrades the body and its passions. This error is identifiable in history when one considers laws instituted by the Roman Catholic Church that priests should remain celibate. However, the Bible clearly teaches that marriage is God's normal plan for his children (Genesis 2:18; Proverbs 18:22; 1 Timothy 3:2; 4:1–3; 5:14; Hebrews 13:4). The idea that there is anything unclean or polluted in sexual relations in the marriage relationship is wrong.

---

[117]Thiselton. A. C. *The First Epistle*, p. 518.

Widows – 1 Corinthians 7:7–8

Having laid down the general principles mentioned in 7:1–7, Paul goes on to deal with specific classes. He begins with the unmarried, and the widows. The "unmarried" refers to all those (male and female) not bound by the marriage tie. The "widows" receive special mention, possibly because of their vulnerability and temptation to remarry.

Those advocating asceticism were most likely suggesting that the widows should remain single and not remarry. Paul agrees with them, but infers that this depends on whether that person has the gift of celibacy. If they do not have this gift, they will not have power over their passions. Therefore, it will be as if they were married.

Believers who are married – 1 Corinthians 7:10–11

"Not I but the Lord" is a phrase that denotes a command specifically given by Jesus. In Matthew 19:4–6, Jesus reminds the Pharisees that God's original intent was that marriage be a lifelong union, a covenant relationship. When a couple unites in marriage, they become "one flesh," (this aligns divorce with the violence of something like mutilation, amputation, or dismemberment), a "linked pair, partnered for the needs, responsibilities, and eventualities of life."[118] Jesus answers their next question on Moses permitting divorce by reminding them that it is clearly not God's will for marriages to be dissolved, and most certainly not for the sake of remarriage to another. However, God knew that sinful human beings would at times so distort a relationship He intended to be good that it would become destructive and harmful.

Another alternative for Gods allowing divorce could have come as an effort to protect and ensure some form of decency within the proceedings of getting a divorce. It is possible that, if God had not intervened, the people would have run riot in this area. It follows

---

[118]Idid.

then that Jesus saw divorce and remarriage as falling short of God's ideal. His thoughts were contra to those held at Corinth. They thought of divorce as a means to attaining greater holiness. He saw the practice as sinful (Mark 10:1–12, Matthew 5:31–32 and its parallel, Luke 16:18.).

With this in mind, Paul's directive was that the wife should remain as she is and not seek divorce, but if she has disobeyed this command, then she must remain as she is[119] and not commit adultery by marrying another. If she finds her unmarried predicament unsatisfactory, she must reconcile with her husband. The same injunction applies to husbands as well.

This brings us to Jesus' comments on Divorce and Adultery in Matthew 5:32.

Ancient Jewish (Greek and Roman) culture almost universally permitted remarriage on the grounds of marital unfaithfulness. In other cases, divorce causes adultery.

In Matthew 5.32, Jesus says: "But I say to you that anyone who divorces his wife, except on the ground of unchastity, causes her to commit adultery, and whoever marries a divorced woman commits adultery." Of particular interest are the words, "causes her to commit adultery," and this by his divorcing her.

The problem with his "causing her to commit adultery" is that the woman might not remarry. Thus, how can she be an adulteress? The intended meaning of "adultery," as used in this passage, explains the confusion.

Jesus is partially quoting from Deuteronomy 24:1. At that time and in the prophets, adultery commonly referred to the "breaking of the covenant with God" (Jeremiah 5:7; Ezekiel 16:32; Hosea

---

[119]In ancient times, marriage and childbirth were very different to our experience of it today. Firstly, marriages took place when the girl was around thirteen years of age. Secondly, marriages seldom lasted more than a decade or two since a woman's life expectancy was between twenty and thirty years. This might be because 1/5 of mothers died giving birth. Pantel, P. S. *A History of Women in the West*, pp. 302–10.

2:4). Thus, it is possible that the "adultery" referred to in Matthew 5.32 is a metaphorical adultery representing infidelity to the life-long covenant nature of marriage, i.e. by divorcing her, the divorce itself creates adultery. In this sense, adultery carries the meaning of "breach of faith." In many languages, the word for adultery and "breach of faith" are the same. For example, in Afrikaans, a language closely associated with Dutch, the word for adultery is "trou-breuk" (literally translated "marriage break").

The fact that this "causing to commit adultery" only applies in the absence of marital unfaithfulness now also makes sense from the opposite position of the woman having been unfaithful. This is because she has already committed the physical act of adultery, and as such has undermined one of the most fundamental elements of a marriage—sexual exclusivity. Therefore, the man would not be causing her to commit adultery; she would have done so already. However, what then do we make of the second "and whoever marries a divorced woman commits adultery" (5:32b)?

Nolland suggests that the translation should rather read, "a woman who has gained a divorce," thus suggesting a woman who has engineered a divorce by provoking her husband.[120] In this case, where divorce is heartless, Jesus goes on to rebuke the man who intends to marry a woman who is prepared to abandon her covenant marriage like this.

Many other passages deal with the marriage/divorce debate, but an in-depth study of them is beyond the scope of this book (Mark 10:1–12 and Luke 19:1–12).

Christians married to unbelievers – 1 Corinthians 7:12–16

It is likely that some of the Christians at Corinth genuinely believed that to remain in a marriage with a pagan would defile them, hence the desire to divorce. Paul commences with the words "I not the Lord" and "rest." The former does not imply that his instruction

---

[120]Nolland, J. NIGTC. *The Gospel of Matthew*, p. 246.

should be taken lightly (lacking authority), or that they were contrary to those taught by Jesus, because he has the Spirit of the Lord (7:40), i.e. he is inspired by the Holy Spirit. Rather, it means that the Lord did not issue specific instructions about mixed marriages. The "rest" in this context refers to couples that married before one of them became a Christian in marriage.

According to Paul, divorce in this type of relationship hinges on the attitude of the pagan partner; if the unbelieving partner is willing (*syneudokei* "agrees with") to continue the marriage, then the believer should not seek a divorce.

Paul explains that believers are "saints"; they are "set apart" (sanctified) for God; the basic idea being sanctification to God, not moral uprightness. It does not require being a Christian to do the latter. This implies that being a "set apart" believer in no way diminishes by remaining married to a non-Christian. In fact, Paul believes the situation to be quite the contrary. The good in the Christian side of the marriage prevails against the evil on the pagan's side; hence, his statement that the unbelieving husband is sanctified by his wife. It is a scriptural principle: the blessing that flows from fellowship with God extends to others (Genesis 15:18; 17:7; 18:26), i.e. in this case, the unbelieving husband or wife is more likely to turn to Christ while in a family with a Christian present. This principle includes children. However, his comment "otherwise your children would be unclean, but as it is, they are holy" is obscure.

The way Paul speaks in the second half makes me think that he used this issue of children as final evidence in his argument. It is almost as if this issue was self-evident to the Corinthians judging by the way he reasons – "By the way, you know your unbelieving partner is sanctified in the relationship because your children are holy." In other words, "if your children are sanctified, which you already know to be true, so is your unbelieving spouse." However, what was it that was evident to them and not to us? Fee suggests that the usage of "holiness," mentioned here, is similar to Paul's metaphor in Romans 11:16:

If the part of the dough offered as first fruits is holy, then the whole batch is holy; and if the root is holy, then the branches are holy. The "consecration" of the part, in the sense of "setting it apart for God," "sanctifies" the whole. Israel is not yet converted, but because the "first fruits" and "root" were "holy," that is, because Israel was originally thus "sanctified" unto God, the Israel of Paul's day, though still in unbelief, was nonetheless "holy" in this special sense. Precisely, because they belonged to God in this special sense, Paul hoped for their eventually coming to faith.[121]

In the current case, if the Corinthians believed that their children became "holy" for the reasons mentioned above, and we know they did, then the same logic applied to their spouse's holiness. The spouse experienced a believing partner who offered input and a lifestyle different from the typical society of unbelievers. At the very least, this difference would require the non-believer to sit up and pay attention.

The case becomes different if the unbeliever is unwilling to continue in the marriage. Paul says that if the unbeliever wishes to end the marriage, the believing partner is free to do so, (they are not bound or "enslaved" to try and fight to maintain the marriage, especially in the case where the unbeliever is causing great distress within the marriage) for the sake of peace.

---

[121]Fee, G. D. *First Epistle*, p. 301. "Irenaeus notes that Paul's treatise on the mystery and generosity of God's unstoppable electing grace focuses on the derivative holiness of Gentiles from Israel's elected, privileged status as the people of God. Similarly, the 'union' with the holy makes an inclusive extension of the holy. Irenaeus thereby treats 1 Corinthians 7:14 in the context of (i) the OT (Abraham, Moses, Rahab, Hosea, the call of 'a people who are not'); (ii) the electing, generous grace of God; (iii) cross references with Paul's thought in Romans 9–11; and (iv) the efficacy of 'union' instantiated most fundamentally in union with Christ. Thiselton. A. C. *The First Epistle*, p. 531. Therefore, imagine that the parent is Israel and the children are Gentiles grafted into the tree.

A number of hermeneutical errors have arisen from these verses. Many have used 7:14 to suggest that babies/young children are Christians until they are old enough to decide for or against Christ, as well as to justify infant baptism. The problem is that the verse does not imply this, but merely suggests a stronger opportunity of "influencing" the other members of the family to a potential life in Christ. The fact that Paul allows a believer freedom to accept a divorce in the name of "peace" does not mean that he is also permitting remarriage. Remember that he is talking to those who want to divorce to prevent defilement, these people have no intention of re-marrying. It would be erroneous to use a passage not addressing the issue of remarriage to add weight to the argument in favour thereof.

These are serious issues with significant ramifications. Solving them would require a number of other texts. One would have to look at a much larger body of scripture in search of clearer answers to them.

I'll say it again, "Remain as you are" – 1 Corinthians 7:17–24

This section serves as a bridge between 7:1–16 and 7:25–40. It offers a general method of looking at the four situations dealt with in 7:1–16.

The issue at hand is the Corinthians concern over a change in status; they wish to serve God correctly because of coming to Christ. They are of the opinion that to do this, they need to alter their life circumstances.

However, Paul mentions on three occasions that a person should not seek a change of position because they have been saved (he is not addressing people involved in an obvious sinful lifestyle requiring repentance). God had called them as they are and in their current circumstances. The main point is that they should not seek change for the sake of spiritual significance.

Verses 18–19 contain two examples, viz. "circumcision" and "slavery."

There were Jews and Gentiles in the Corinthian church. The Jews saw the uncircumcised as outside the covenant of God, whereas the Gentiles considered circumcision a matter of scorn, the mark of a despised people. Paul explains to both groups that circumcision is irrelevant to their status.

Then there were those who were slaves.[122] The slave in Christ had entered a glorious new freedom from sin as a child of God. This divine freedom was more important than the outward circumstances of his or her life. Thus, the slave saw him/herself as the Lord's freed person, even though on the outside, s/he was still subject to slavery. On the other hand, those who considered themselves free were bought with a price; their life was no longer theirs. Again, the point is that outward circumstances are irrelevant to their status. "A Christian does not have to seek 'the right situation' in order to enjoy Christian freedom or to serve God's call effectively."[123]

Many Christians struggle because they feel that they need to change their jobs or go into full time ministry at the point of salvation. However, look at Paul's point in this section. One can serve God in a variety of places. It is not necessary to leave one's station in life simply because you convert to Jesus Christ.

Virgins – 1 Corinthians 7:25–38

Thus far, Paul has offered advice to the married, unmarried (7:2–7) or widowed (7:8–9), those thinking of divorcing (7:10–11), believers married to unbelievers (7:12–16) and those who seek to move up in life, i.e. the slave who wishes to be free (7:17–24). Now he addresses the virgins. The first challenge is to determine who these "virgins" were. Some of the theories are that they were:

- Engaged couples, women, in particular;[124]

[122]There were many "lower class" types in the church, thus making his example of slavery apt (1:26).
[123]Thiselton. A. C. *The First Epistle*, p. 545.
[124]Elliott. J. K., *Paul's Teaching on Marriage in 1 Corinthians: Some Problems*

- A virgin male;[125]
- Couples involved in "spiritual marriages," i.e. marriages with no sexual intercourse;[126]
- Virgin daughters given in marriage by their fathers;
- Unmarried men and women engaged to be married; and
- Young widows and widowers previously married once.[127]

In my opinion, number five is the most plausible. The ascetic spiritually elite were likely pressing home the idea of celibacy in the name of being "holy." This was making the couples doubtful about getting married.[128]

Our next problem involves answering the question, "what were the Corinthian Christians saying that required correction?" Something like this, "It is well for a man not to touch a woman" (7:1).

Given their view of sex and the body, surely they would have been saying that it is better for the couple to refrain from marriage. Their reasoning might have been that it is more difficult to abstain from sexual relations if one is married.

This section is different to the others. Firstly, it appears that Paul is offering advice here and not a specific authoritative teaching. Even so, it is important. Secondly, Paul does not quote the Corinthians position as he did elsewhere, most likely because he agreed with them – do not get married; albeit for reasons contrary to theirs! However, this "contrary reason" is where he must face yet another sticky situation. On the one hand, he agreed with their sentiments, but on the other, he did not want to come across as supporting a dualistic mindset.

Considered, pp. 219–225.

[125]Bound, J. F. *Who Are the "Virgins" discussed in 1 Corinthians* 7:25–38, p. 85.

[126]Hurd, J. C. *Origins of 1 Corinthians*, pp. 176–180.

[127]Ford, J. M. *Levirate Marriage in St Paul*, p. 362.

[128]It is also possible that this group consisted of couples "spiritually married" who were interested in having sexual relations. Thiselton. A. C. *The First Epistle*, p 568.

His advice is based on three important considerations; the "present crisis" (7:26), that "time is short" (7:29), and "devotion to the Lord" (7:35).

Firstly, it is because of "the impending (present) crisis." It is not clear what this "crisis" was. Some believe that it referred to eschatological events, i.e. the thought that immanent tribulation awaited them because the Second Coming of Christ was near. Others believe that these words referred to some persecution or famine they were about to face. Chances are that these terms did carry an eschatological overtone. However, they did not refer to Paul's expecting the Second Coming of Christ immediately.[129] Although we cannot be sure what to make of this text, we can be certain that Christians who seek to remain faithful to the gospel will incur times of persecution and suffering, including loss of possessions, homes and friends. It is most likely that Paul's advice to "remain single" was intended to spare families from these difficulties.[130]

Secondly, because the "time is short." The word "time" (kairos) here refers to the quality of a particular time and not time as chronological duration. It also refers to a "point of time that has a special place in the execution of God's plan of salvation"[131] i.e. a golden opportunity, for example, Paul's vision of a man summoning him to come to Macedonia to help them (Acts 16.9). What this means for us is that our lives and activities must be held loosely to allow for eschatological realities.

In 7:35–38, he reverts to discussing marriage and singleness. He qualifies his statement pointing to the advantages of celibacy by

---

[129]I do not agree with the notion that Paul believed the Second Coming was about to occur for the reason that he was writing under the influence of the Holy Spirit. Would the Spirit allow such confusion? Paul, "regularly used end-of-the-world language metaphorically to refer to that which they well knew was not the end of the world". Caird, G. B. *Language and Imagery*, p. 256.

[130]Luther. M. *Works*, pp. 28:49.

[131]Cullmann, O. *Christ and Time,* p. 39.

making it clear that marriage is a blessing. There is no sin if the virgin gets married (7:36).[132] There has been a lot of debate about whether Paul is speaking to a father about his virgin daughter or speaking to an engaged couple. Most modern translations, NRSV, REB, NIV, NJB, NASB and most scholars believe it to be the latter.

In 7:37, Paul again stresses his preference. However, if the desire is for marriage, it is of critical importance that the couple make the decision without influence. The person/s must make the decision from conviction, free from the influence of others. He stipulates four conditions pointing to freedom of decision:

- The person has concluded by him or herself that this is the right course of action;

- There are no constraints imposed by other people's beliefs, expectations, and pressures;[133]

- He has control, (*exousia*) "authority," that is the right to give effect to his own decision. Slaves, for example, would not have had this right; and

- He has reached his decision independently through personal conviction, to respect her virginity.

Paul concludes that a person who marries does well, but if they remain single, it is better (baring in mind the circumstances – 7:38).

Finally, the focus reverts to widows.

Widows who want to marry – 1 Corinthians 7:39–40

They too are free to remarry. However, as is the case with virgins, they would do better to remain single. His one non-negotiable instruction on remarriage is that they get married to another Chris-

---

[132]This is obvious to Paul. Thus, it is likely that he is repeating something the Corinthians had been suggesting, i.e. marriage is sinful.

[133]Bruce, F. F. *1 and 2 Corinthians*, p. 76.

tian.[134] The words "only in the Lord" imply this. The mere thought of trying to live every day with someone who cannot share your dreams and beliefs is foolishness in Paul's eyes.

What! No divorce and remarriage?

This is a very sensitive topic touched on previously. Should you wish to study this issue in more depth, you will need to include other important biblical texts, such as Genesis 1:27, 2:24; Deuteronomy 22:13–21, 24:1–4; Malachi 2:16; Matthew 19:3, 9; Mark 10:2–9 and Luke 16:18.

I can do no better than to agree with Kaiser in his comment on Mark 10:11–12. "Legislation has to make provision for the hardness of men's hearts, but Jesus showed a more excellent way than the way of legislation and supplies the power to change the human heart and make his ideal a practical possibility."[135]

Questions and Thoughts for Reflection

1. Paul's major lesson to the church at Corinth was "to remain as you are". In their case, it was to do with relational matters. Those who were becoming Christians or seeking deeper spirituality wanted to change something significant about their lives to achieve it. This is something that happens quite commonly today, particularly with people who are newly reborn, and in the context of their present "careers". (Make no mistake, the

---

[134]Note that the text in 2 Corinthians 6:14 referring to being "[unequally] yoked together with unbelievers" is not addressing the topic of marriage and should not be used, first and foremost, to justify steering clear of marrying an unbeliever. Paul here is providing a general rule of not becoming involved in the cultic lifestyle of the city. The concern here is to prevent the Christians from compromising the integrity of the gospel and their faith. For a passage supporting the notion of steering clear from marrying an unbeliever, see (7.39).
[135]Kaiser, W. C. *Hard sayings of the Bible*, p. 431.

problem still manifests itself in relational contexts as well.) The problem manifests when the reborn Christian feels that they should go into full time ministry or become a missionary in order to serve Jesus. While this might be an authentic change brought on by a "calling" in a tiny percentage of cases, most of the time it stems from incorrect thinking. Let me illustrate this. Imagine a chocolate cake sliced into pieces. This cake and its pieces represent the way many Christians live their lives today. There is a piece for the job, another for family, entertainment, children, sleep, quite time, church and so on. The problem is that one should not live Christian life like this i.e. in a fragmented fashion. It is this sort of mindset and behaviour that drives some to believe that "I should go into fulltime ministry, because that is the only way I am going to get to serve Jesus wholeheartedly". But, (staying with illustrations) one should rather think of a person's life as represented by a pond. Into this pond, a stone is then dropped, resulting in ever widening ripples. The stone is Jesus and the ripples, representing his vision, mission, values, priorities and practices, slowly begins to permeate ALL of the person's life. When a person realises that they can experience Jesus in all facets of their lives, there should be no need to enter fulltime ministry or the mission field. This might surprise you, but wherever you find yourself presently, that is most likely where God wants you to be in fulltime ministry and mission. Lastly, there is one exception to Paul's teaching on "remain as you are". If a person is living a sinful life or involved in a "shady business", then they certainly need to change.

2. Some of the Corinthians were advocating a lifestyle of celibacy within marriage. What does Paul say about celibacy and their practice of it? Turning aside from their erroneous motivations for celibacy, it is worth noting that in many cultures today, celibacy is frowned upon, or at least the individual living as such is

thought "a bit strange". However, from Paul's writings, celibacy is clearly just as much of a gift from God as is marriage. Therefore, Christians are to extend equal respect to both gifts. Furthermore, irrespective of the gift we find ourselves with, we will still encounter times of severe strain, but we can rest assured that the Holy Spirit will be there to support us if we will only turn to him. The problem arises when we try to live out a gift God has not given us. The Roman Catholic priests are a case in point. For millennia, those who wanted to be priests in this denomination were required to remain celibate, but the problem is that many did not have the gift of celibacy. When this happens, terrible evils such as child molestation, paedophilia, homosexuality, fornication and rape result.

3. What is Paul's advice to the widows about celibacy and marriage? Would you say that this advice is still appropriate today?

4. What did Jesus teach about marriage and divorce? See Matthew 5:32, amongst others. If a friend of yours came to you and asked your opinion on whether s/he could remarry, how would you respond using John Nolland's interpretive explanation? Given your context, what would you say is the major reason for divorce? Some of the major causes include differing perspectives about money, immaturity, sexual problems, parents-in-law, alcoholism, jealousy, irresponsibility and idealistic presentations of marriage through the media, which cannot possibly exist within reality.

5. What two reasons does Paul give as to why virgins should not marry and what do they mean?

Chapter Ten
Food Sacrificed to Idols and Paul's Apostleship

This portion of scripture seems far removed and not applicable today. Unless you live in some parts of Africa or Asia, you will probably be unaccustomed to the practice of eating meat sacrificed to idols. Chances are that if you encounter this practice, you would either stay well clear or consider it irrelevant and eat as usual. Some of you might have heard about Jews steering clear of certain foods, since they consider them "unclean," or, more applicably, perhaps you have heard of "halal" foods before.[136] Similarly, many of us may have felt a pang of uncertainty when a Hindu colleague may have given us a gift of food at Divali – the Hindu New Year. The question is: may we share food in celebration of another "god"?

Although food issues might seem trivial to some in the West, this was not the case for those in Corinth where there were numerous complicating factors. Further, this text contains many key principles for proper Christian living. You would do well to take note and apply them.

---

[136]Halal is an Arabic term meaning "permissible" in the eyes of Islamic law. "Muslims are allowed to eat what is 'good' (Qur'an 2:168) – that is, what is pure, clean, wholesome, nourishing, and pleasing to the taste. In general, everything is allowed (*halal*) except what has been specifically forbidden." Available [Online] at http://islam.about.com/od/dietarylaw/a/diet_law.htm

Socialising at Idol Temples

Corinth was a city where social gatherings were intermingled with religion, particularly worship services.

These worship services were held for many reasons: to sacrifice to a god, births (birthdays), funerals, coming of age parties, marriages, times of good fortune, regular seasonal feasts, political debates, and election victories.[137] People would invite their friends to join them at the temples (high places) where they would worship and celebrate. Therefore, to dissociate oneself from sacrificial meals meant turning your back on a social life or even societal rejection. It could have also meant the loss of business and material resources. Emperor worship was also popular and Roman Citizens had a special right to participate in the regular imperial festivities. Missing these festivities could have got you noticed and spelled trouble. One can see that these services were an important affair.

Nevertheless, why was it evil for them to participate in these feasts? Well, they were not just eating food sacrificed to some "god". These festivities exposed them to immorality, idolatry, gluttony, and sexual orgies. Worship in those times was significantly different from our worship. They never went to a temple to sing or listen to a sermon, and neither did they go simply to offer sacrifices or pray.[138]

These feasts often involved sacrificing many animals (1 Chronicles 29:21; 2 Chronicles 29:33; 30:24). Meat not burnt in the sacrifices went elsewhere. Some of the meat went to the priests while the rest was prepared for eating in the presence of the deity. The leftovers ended up in the market place (*Agora*) and butcheries (10:28 and then 10:25).

Archaeological evidence substantiates the existence of these feasts. For example: "Apollonius asks you to dine at a table of the

---

[137]See also Exodus 32:6; 34:15; Numbers 25:1–2; Hosea 4:11–14; Matthew 21:23; 26:55; Acts 3:1, 5:42; Luke 4:16–19, 18:10, 24:53.
[138]The Jews by comparison confined themselves to praying, worshipping, praising (singing), proclaiming the word, teaching, and reading scripture.

lord Sarapis on the occasion of the coming of age of his brothers in the Thoerian [temple]."[139] "Apion asks you to dine in the house of Sarapis at a table of the lord Sarapis on the 13th from the 9th hour."[140] "Chaeremon asks you to dine at a table of the lord Sarapis in the Sarapian [temple] tomorrow, which is the 15th, from the 9th hour."[141]

Two of Lord Serapis' temples were located at Corinth.

Christians amidst Idols

The phraseology of the passage suggests that Paul's answer was one of a series of questions addressed to him by the Corinthian church. They were uncertain as to the morality of certain practices by some in the church, and so Paul aims to address their query. However, what was the situation disconcerting to them?

It seems that the Gentile Christians had reverted to their old ways of fellowshipping/eating at the temples, in spite of Paul forbidding it in a previous letter. Their reasoning for doing this was as follows:

- They considered themselves possessors of "knowledge" in the sense that they knew there was only one God. Therefore, idols were a lot of nonsense (8:1, 4). Thus, if the idols were irrelevant, their going to the temple was simply to enjoy themselves with friends, no harm done. Paul would have agreed with this argument.

- They were also aware that food, in itself, was of no concern to God, which Paul would have agreed to as well (8:8).

- There is a possibility that the Corinthians thought that they were immune from committing apostasy because they regularly participated in the Lord's Supper (10:1–4).

- It is likely that they also thought it a good idea that the "weak"

---

[139]Papyrus Oxyrhynchus. 1484.
[140]Ibid. 1755.
[141]Ibid. 110.

Christians extend themselves by attending these feasts to strengthen their faith. Of course, the danger was their inability to discern what was right and wrong, thus exposing them to potential idolatry.

- Some in the church thought little of Paul's authority. This was because he would not accept money from them, and it appeared that he led a hypocritical lifestyle, i.e. he would refrain from eating food sold at the market place with Jews but gladly tuck in when with the Gentiles (9:19–23).[142]

The first paragraph states that some had returned to the feasts. The main problem had to do with where the food was being eaten, namely idol temples. However, a secondary problem was whether one could eat meat from the market place (at home or with friends) originally sacrificed to pagan gods in the temple (10:25). Considering the number of animals slaughtered for these feasts and the number of "gods" available to worship, it is reasonable to suggest that most of the meat sold in the market place had been offered in worship to a "god."[143] It is also reasonable to assume that it might have been difficult and possibly expensive to locate meat from other sources. If this is true, then, like the Corinthians, we may share a concern as to where issues of convenience overlap moral issues. Should we adopt a pragmatic approach or should we take an approach of abstinence? Consider a modern day example like television: many programs on television have immoral overtones – should we then avoid television? The Corinthian church faced a similar conundrum.

Briefly, there was a concern that those who consumed this meat were eating what belonged to the devil. The Jews forbade the practice of eating any of this meat sold at the market place. They solved

---

[142]This summary has been a paraphrase out of Fee, G. D. *First Epistle*, pp. 361–362.

[143]This is also supported by the fact that the Roman Government would only permit the priests to butcher the meat.

this problem through kosher foods.[144]

Thus far, we know what the two problems were:

- Eating food at the idol temples; and

- Eating meat previously offered to an idol in either one's home or the home of a friend.

However, did Paul forbid both these practices like the Jews did?

According to 10:25, Paul states that it is acceptable to eat meat sacrificed to idols bought in the market place. However, he forbids going to pagan temples because eating there is tantamount to "drinking the cup of demons." Thus, from Paul's perspective, the real problem is the latter.

It is strange though to think that the Christians wanted to visit an idol temple in the first place. What could possibly have been the attraction? Well, the temples were actually a form of "restaurant?" Some who had converted to Christianity did not want to give up their previous social lives.

Let us not put the cart before the horse though. This is a lengthy section and deserves some time considering Paul's approach to the problems.

His answers tackle the problems we have looked at in five sections.

1. He deals with their preoccupation with "knowledge" and "rights" by emphasising that "Love" and "what is best for others" should govern behaviour, not how much one "knows" (8:1–13).

2. He deals with the validity of his "apostolic rights." He has the "rights," but he has chosen to give them up for evangelistic purposes (9:1–27).

---

[144]In Hebrew, "Kashrus," from the root kosher (or "kasher"), means suitable and/or "pure", thus ensuring fitness for consumption. The laws of "Kashrus" include comprehensive legislation concerning "permitted" and "forbidden foods". Available [Online] at http://www.koshercertification.org.uk/whatdoe.html

3. He addresses their false security of sacramental protection. His warning comes in the form of a reminder of the tragedies that befell Israel in the wilderness (10:1–13).

4. He tackles the real problem: they are eating at the idol temples (10:14–22).

5. He advises them on what they should do about eating meat sacrificed to idols, sold in the market place, together with certain principles of Christian freedom (10:23–11:1).

We will deal with Paul's response to sections 1, 3 and 4, and then look at sections 2 and 5.

Free to Love and Protect – 1 Corinthians 8:1–13

"What is best for others" should motivate how we think and live.

Food related to Idols – 1 Corinthians 8:1–6

Paul begins with the root of the problem – "knowledge versus love" (8:1–3). The statement, "all of us possess knowledge" (8.1) was very likely a quote coming out of the church. The elevation of knowledge as an end in itself was probably the result of the influence of proto-gnostic thinking. Those who had *gnosis* (knowledge) were a special elite group, elevated above the majority, who did not have such *gnosis*. Paul agrees that knowledge is important, but the real issue is, do you "love" your neighbour who may be offended by the exercise of your superior "knowledge", because, knowledge without love puffs up the ego; it makes a person proud, and knowledge is partial. "Anyone who claims to know something does not yet have the necessary knowledge" (8:3). Human knowledge is at best incomplete. Therefore, there is no justification for priding oneself over another when you know so little (in comparison with God). In contrast with this, love has a permanent character, and "it builds a person up." The important thing is not that we know God, but that

He knows us (2 Timothy 2:19).

Paul then returns to the subject of idol meats (8:4). He agrees with the Corinthians that "no idol in the world really exists," i.e. they are manmade figments of the imagination.

However, to a pagan who regularly participated in these feasts, an idol (an object) was a "god," a "lord." These "gods" had a reality for them, and there were many gods (Deuteronomy 10:17; Acts 17:16–23).[145] Paul explained this to the "strong in faith" as part of his argument to convince them not to go to the temples to eat, thereby causing younger Christians to sin (8:11). We will return to this below.

Think before you Act – 1 Corinthians 8:7–13

Thus far, we know that "love" is more important than our need to express our freedom of rights in the name of "knowledge." In this portion of the text, he goes on to demonstrate the use of love through respecting the weaker Christian.

The "strong" had professed that there was only one true God, and they took great joy in being able to exert their newfound freedom by going to the idol temples to eat. However, the weak did not see things in the same light.

There were many new converts in Corinth who had eaten food sacrificed to idols all their lives. They also believed that in their eating at the temple that there was a spiritual side to the supper. They did not think of the food as only a means of socialising. They lacked the knowledge that depersonalised the spirituality of the event.

Thus, what was purely social for the mature contained a spiritual

---

[145]Christianity is monotheistic, meaning belief in one God. Pagans, being pantheistic (belief in many gods), had the tendency to divide creation up amongst their gods and goddesses; for instance, Artemis, the goddess of forests and hills and Zeus, the god of the sky and thunder. A modern day example of a pantheistic religion is Hinduism ("modern" in the sense that it exists today).

element for the weak, and that is where the danger lay. Their heads were telling them that there was only one God, but their hearts needed convincing. Therefore, by returning to idolatry, their consciences were being defiled (tainted, stained) and so too their relationship to Jesus. In being a part of leading others into this situation, they were also sinning against Jesus.[146]

Paul uses himself as an example to end off with (8:13). He explains that the "strong" must adapt their behaviour to the conscience of the weak. To Paul, the well-being of the Christian and the church is what counts. He would rather be a vegetarian than eat meat if it might cause a brother or sister to sin.

Stay Away from Idol Temples – 1 Corinthians 10:1–13

We are going to skip (9:1–27) for the moment, as it deals with Paul's "rights" and "freedom" as an Apostle. We will look at the connection between him and these portions on idols and temples in the pages ahead.

Previously, Paul had argued in favour of the weak. Now he aims his attention at those who assume they are strong. He warns them by referring to some horrific examples from Israel's history. He then explains why idol temples are a "no-go-zone" for Christians.

Israel was almost wiped out – 1 Corinthians 10:1–5

In 1 Corinthian 10, Paul utilizes a style of preaching called *midrash*,

---

[146]"Since, through participation in the death of Christ crucified, the believer becomes identified with Christ, Christ identifies himself with those whom he has consecrated (1:2), enriched (1:5), and purchased as his own (6:20), who are shrines of the Spirit (6:19). The previous verse (8:11) has shown that what is at stake is the self-assertive stance of 'the strong' bringing 'the weak' for whom Christ died face-to-face with destruction. The solemnity and dire seriousness of this emerges in Paul's ringing declaration that [in behaving like this, they actually] sin against Christ, who identifies himself with 'the weak.'" Thiselton. A. C. *The First Epistle*, p. 655.

"rabbinical metaphor" or "parallel." Rabbinical exegesis often compared one event with another. Another example is Paul's references to Sarai and Hagar paralleling the New Covenant and Old Covenant in Galatians 4, although there is no direct link between them. In 1 Corinthians 10, Paul is comparing the Christian journey with the journey of Israel in the wilderness on the way to the Promised Land.

This section seems out of place, but it actually ties in beautifully because the "strong" Christians thought that they were safe from apostasy because they participated in the "sacraments." Of course, they were completely wrong and would need correcting. Hence, Paul launches into a comparison between Israel's wilderness event and their walk with Jesus. This is the reason why he refers to the examples from Israel's history: "and all were baptized into Moses in the cloud and in the sea, and all ate the same spiritual food, and all drank the same spiritual drink. For they drank from the spiritual rock that followed them, and the rock was Christ" (10:2).

The Israelites experience with the cloud and the Red Sea united Israel to Moses because they were all baptised into him (Exodus 13:21–22; 14:21–22). "Baptism signifies being bound up with the one in whose name, or in whose sphere of influence, a person is baptized … [Thus, the Christian baptism] signifies above all else identification with Christ, especially identification with Christ's saving death and resurrection (Romans 6:3–11)."[147] The point is that God judged the Israelites for their sins in spite of their sharing in a common baptism.

His next element within the comparison relates to the "food" (Exodus 16:4 and 13). It was spiritual food that God had given and thus had its origin in heaven. Similarly, the bread the Corinthians ate at the sacrament was Christ-initiated and therefore, also heaven-sent.

Finally, he refers to the spiritual "drink" (Exodus 17:1–7 and

---

[147]Thiselton. A. C. *The First Epistle*, p. 724.

Numbers 20:2–13). Moses got water from the rock at the beginning and the end of the Israelite's journey through the wilderness. The Israelites had a legend that the rock had travelled with them the whole way through the wilderness. Paul takes their legend and refers to Christ as the rock that followed them, giving them water through the wilderness. He transfers to Christ the title of "the rock," which was another name used for Yahweh (Deuteronomy 32:15; Psalm 18:2). Similarly, the Corinthians "drink" (wine) was Christ initiated and heaven-sent.

In 10:5, Paul shows the Corinthians the cold truth of what happened to people who had also partaken of a sacrament very similar to theirs. Even though the Israelites had such vivid manifestations of God's power and goodness, all but two of them failed to enter the Promised Land. God's wrath came upon them because they had indulged temptation and ended up sinning against God.

You are on dangerous ground – 1 Corinthians 10:6–13

Paul offers four examples of the way "the chosen" Israelites desired after evil things. "Some have suggested that misdirected desire underlies all four of the examples, while worldly self-indulgence or "sensuality" leads to (i) idolatry and (ii) immorality; unbelief leads to (iii) doubt, which puts God to the test, and (iv) despair, complaint, or murmuring."[148]

Right from the outset, people who participated in idol feasts knew what they were letting themselves in for. In 8:7, Paul mentions the words "and they rose up to play." "Play" in this instance most likely referred to "letting their hair down" with overtones of idolatrous dancing to the golden calf, amongst other things.

"Paul singles out one sin in particular within this context, sexual immorality. The immorality represents the second of the four failed tests, which characterized Israel in the OT wilderness traditions and

---

[148]Edwards, T. C. *A Commentary on The First Epistle to the Corinthians*, p. 248.

very likely refers to temple prostitution."[149] As a result, the Book of Numbers states that judgement came on the people as a plague that wiped out 24 000 people (23 000 in 10:8).[150]

The third example (warning) is that of putting Christ to the test. The words "put Christ to the test" mean, "to see how far one can go." Israel did this in the past when they tried to play off God's protective love against their wilful craving after food, and God sent deadly snakes among them (Numbers 21:5–6).[151] In a similar fashion, the Corinthians were treading this fine line by thinking they were safe from spiritual harm at these temple feasts. "They presumed to force God's hand to preserve them by putting his love and salvation to the test (10:23)."

The fourth component deserving of God's punishment was the Israelites "grumbling" against God (10:10), something closely linked to their "testing" God. The Israelites complained about God's provision and wanted to return to Egypt (Numbers 14:2; 36), the result, they died (Numbers 14:12, 36–37).[152] The Corin-

---

[149]Wolff. C. *Der erste Brief des Paulus an die Korinther*, p. 219. Note that improper sexual behaviour and idol worship were closely associated with one another. Paul chooses an incident where Israel was infiltrated by paganism, when Israel "began to indulge in sexual immorality with Moabite women" and "joined in worshipping Baal of Peor" (Numbers 25:1–10).

[150]Paul quotes a figure 1000 less than the figure mentioned in Numbers. A possible explanation for this is that both figures are round numbers, and Paul may be making some allowance for those slain by the judges and not the plague (Numbers 25:5) as well as those slain the day before.

[151]This should be a lesson to all Christians; some of us think that because Christ has died for us, we are somehow immune to this level of punishment. The Israelites tested God and encountered deadly plagues and snakes as a result, but we think, "that is Old Testament, things are different now". However, the account of Ananias and his wife Sapphira are in the New Testament, and look at what happened to them; they died because they lied to the Holy Spirit (Acts 5:9). Let this be a warning to us!

[152]"In context the concept is not petty complaints as such, but the constant grudging, carping, querulous moaning which transformed the bold, glad

thians were now complaining against Paul for the right to return to the idol temples. The Israelites complaining against Moses and their complaining against Paul are tantamount to complaining against God. This grumbling might have additionally stretched to possible comments the "strong" were making about the "weak" (poor).

These events should serve as a reminder to us. The Corinthians were confident in themselves and their covenant with God. However, so were the Israelites and look what happened to them, "So if you think you are standing, watch out that you do not fall" (10:12; Proverbs 16:18), or to put it another way, when you are self-confident, you are in grave danger of falling.

Part of the complaining probably resulted in Paul's raising the issue of "temptation" (test, trial – 10:13). It could have been that peer pressure to participate in these feasts, directly or indirectly, and their need to socialize with friends, was causing unbearable temptation in their eyes.

Paul counters this idea by suggesting that God, in His faithfulness, always provides his people with a way out; allowing a situation to stretch beyond their limit is not an option for him. However, the fight against temptation is never a one-sided affair. A person must decide of "their will" to turn away from what is tempting them on an on-going basis and cling to the promises of God. Furthermore, they should not expect God to remove their temptations. Rather, their ability to resist will prove their usefulness to God. A similar idea is in mind when Jesus experienced temptation in the desert (Matthew 4:1–11).

---

self-perception of those whom God had redeemed from Egypt for a new lifestyle into a self-pitying, false perception of themselves as 'victims' on whom God had weighed heavy burdens and trials, in contrast to a fantasy life of ideal existence in Egypt or the world." Thiselton. A. C. *The First Epistle,* p. 742. 1 Corinthians 10:10 is taken from Numbers 16 where overthrowing the company of Korah is addressed (Numbers 16:1–39).

Beware of Idolatry – 1 Corinthians 10:14–22

Paul's point is: "flee from the worship of idols" (10:14). The only course is to have nothing to do with them. You will recall that the Corinthians thought themselves wise (Chapters 1–4). Now Paul appeals to their claims, suggesting that they are sensible people who are able to make valid decisions.

The evidence Paul gives about the sacrament serves to prove the inherent danger of their eating sacrifices made to idols. By attending temple meals, they were participating in and fellowshipping with the "deity" being honoured. He proves this by drawing a comparison between the Lord's Table of worship, and the sacrifices made to demons.

In Holy Communion, there is a participation in the Blood of Christ. Those who receive the cup receive Christ as well as binding themselves together in fellowship with Him. A spiritual process takes place by faith. The receiving of the loaf is also a participation in the Body of Christ (1 Corinthians 10:16).

Paul shows the Corinthians that it was common knowledge to the Israelites, who when they ate the sacrifices made to God, wilfully participated at the altar. Therefore, those who received the food of sacrifice entered into fellowship with all the altar stood for (1 Corinthians 10:18).

The problem was that when the "strong" shared food in this context, they were fellowshipping with and worshipping a deity, which their friends believed to be present at the feast. Moreover, what is worse, although these were false idols, something very real was lurking in and around them: "demons" (1 Corinthians 10:20, see Israel's History – Deuteronomy 32:16–17).

Thus, "You cannot drink the cup of the Lord and the cup of demons. You cannot partake of the table of the Lord and the table of demons" (1 Corinthians 10:21). They could not bind themselves to Christ and then bind themselves together with demons as well. This was a spiritual impossibility. Surely, those who have accepted the Lord's invitation (Christians) cannot in good conscience also accept the invitation of demons (Pagans)? Do you recall my paint-mixing example? Your purple (royalty) life in Christ mixed with yellow demons turns you brown. You have lost the beauty of purple.

However, what if those participating in the feast did understand what they were doing? Well, then they were wilfully provoking the Lord to anger (Exodus 17:7; Deuteronomy 6:16), not a wise move considering humanities history with God.

I <u>Am</u> an Apostle – 1 Corinthians 9:1–27

On a first reading of Chapters 8–10, you might think that Chapter 9 is a separate subject. Some assume that Chapter 9 was an insertion from another letter Paul wrote, but this is incorrect. Previously, you read of how the "strong" in the church asserted their "rights" (freedom) even when it meant harm to others; although they did not think that they were doing any harm. By this, they demonstrated their inability to allow "love" to be "the" guiding principle of their behaviour towards others. Paul's request to the "strong" in light of this error was to forgo certain things, even though they were entitled to them. The link with Paul's "apostolic rights" thus comes in when he demonstrates similar behaviour by foregoing those rights to achieve an objective as well.

As has been the case with other Chapters, Paul here responds to a problem among them. To find it, consider these words in the first three verses beginning Paul's defence: "Am I not an apostle?" "At least I am to you" (9:1–2). Moreover, "This is my defence to those who would examine me" (9:3). It seems as if the problem centred on people doubting his apostolic authority for two reasons. Firstly, he was refusing their offer of material remuneration and secondly, they saw his different eating habits among the Gentiles and Jews. He would eat certain food with one group while refusing to eat with the other.

Paul responds as follows: firstly, there is the issue of his "rights"

(9:1–18), then he explains his social behaviour, which differed according to whose company he was in (Gentiles or Jews – 9:19–23), and finally, his urging for self-discipline in which he stands as an example (9:24–27).

The Rights of an Apostle – 1 Corinthians 9:1–18

In this section, Paul has certain objectives in mind.

- To inform the Corinthians of his true rights as an apostle, and that he is deserving of those rights (9:1–12a)

- To explain why he has given up his rights to financial support (9:12b–18).

He begins with four rhetorical questions, two of which serve to highlight the "qualifiers" for apostleship:

- He had seen Jesus Christ. Apostles were authoritative witnesses to the facts of the gospel and more especially to the resurrection (Acts 1:21; 2:32; 3:15; 4:33; 22:14 and 26:16). Therefore, because Paul was not one of the original 12, some might have questioned his apostolic credibility. However, on the Damascus road, the Lord appeared to him, thereby qualifying him as a witness to the resurrection (Acts 9:1–9);[153] and

- He was the founder of their church. This was more convincing than the former defence, especially as they doubted his apostolic authority. The irony was that if they doubted his authority, they were also placing their existence as a church and as individual believers in jeopardy, since Paul was the instigator of their belief in Christ and the church at Corinth. Therefore, they were proof of the apostolic work done by

---

[153]Fee suggests that this was more likely a genuine resurrection appearance and not just a vision. "Paul must have considered himself commissioned in some manner since numerous people had witnessed the resurrected Christ" (see Galatians 1:16). Fee, G. D. *First Epistle*, p. 395.

him. The word "seal" (9:2) served as a mark of ownership. One could also see it as a mark of authentication. If the Corinthians saw their church as authentic, they had to admit that their founder was too.

Having verified his apostleship, he follows with certain technical legalese to defend his claim to use the rights afforded an apostle if he chooses. He begins by establishing what rights are important in this context.

Paul asked his antagonists three questions (9:3–6):

1. "Do we not have the right to our food and drink?" (9:4)[154]

2. "Do we not have the right to be accompanied by a believing wife, as do the other apostles and the brothers of the Lord and Cephas?" (9:5)[155]

3. "Or is it only Barnabas and I who have no right to refrain from working for a living?" (9:6)[156]

Following on from these issues are the basis for these rights.

Consider the right to financial support (food and drink). The Corinthians appeared angered by Paul's refusal to take money from them for his ministry (2 Corinthians 11:7). This would appear strange to us. However, it was customary for sophists and the like to support themselves through charging sums of money, staying in wealthy households, working or begging (those who had to work were probably not very good at their rhetoric and not accepted in their field, let alone those who had to beg).

---

[154]By "right to food and drink" is meant, "have not we the right to eat and drink what we please – and to do so at the expense of the community?"

[155]"Two issues were possibly being addressed here. First, he is dealing with the issue of his right to receive support from them, but second, his way of life, choosing to remain single, is different from most others. Could it be that the Corinthians considered his not being accompanied by a wife to mean that he was not a genuine apostle?" Fee, G. D. *First Epistle*, p. 403.

[156]Luke, in Acts 4.36–37, mentions that Barnabas gave up his source of income to help the church.

Secondly, and more to the point, it was very much a "you scratch my back, and I yours" society. I guess things have not changed much. The problem amongst the influential in Corinth was that they had no handle on Paul, thus they could not manipulate him. They could not obtain any worldly benefits from him like increased attention or status, and neither could they climb the ladder of significance within the church through him.[157]

He draws on the examples of a soldier, a man who plants a vineyard and a shepherd. The point being that they all draw sustenance from their occupation and so too, can an apostle. Further, this is not just a principle established out of kindness for the one who works. The law specifies it, and the law is authoritative. After all, consider what Moses said, "You shall not muzzle an ox while it is treading out the grain" (9:10).[158] Now if God could show this sort of mercy to an ox, surely the worker was also entitled to a share in the fruits of his labour.

Paul believed that this principle applied foremost to the preacher. The Christian worker, be he a ploughman or a reaper, must do his work with vigour and hope because God will provide for his needs

[157]"At that time Paul's behaviour and those in power's response could have led to the Corinthian's assumption that his reluctance to take advantage of an apostle's 'right' implied that the 'right' itself was in question, i.e. either Paul was not a true 'apostle,' or he had somehow compromised the leadership role which invited such entitlement." Thiselton. A. C. *The First Epistle*, p. 663. It is also possible that they surmised that Paul's restriction on his eating habits (he would never eat meat again if his eating proved detrimental to the well being of a Christian brother) proved that he was not a true apostle because he would never have allowed himself to be restricted in this manner.

[158]In ancient Israel an ox was often used in threshing. The ox did this by trampling the corn, thus shaking the grain loose from the husks. Then the mixture was thrown into the air where the breeze would blow the chaff away, leaving the heavier grain to fall straight back down. Now the Law (Deuteronomy 25:4) provided that an ox treading the grain should not be muzzled while on the job. This meant that he could eat some of the grain he was trampling.

from the first fruits of his labour. He ends his argument by reminding them of words originating out of the Jesus tradition; "the Lord commanded that those who proclaim the gospel should get their living by the gospel" (9:14; Matthew 10:10 and Luke 10:7). Paul established their church. Therefore, he was fully entitled to share in any harvest that came from what he had planted if he desired. His illustrations of people who work at the temple, and altar, clarify his argument. These two examples deal with those dedicated to working for God, specifically. Those who do the work of administering the sacred rites get their food from the temple and those offering sacrifices on the altar eat a portion of the offering (Leviticus 10:12–13; 24:9; 27:21; Numbers 3:48; 5:9). The temple referred to here was most likely the one in Jerusalem. Earlier on, in Chapter 3 and 6, he had reminded them that the church and individual Christian were "temples" of the Holy Spirit. Therefore, the parallel here could well be that what applied to the temple workers also applied to the "gospel worker."

He has explained that he deserved the "rights" of an apostle, but he followed this by explaining why he had not exercised those rights.

Paul's "rights" and a higher purpose – 1 Corinthians 9:15–18

What are his rights? Quite simply, "to be able to boast"! Do not read this wrongly. Keep in mind that Paul has made it his life's ambition to "glory in the cross" (1:18–31). Paul's central point was: he boasts in his freedom to provide the gospel with "no strings attached" just as Christ provided free salvation; that his life and ministry are a reflection of freedom offered through Christ and because nothing hinders his ministry of spreading the gospel of Jesus Christ. He believed so firmly in this that he would rather die than change it.

However, he clarifies his boasting by explaining that preaching the gospel is not a matter of boasting. There is woe for him if he does not do it (Jeremiah 20.9). He states that if his preaching was voluntary, he would merit a reward; but as it so happens, he has no choice. He is a slave to Christ (9:17, 7:22; Romans 7:25). Paul believed that he could not claim anything for himself. He had done no more than was expected of him.

Finally, he replaces the word "boast" with "reward." It is his reward (pay) to work for no pay (9:18).

Paul's Freedom – 1 Corinthians 9:19–23

In this section, Paul continues to defend his apostleship. Previously, he dealt with the issue of not accepting payment from them. However, the Corinthians had also taken offence with his varying conduct within certain social settings. They had observed that he behaved differently when visiting with Jews or Gentiles. They were not about to listen to him dictating whether they could eat meat at an idol temple when he apparently lived a hypocritical life.

As a result, in this section, he aims to show them that evangelism is his motivator. He believed that he had the authority (rights) and the freedom to be able to act as he saw fit in different company to achieve the best results for the gospel. Ironically, the Corinthians had misinterpreted Paul's strength (freedom to do or not to do) as a weakness. Paul was of the opinion that true Christian freedom rested on "not being mastered" by anything[159] (Acts 16:1–3; 21:23–26; 1 Corinthians 6:20–22; 9:19; Colossians 1:23). To win over the Jews, he conformed to the practices that would enable him to win those under the law. To those not under the law (Gentiles) Paul came out from under the law. He met them on their home turf (Acts 17:20–25). Coming out from under the law incidentally did not mean that he became lawless, he was not free from God's law, but was under Christ's law. He was committed to ethical ends in the service of God (Romans 7:22; Galatians 6:2). It is also interesting to note that Paul refers to himself as a "servant" and not a "slave." There is a big difference between the two, particularly concerning

---

[159]He circumcised Timothy and he participated in a ceremony of purification to prove that he had not abandoned the law (Acts 16.3).

the areas of "freedom" and "mastery".

His behaviour brings us to an interesting question. In Galatians 2:11–16 Paul criticised Peter for siding with the Jews. What was the difference, if any, between Peter's actions and Paul's (Acts 16:1–3; 21:23–26)? Paul pandered to the Jewish custom because he was motivated to win people for Christ (present a free gospel); Peter's motivation was fear (Galatians 2:12). He pretended to be something he was not (hypocrisy; Galatians 2.13) out of fear for what the circumcision group might think or do.

Paul also adapted to the "weak." When he refers to the "weak," it is within the context of evangelism (9:22b). Thus, the "weak" were likely non-Christian. He is talking about "winning converts." It is reasonable to assume they were "weak" because of their reliance on owners or employers; they were in a predicament where they could not exert their opinions or behave as they wanted to without significant consequences. Therefore, when Paul identifies with them, he means that his right to living like an expert and teacher was set aside to live like an artisan. Of course, this was hardly characteristic behaviour for an apostle in the eyes of the Corinthians.

In short, Paul has become all things to all men. He is free to be a slave and a servant to all for spreading the gospel. He is prepared to go to extreme lengths to meet the people where there is no principle preventing him. His attitude shows an astonishing elasticity of mind and flexibility in dealing with different situations in a very difficult arena. As such, it does not seem that Paul was compromising his beliefs with a view to evangelising, but rather that he would limit his own freedom to meet people in the emotional and spiritual place where they found themselves.

On a practical note, what kind of Christian are you? Are you repulsed by sinful people and thus keep your distance? Would you associate with Moslems or Hindus? Are you sufficiently familiar with your freedom in Christ to be able to draw alongside any person to meet them on their turf to share the gospel with them (without sinning of course)? The trick is to know where to draw the line, i.e.

how far should one go.

The Christian athlete – 1 Corinthians 9:24–27

Up until now, Paul has made three things clear.

1. He has the full rights of an apostle.

2. When he did not use them, it was for evangelistic purposes.

3. He has used his freedom as a true reflection of the gospel.

However, there was still a question regarding the Corinthians lack of self-discipline in their walk with the Lord (idolatrous eating in pagan temples).

He chooses their knowledge and awareness of the Isthmian Games to exhort them on this matter. The games commonly involved the disciplines of running, jumping, wrestling, boxing, javelin and discus throwing. He makes use of the metaphors of running and boxing. Like the runner, Christians must also give of their best (9:24). Christian life is extremely challenging (9:25). A competitor had to go into rigorous training during which time he had to be "moderate in all things" and after all this training, his reward, if he won, was a crown that would not last.[160] In contrast, how much more worthwhile is the Christian life than this? The Christian competes to receive a prize that lasts forever (2 Timothy 4:8; James 1:12 and 1 Peter 5:4). All of the strenuous discipline an athlete had to put in just to receive a fleeting reward is a strong rebuke to the half-hearted Christian today.

How often do you see a person slaving away, disciplining him or herself to the extreme, merely to get something that soon changes or passes away? Consider areas like dieting, exercising, getting a better house, more money, a smarter car, a better golf handicap, or a degree.

Paul refused to be in bondage to his bodily desires. Words like

---

[160]Isthmian Game's victors would receive wreaths and possibly a statue or ode.

"beat" and "slave" (9:27) leave no doubt as to the strength of his convictions. The way Paul speaks gives one the impression that he considered the material body evil. This is an error because what he actually means is that the body must be placed under strict control because it has a predisposition toward evil. It must be mastered and not be the master. The physical members of one's body can either be offered to sin for use in its employment; or they can be offered to God, for use in the service of righteousness.

Finally, Paul's use of the words "I, myself will not be disqualified for the prize," does not imply the loss of salvation. Rather, he disciplines himself to "stand the test" of surrendering all for the sake of the gospel to attain a prize that is beyond salvation.

This final reminder is important. Let love guide you and always be willing to surrender your "rights" when it will benefit others in terms of drawing them closer to Jesus Christ.

The Practical Outcome of Christian Freedom – 1 Corinthians 10:23–11:1

Looking at it from another angle, the "strong" were also in danger for treating demons casually. I mentioned above that the Christians "in the know" felt protected from demons when they participated in idol feasts. If a knowledgeable Christian could go and eat without the danger of hindering another's faith, it would be fine. The problem with this attitude was that the events of 10:1–22 severely warned against doing this. Thus, the reason for not participating in an idol feast was twofold: "you will not be acting out of love and, by eating there, you are fellowshipping with demons."

Paul has been dealing with the question of food sacrificed to idols for approximately three Chapters (8:1 onwards). He has now come to the place where he must sum up with practical advice and precept (10:23–11:1).

It is time for a quick recap!

Paul has tackled two problems concluding that:

- The Corinthians must not eat food sacrificed to idols in the idol's temple.

- Paul did not give up his rights as an apostle simply because he refused financial support.

Paul still had to discuss the matter of eating idol food in general; should they eat such food or not? What happens if all the meat at the market is idol sacrifice related? Should they buy this meat to use in their homes? What happens if friends invite them around and dish up meat sacrificed to idols? These are some of the questions requiring a response.

He begins by repeating a statement he has already made under another section (6:12) with one added difference – "but not all things build up." Christian freedom is important, but not at the expense of another. In these circumstances, it is more important to avoid such actions than to assert one's rights. The guiding principle should be, "Do not seek your own advantage, but that of the other" (10:24; see also Matthew 7:12 and Philippians 2:3–4). The point of these verses relays a message of deep, sincere concern for the well-being of others.

Paul tackles their problem within two distinct settings: firstly, in 10:25–26 and secondly, in 10:27–28. The first setting is within one's home. The second is when you go to a friend's house.

The Christians in Corinth faced a dilemma. Firstly, it would be almost impossible to identify all of the meat sacrificed to idols. Paul sees no point in raising the issue of conscience because, in his eyes, a Christian could eat anything sold at the meat market based on the judgement made in the Psalms, "The earth is the LORD's and all that is in it, the world, and those who live in it" (Psalm 24:1). This stands in sharp contrast to the Jewish approach. Judging by Paul's response, one can see that he was serious about an idol being nothing. Ultimately, idol food is as much the Lord's as any other food.

Therefore, what should their response be if someone invites them to dine at their house? The same principle applies whether they eat at a friend's house or their own house (10:27). There is one exception to the basic principle (eat anything you like). When "someone says to you, 'This has been offered in sacrifice,' then do not eat it, out of consideration for the one who informed you, and for the sake of conscience – I mean the other's conscience, not your own." (10:28–29, 32–33). In this case, the meat is no longer a good gift from God. Someone has noted that it was the product of idolatry (meat sacrificed to an idol) and objects to this. Therefore, to eat the meat in the eyes of the one who pre-warned you would be to show approval of idolatry, at least in that person's opinion. For the sake of the other's conscience, the "strong" person should refrain from eating the meat[161] (Romans 14:1–18).

In 10:30, Paul refers to his statement in 10:26 (based on Psalm 24:1). His statement in 10:31 is a repetition of 10:25–30.

The principle is clear. A Christian should not be concerned about

---

[161] The following arguments pertain to whether the "other man" was a non-believer or a weak/young Christian. He says that, "it is not easy to see how a non-Christian's conscience could enter into the matter. It is therefore best to suppose that we have to do with a second Christian guest, whose weak conscience, permitted him to attend the meal, has led him to make inquiries of his host or in the kitchen, and who, using the most courteous words available, now passes on the fruit of his research to his stronger Christian brother." Barrett, C. K. *The First Epistle*, p. 242. Alternatively, Fee suggests "that Paul intends a non-believer because of his deliberate change of words for idol food. In other places Paul uses the word 'eidolothuta'– food sacrificed to idols. Apparently Jews and Christians only used this term and its intention of use was to belittle idolatry. On the other hand pagans used the term 'hierothuta'– food offered in sacrifice or sacred food. This latter term is what Paul's speaker had used. It is difficult to imagine a 'weak Christian' using such a term when idolatry would have been the issue for him." Fee, G. D. *First Epistle*, pp. 483–484. I tend to favour Barrett's opinion of it being a weak Christian. The reason being that Paul has been addressing the church about not causing the weak Christian to stumble. I have difficulty thinking why this section would be different. Ultimately, whichever way the pendulum swings, the principle of placing others before ourselves remains crucially important.

his rights, but rather with giving all the glory to God. It is easy to carry out, just show tender concern for all, viz. Jews, Greeks, and the Church of God.

If I had to summarise these three Chapters into one sentence, it would be, **"love your neighbour!"**

Questions and Thoughts for Reflection

1. Paul uses himself as an example to end off with (8:13). He explains that the "strong" must adapt their behaviour to the conscience of the weak. To Paul, the wellbeing of the Christian and the church is what counts. He would rather be a vegetarian than eat meat if it might cause a brother or sister to sin. How do these principles apply today? Consider the following examples:

    1.1. Your friend Joe has recently become a Christian through your witness. He comes out of a rough background and has a drinking problem. He looks up to you because you have introduced him to a new life. One day, you invite him over for dinner together with a number of your other friends. Come dinnertime, your friends pull out their bottle of wine (not knowing Joe's background), which ends up in Joe's hands. Inwardly, he wrestles with the matter and concludes that because other Christians are drinking wine, he can to. Need I say anymore? If you knew that one of your recently converted friends, or simply a guest invited to your party, was previously an alcoholic, would you refrain from having any alcoholic beverages? It is about counting the costs. It might well cost you all some fun and enjoyment not having your favourite beer and wine on hand, but imagine how much it could cost that ex-alcoholic if he goes back to drink?

    1.2. Millions of Christians worldwide celebrate Christmas. However, many Christians are aware that it is highly unlikely that Christ was actually born on Christmas day, but celebrate His birth at this time anyway. I would also imagine that a number of Christians are aware that Christmas had strong ties with Paganism before Jesus' time. For instance, the ancient Babylonians celebrated the Son of Isis (Goddess of Nature) on December 25 while participating in many unsavoury practices. The Northern Europeans celebrated their winter solstice known as "Yule", which was symbolic of the pagan Sun God on the 25th as well. Then there is the matter of many items used in the Christmas celebrations, like the Christmas tree, which also has pagan origins. Now, you have friends who have recently become zealous new Christians. You and your family are aware of some of Christmas' pagan origins, yet you still dust off the old Christmas tree and keep the secret that Santa Clause goes around on Christmas Eve breaking the speed of light trying to deliver all of his presents. Your zealous friends, however, have come to find out that Christmas is not when Christ was born, and that it represents a host of ungodly practices. When they come to visit, they are surprised that you still entertain the idea. This sort of thing can mislead people. Therefore, would you be prepared to forego your tradition to protect them and make a point of honouring Jesus?[162]

With respect to 1.1 and 1.2, to put it another way: do your rights, or the rights of others, govern you? Evidence from Western society certainly suggests the former. Your lifestyle should always be, "what is best for those around me and how can I facilitate that?" not "what can I do to ensure my happiness or my freedom of rights?" Do not

---

[162]An alternative would be to sit down with them and carefully explain that Christmas, while not being the date of Christ's birth, is still a time that you use to celebrate his birth. But, this does not explain away pursuing the Santa traditions.

get me wrong here! There is nothing wrong with seeking happiness, but it should never be at the expense of others. There are many occasions in life that I call "border line situations," because neither God nor the government prohibits them. However, they are situations that may lead to a new Christian stepping across into an area that does break the law, or causes him/her to stumble in their Christian walk. One must also consider the un-believers around you. This brings to mind what Ghandi said, "I like your Christ, I do not like your Christians. Your Christians are so unlike your Christ." This is a shocking testimony against Christians! I will leave you with this thought; "what example are you setting for onlookers on a daily basis"?

2. Where does temptation/s lie for you? Where are you weakest? Think about it carefully! The three major categories are money, sex and power. The truth is that most temptations we face are offshoots of these in some manner. Whatever it might be, the solution is a practical move on your part (see also 10:13, which I highlighted earlier). If it is sexual, consider Joseph's practical response, he got up, turned around, and ran out of there (Genesis 39:11–12). There is nothing complicated about it! If it is money and you stand to save a lot in Tax from not declaring certain things, take a quick practical step, write down exactly what it should be and mail it. Again, do not waste time and ponder the issue. My belief is that the more time you spend thinking about the temptation, the greater your chance of falling prey to it. Do not dance with the Devil!

3. There are numerous churches today calling their leaders "Apostle so and so". Is this behaviour accurately in line with scripture? Develop a reasoned response and do not just say "yes" or "no". Based on Paul's criteria, what would he have said about this practice? Try to answer these questions before you read any further. In answering these questions, I strongly agree with Fee

in that, "given the two criteria Paul used, there cannot be Apostles in the sense that he defines his ministry; a 'guarantor of the traditions'. However, from a functional perspective of planting churches in unchartered territory, there certainly are apostles today."[163] Something else requires comment here, and it comes back to leaders being called "Apostle so and so." Fee's statement suggests that an apostle is a function within the body of Christ. But, by calling someone "Apostle so and so", you are changing a function into a title. Why is this a big deal? Well, Paul actually addressed a similar issue in Chapter 3 and 4. At the heart of the matter, we are talking about two totally different ways of viewing leaders. The view that holds that "apostle" is a function is in line with leaders being identified as servants and stewards. The view that holds that "apostle" is a title is inline with the Corinthians perspective of exalting leaders to places of honour and status. This is no place for anyone other than Jesus.

4. I mentioned earlier that Paul criticised Peter for siding with the Jews. Apparently, Paul pandered to the Jewish eating customs because he was motivated to win people for Christ (present a free gospel). Peter, on the other hand, was motivated to act otherwise with different groups out of fear (Galatians 2:12). This does provoke an important question, "How far may we compromise our beliefs with a view to evangelism?" What motivates the way you behave or present yourself as a Christian, around immature Christians or unbelievers? Are you a Peter or a Paul? Imagine you are in your work environment. Others within the office are often vulgar and tell filthy jokes. Do you laugh with them, or quietly remove yourself from the situation? If you were an unbeliever in your office (the "fly on the wall" scenario), would you be able to pick up that there is a Christian in your midst if that person behaved like you presently?

---

[163]Fee, G. D. *First Epistle*, p. 395.

Here are some additional questions worth considering.

5. What were some of the practices that took place at one of these idol temple sacrifices in the OT?

6. Why did Paul prohibit them from eating at an idol temple?

7. How does Paul use the "sacraments" to prove the inherent danger of their eating at idol temples?

8. Why did the Corinthian's doubt Paul's apostolic authority?

9. What, according to Paul, is the principle of Christian freedom?

10. How did Paul demonstrate his freedom?

11. Explain the guidelines laid down by Paul in dealing with matters of indifference.

Chapter Eleven
Behaving Appropriately
in Worship

You arrive early for church and take your seat near the back. As you sit there contemplating your Lord, a group of women dressed in bathing costumes, full costumes, but bathing costumes nonetheless, enter! What's more, you notice one of the women happens to be your wife or 18-year-old daughter. How would you feel? Shocked, embarrassed, distracted, lustful or angry? At the very least, I would imagine most being distracted. But, this might not have been the case if your church met regularly on a Jamaican beach.

The Western cultured person just does not do this or expect to see this in church. Similarly, those within Corinth (men and women) would have found it shocking to see women within a church service without their head coverings on.[164] Therefore, imagine being the minister in that church, having to deal with offended folk, and the feminists (bathing costume women). You do not want to upset or chase anyone from the church. Bearing this in mind, how would you solve the problem and convince these women to wear

---

[164]A situation not entirely different occurred during the 1970's hippie revival in one Cape Town church. None of the new hippie converted ladies wore bra's, many did not wear shoes, and none of the men wore ties. The Pentecostal elders wanted the men to come to church in suits, with ties. It took a long time for the two "cultures" to find each other.

acceptable clothes to church? Let us look at how Paul dealt with a similar situation and hope you never have to deal with something similar.

1 Corinthians 11:2 begins an entirely new section. It includes all the sub-sections in 11:2–14:40. The commonality between all the problems described in these Chapters is that they all have to do with "public worship services."

1. Concerns over women's head-coverings or hairstyles in public worship services (11:2–16).

2. The abuse of the poor while participating in the Lord's Supper (11:17–34).

3. The abuse of the gift of tongues in public services (11:12–14).

However, note that these next few Chapters continue with the overarching theme that ones "right of freedom" should not override love and respect for others.

This first section on "head covering" is fraught with misinterpretation and misapplication. It is a difficult section because it deals with a custom foreign to the Western world, about which we know very little.

The way things were

We know that women participated in the public worship services, and it was the prevailing custom for women to pray or prophesy with their heads covered. Those women who did not comply were going against the custom. It caused some commotion. The question is: what did it mean to "have your head covered" and should these women stop doing it?

The literal translation of "head being covered" is "having (whatever the covering was) down the hair" (11:5, 6, 13, 15). There are a number of possibilities as to what this covering was: some form of veil, her long hair or her long hair let down. The traditional interpretation, and the one I still hold to, is that the covering refers to some sort of "veil." Note that none of the options is without fault but the "veil" and "letting her hair down" carry the least number of difficulties. In the case of the latter, I feel that verse 6 opposes it: "If a woman does not cover her head, she should have her hair cut off." Some other translations put it as: "If a woman does not cover her head, it is just as though her head was shaved." The point is that both these verses assume that her hair was already long – "she should have her hair cut off" or "it is just as though her head was shaved." This implies that even though her hair is long, she remains uncovered.

Therefore, if the covering was not hair, the veil remains as the only possibility. The veil would have most likely concealed her hair and the upper part of the body (shoulders).[165] As to why women were reluctant to wear it; well, there is no certainty. It could be due to their over-realized eschatology. Their belief in the Kingdom coming in its fullness would imply things, such as "we are like the angels who do not marry." Furthermore, in this Kingdom, there were no sexual distinctions; therefore, they did not need to wear a veil because they had their authority.

To add a little extra background, Paul mentions the traditions, which they were apparently adhering to. (I say, "apparently" because clearly this was not entirely the case.) The best way to understand the argument is to determine if those who raised the issue with Paul had said, "Paul, we are adhering to the traditions (head covering) but our women are not."

Paul's dilemma was to maintain the tradition in order to prevent social disruption. Somehow, he would need to persuade the women to temper their newfound freedom without upsetting them, while correcting the men at the same time. Not an easy task considering firstly, he had personally stated that "There is no longer Jew or Greek, there is no longer slave or free, there is no longer male

---

[165]There is little evidence that it might have been a veil with tiny slits for the eyes, as is customary in contemporary Moslem communities.

and female; for all of you are one in Christ Jesus" (Galatians 3:28) and, secondly that the culture of the day fully subscribed to women wearing veils!

Thus, how does he do it? His argument is both theological and cultural, which is something we ought to bear in mind these days too.

Firstly, he covers the basic theological statement "But I want you to understand that Christ is the head of every man, and the husband is the head of his wife, and God is the head of Christ" (11:3). This suggests that there is a divine order. In 11:4–6, the solution to the problem is that women should revert to old ways. Then, in 11:7–12, the root of the theological argument rears up, namely that a woman is the glory of man, and that man is the "head" of the woman. Further, man came from women and vice versa. Lastly, in 11:13–16, he refers to their socio-cultural situation by drawing on analogies from nature and church-related socio-cultural customs.

He begins by offering the Corinthians sincere praise. It is possible that the Corinthians had shown Paul, in some way, that they had remembered the "teachings" and "traditions" he had passed onto them. These "traditions/teachings" were the central truths of the Christian faith communicated verbally before the emergence of Christian literature.

The theological argument – 1 Corinthians 11:3, 7–12

Clearly, Paul's reason for maintaining the status quo has to do with the "divine order" (11:3).[166] A similarity exists within the relation-

---

[166]In the first century Middle East a veil covering was a symbol of the divine order of authority established by God (11:3). It was also a sign of respectable womanhood and modesty; something a wife/woman might wear to affirm herself as a woman of dignity. It is reasonable to think that most respectable Roman, Greek and Jewish woman wore a head covering in public. Aline Rousselle and Dale Martin have shown that for a married woman in Roman society to appear in public without a hood sent out signals of sexual availability or at very least a lack of concern for

ship between a husband and his wife,[167] Christ and man, and God and Christ. It appears as if the term "head" is reflecting this relationship.

It is vital to our understanding of this section to determine what the metaphorical meaning of the word "head" is (11.3). In the Greek Old Testament, this word *kephale* had hierarchical connotations. For instance, in Judges 10:18, "The commanders of the people of Gilead said to one another, 'Who will begin the fight against the Ammonites? He shall *be head* over all the inhabitants of Gilead.'" However, at the time of Paul's writing, the Greek language included the meaning of "head" as "source," as in "the source of life." Therefore, Paul's intent is not hierarchical or authoritarian (who has position over whom), but *relational* (the unique relationships predicated upon oneself for being the source of the other). Thus, Paul is more interested in the fact that the woman is the man's glory. If she is not with him, he remains incomplete, and to blur this relationship would bring shame on her head.[168] Paul wants them to be who they were made to be, thereby honouring God; trying to be someone or something other than yourself does not.

In this instance, *God the Father is the origin of Christ's authority. Christ is the origin of man's authority, and man is the origin of woman's authority.* This does not mean that man is the origin of women because God is the origin of women. The portions in italics above represent the point of 11:3 and form the basis of Paul's entire argument (see also Colossians 1:16).

Another puzzling word within 11:7 is "glory." Why is a woman not the "glory" of God? This is a difficult statement. The word "glory" has many different applications. Consider the following

---

respectability. Duby, G. and Perot, M. (eds.) *A History of Women in the West, I: From Ancient Goddesses to Christian Saints*, pp. 296–337.

[167]There is some debate as to whether "man and woman" or the smaller category of "husband and wife" are being addressed here. I am of the opinion that both are being addressed.

[168]G. D. *First Epistle*, pp. 503–504.

texts: 2 Thessalonians 1:9; Hebrews 3:3; 9:5; 1 Peter 1:24; 2 Peter 2:10 and Jude 8). It seems as if the word "glory" relates to a spiritual context.

The following extract taken from "The Message" on the Corinthian text is helpful.

> By the way, don't read too much into the differences here between men and women. Neither man nor woman can go it alone or claim priority. Man was created first, as a beautiful shining reflection of God – that is true. However, the head on a woman's body clearly outshines in beauty the head of her "head," her husband. The first woman came from man, true – but ever since then, every man comes from a woman! Moreover, since virtually everything comes from God anyway, let's quit going through these "who's first" routines.

Therefore, he is suggesting that to be the "glory" of man is a good thing. It is like a king without a crown or a crown without a king. A king without a crown (crowned at his coronation) is not a king, and a crown without a king is a piece of jewellery. However, together, they have a purpose and reflect the full majesty of those whom and for what reason they were created.

Let us move on to 11:10. Two phrases obscure the meaning of this text. The first is the use of "a sign of authority" instead of "veil." Translations vary on the wording here. Variations range from "sign of the authority" (NJB; NIV); a "sign of submission" (NAB); "symbol of authority" (NRSV); to "sign of her (the woman's own) authority" on her head (REB). My opinion is that the correct translation is the last. Consider the following:

> Numerous scholars suggest that prophetesses suffered "peer-group pressure to throw aside their hoods ... in the name of gospel freedom and gender equality. Paul insists, however, that they keep control of (how people perceive) their heads, because the issue here ... remains that of assertive autonomy (I

have the right to ...) versus self-control ... The translation "to have" does not always have the force of power over; it often denotes control of something as well as on something, i.e. if a woman exercises the control that exemplifies respectability in Roman society, and retains the semiotic code of gender differentiation in public, "with the veil on her head she can go anywhere in security and profound respect." This extends to the act of using prophetic speech in public worship, but ... is not restricted to being specifically a sign of "authority" to use prophetic speech as such.[169]

The second obscure phrase is "because of the angels." The puzzling issues include, who are these angels and why should the women behave in a certain manner because of the angels? Here are some suggestions.

Could it be that the angels were the "Sons of God" who raped the daughters of men? Against such potential attackers, women need help. Alternatively, that the word "angels" actually referred to apostles (Rev. 2:1)? Lastly, it might be that the women were insisting that they had authority and were already like angels, or perhaps speaking the language of angels (13.1).

I am doubtful about the first two. Firstly, if women really were in danger of attack and rape by bad angels, how would a veil protect them? Secondly, was this the only time that lustful angels would prey upon the women – while at worship? I would think that worship services would be the last place they would dare attempt anything. As regards the second option of "apostles"; the Greek word for "angel" is *aggelos* (messenger) and for "apostle," *apostolos* (sent one). The word used in 11:10 is *aggelos*, thus it is unlikely that the "angels" were "apostles."

In my opinion, the third option is most likely. The argument develops along these lines. Women approached Paul believing that they had authority to be without a cover because they were like the

---

[169]Thiselton. A. C. *The First Epistle*, p. 838.

angels (their new-found state) or perhaps because they were already speaking the language of the angels. If this is correct, Paul's argument would have taken a slight turn, viz. He has just supported the notion that men should not wear a head covering, and vice versa for women. However, now he turns and supports the women to the tune of their right to freedom. However, he suggests that because the woman is dependent on the man, she should sacrifice the exercise of this freedom for the sake of the tradition, at least for now.[170]

Why should they behave in this manner "because of the angels" – because they will judge angels in the future? This should motivate us to judge rightly as well (6:3). In respect to the meaning of "judging angels," please refer to my John Deere illustration in (6:1–6).

Therefore, the women's authority should motivate them to use their authority properly with regard to covering their heads now. She has the right to do with her head what she wills, but like Paul, she must give up this right for the common good.[171] Verses 8–9 and 11–12 follow suit.

1 Corinthians 11:8–9 focuses on "what has existed from the beginning of creation." I tend to think that Paul was aiming these two verses at the women because they had misunderstood their new-found freedom. He reminds them that they came from man. They were co-dependent (Genesis 2:21), but created as a suitable helper for man (Genesis 2:18), to complete him. However, after reminding them of this fact, he then warns the men not to exaggerate the significance of their being created first either (11:11–12). The Lord established a partnership between the genders in which neither could exist without the other. A woman may have initially come from a man, but ever since that first occasion, men have come from women. Ultimately, both are created by God – He is their origin.

This is the end of Paul's theological argument.

---

[170]Fee, G. D. *First Epistle*, p. 522
[171]Keener, C.S. 1 *and 2 Corinthians*, p. 94.

The cultural standpoint – 1 Corinthians 4–6; 13–16

There are three reasons Paul uses to encourage the women to continue with the existing custom:

1. By uncovering herself, the woman is dishonouring her "head" and bringing shame upon her husband and herself.

2. Paul's metaphor from nature teaches that a head covering is the correct way.

3. The wider church simply knows no other way.

Let us take a closer look at these passages.

The area of uncertainty in 11:4 lies in the meaning of the word "head" used twice. The first meaning of "head" refers to a man's head, but the second is less certain. In the latter, it could mean "man's head," "Christ's head," or that it is both "Christ and man's head." As with other sections, the answer is not completely certain. However, it is my opinion that the third alternative is most likely.

You will recall that we looked at the authority structure initiated by God. A symbolic way (in Corinth) of representing this authority structure was to either wear (woman) or not wear (man) a veil. To go against this custom meant failure to recognise the authority structure established by God. Therefore, in so doing, they were dishonouring themselves, as well as Christ. The veil was only relevant to the culture that interpreted it in this light, most likely the Greco-Roman culture. Jewish men wore head coverings when they prayed, so Paul's argument would have made no sense to a Jewish culture.

In 11:5–6, Paul explains to the women that when they go against the tradition, they dishonour their husband and self. One could compare this to the bathing costume example again or to a pastor whose wife has dyed her hair red and walks around in black skin-tight leather pants, and this in a culturally conservative church. The argument here is purely cultural. Paul says that if she does not wear a veil, she may as well have shaved off all her hair. In those times, shaven women were frowned upon and often taken to be adulterers (a husband who suspected his wife of adultery would shave off her hair, strip her naked and send her out into the street).

In 11:13–15, Paul changes the reason for abiding by the current custom by using a metaphor from nature. His use of the words "the very nature of things" is obscure. Paul must surely mean "culture." If he were literally referring to "nature," the metaphor would not make sense. A man's hair is not "naturally" short unless "unnaturally" cut. The point of these verses comes up in 11:13. It was simply inappropriate, culturally, for a woman to have short hair and a man to have long hair. In the same way, it was incorrect for a woman to unveil herself in a public worship service. A similar norm in Western culture is that we do not believe that a woman should go around with only her eyes peering through slits in a veil.

In the final verse (11:16), Paul makes it clear that he does not intend to argue about this subject. His last ploy has an ethical side to it. "We have no other practice, nor do the churches of God." The point here is that this custom was universal to all Christians in all Greco-Roman churches at that time. The women should respect this.

Questions and Thoughts for Reflection

Over the past few years, there has been much debate about this portion of Chapter 11, especially regarding male/female relationships. How does God see us as relating to one another?

1. Shortly after creation, Adam and Eve disobeyed God. God's first interaction with them and the serpent involves Him delivering a prophecy with different parts pertaining to each of them. To the woman God said, "I will greatly increase your pangs in childbearing; in pain you shall bring forth children, yet your desire shall be for your husband, and he shall rule over you." The prophecy impacts the woman's two primary roles of childbearing and relationship with her husband. It is this second role that I want to draw to your attention. Genesis 3:16 is fraught with interpretational difficulties, but one of the fore-

most biblical scholars on Genesis believes the following meaning with respect to this passage:

> Applied to 3:16, the desire of the woman for her husband is akin to the desire of sin that lies poised ready to leap at Cain. It means a desire to break the relationship of equality and turn it into a relationship of servitude and domination. The sinful husband will try to be a tyrant over his wife. Far from being a reign of co-equals over the remainder of God's creation, the relationship now becomes a fierce dispute, with each party trying to rule the other. The two who once reigned as one, attempt to rule each other.[172]

We see this curse playing itself out throughout history. In the Old Testament, women were treated poorly and not permitted to take part in the activities of men. They had no status or say in matters. Their best chance for anticipating a fulfilled life was if they were beautiful and/or born into a well-to-do family. The prevailing attitude was that the "woman was created for man's enjoyment;" however, Jesus shook the establishment (see Matthew 26:7–13; Luke 7:44–47; 10:38–42; John 4:7–9; 8:3–11; 20:13–17). The ways He allowed women to anoint Him, kiss Him, sit at His feet, hold Him and even just talk to Him, were not publicly acceptable. Nevertheless, Jesus' compassion for women was notable. His behaviour and teaching communicated, "all are one in Christ" (Galatians 3:28). This meant that there was a shift in the "value of women." Suddenly, Jesus was saying that men and women were equal (the curse was being undone); God saw no inequality between them in Christ. This applied to slave or free, Jew or Gentile, male or female. The problem is that Christians do not seem to take cognisance of what Jesus has taught and practiced. There remains serious

---

[172]Hamilton, V.P. *The Book of Genesis Chapters* 1–17, p. 202.

sexism within many cultures today. What about you? How do you respond to the opposite sex?

2. Thiselton suggests that "respect is a key feature of love for 'the other' in Jesus and Paul: respect for the 'other' is the keynote of this passage – for God, for fellow Christians at worship, for the Roman world as it receives Christian's, and not least for the self in terms of self-respect. What aspects of the ministry of Jesus does this reflect? How did Jesus treat outcasts and the despised? The prodigal son in the world of the parable (Luke 15:22) receives back a robe, sandals, and the ring as marks of dignity and respect. Genuine respect nurtures and supports love (13:4–7), which is the desire for the wellbeing of 'the other.' Why does love not despise 'respectability'? This positive effect of mutual respect is not only common to Jesus and Paul. It is also a matter of common sense reflection: 'come to a decision for yourself' (v. 13)."[173]

3. Many people believe that this text was only applicable to that day and age because the problem arose out of a culture very different from ours. However, they would be seriously mistaken. Some scholars entitle this portion of text "Propriety in Worship." Women in the congregation were drawing men's attention away from the Creator and back to the created. It does not really matter how they were doing it, the point is that they were. It is this principle that we can apply. Think of what draws peoples' attention away from the Creator to the created in a church service. For example:

   • The types of clothing we wear
   • Reserving seats for "VIPs" at church services
   • Television cameras
   • People who try to steal the attention of the congregation

---

[173]Thiselton, A.C. *1 Corinthians: A Shorter Exegetical Commentary & Pastoral Commentary,* p. 179.

through performance in worship, preaching, healing, prophesy, etc.

4. Men's roles are changing within modern society. Various factors have resulted in men deferring spiritual authority to women. For example, the fragmentation of families stemming from high divorce rates and unmarried-parenthood has led to "single mother" child rearing. Men raised in a fatherless generation struggle to take up their roles in society as men, since they have had their responsibility deferred to women all their lives. This contradicts how God envisages the role of men. Have you noticed this trend within your society? Has this perhaps impacted you personally – being raised fatherless? How do you think this has affected you or could affect others?

    Here are some additional questions to consider:

5. What was the problem in public worship services in the Church at Corinth (11:2–16)?

6. Why were the women behaving contrary to the culture?

7. What was Paul's theological argument in favour of their continuing with the prevailing custom?

8. What was Paul's socio-cultural argument in favour of continuing with the prevailing custom?

9. Are there issues within your culture that Paul might offer the same advice to?

Chapter Twelve
The Lord's Supper

Paul's letter to the Corinthians now begins to move from the general sphere of church practice into the practical details of church order. The first theme that he addresses under church order is the Corinthians use of the Lord's Supper. From the text, we can see that Paul writes to highlight error, re-instruct and warn them against wrongful actions within their context. Was it possible that the Corinthians were drunk when participating in this rite? Was this leading to some being sick, and even dying for their sin? One wonders whether this is still happening today! Let us find out!

Before we begin, I must mention three things:

1. This text most likely represents the earliest known documented version of the pattern of "Holy Communion." It is thus vital that we understand this teaching and endeavour to practise what Paul preached.[174]

2. Most Christians are very familiar with Holy Communion and participating therein. This can be a danger. Many are tempted to skim over this section thinking they already know it.

3. Some scholars do not believe that Paul was talking about the

---

[174]1 Corinthians pre-dates the publication of the gospels in time, even though the story the gospels tell predates 1 Corinthians.

"Lord's Table" as we know it. There is strong evidence refuting this though. The phrase used to denote "Lord's Supper" (*kyriakon deipnon*) stresses the connection with the Lord, to honour or consecrate Him. Secondly, Paul says, "when you come together, it is not the Lord's Supper you eat" (11:20). He implies that the Corinthian Christians' behaviour makes a mockery of participating in the Lord's Supper. Lastly, if it were not the Lord's Supper, why does he make a fuss of repeating Jesus' words of initiation?

Let us first consider what was taking place to warrant a letter from Paul.

What was the problem?

Why did Paul address the topic of the Lord's Supper? Judging from the tone of his letter, it appears as if those in the church were committing some sort of abuse. You will recall from the previous section on "Women in Worship" that Paul began with commendations for "maintain[ing] the traditions just as I handed them on to you" (11:2). This is hardly the case here. He says, "I do not commend you, because when you come together it is not for the better but for the worse" (11:17).

A good place to start is with what we know.

- Most of the church took part in the supper. Words such as "when you come together as a church" and "come together" suggest this (18, 20, 33, and 34).

- The "Lord's Supper" and a community meal go hand-in-hand. This is the case for the following reasons: When Jesus began the tradition, he did so in the context of a meal (Matthew 26:26–29; Mark 14:22; Luke 22:8–20). There were additional instances in the New Testament linking the two (Acts 2:46; 20:11; 27:35–38). There is no reason to think that they would have broken with this tradition.[175]

- The meal had to do with the church's strong eschatological belief. One of the hopes of the Jews was that they might join in the celebrations at the great banquet in the presence of God. Jesus instituted the Lord's Supper in the context of that hope, "Truly I tell you, I will never again drink of the fruit of the vine until that day when I drink it anew with you in the Kingdom of God" (Mark 14:25, see also Matthew 8:11; 26:29; Luke 13:29; 14:15, 16, 24; 22:29–30 and Revelation 19:9).

- Most people in Corinth were accustomed to worshipping their gods by eating a meal in their presence, i.e. eating at the temple of whichever deity they served. Many of those people were now in the church. The practice of eating a meal in honour of the deity had not necessarily changed. The "god" they worshipped had changed (hopefully)!

Let us clarify what the issue was by considering the abuses and the clues Paul leaves for us in his text (11:17–22).

One way to consider the problems is to view them from two dimensions: A "horizontal dimension" – relations amongst each other and a "vertical dimension" – relations between God and themselves.

The Horizontal Dimension

Holy Communion took place in conjunction with a full meal, commonly called a "love feast" (Jude 12). However, the participants' behaviour towards one another was disgraceful. The wealthier members were most certainly providing all the food, a wonderful expression of love. However, was that their intention?

Corinth was a cosmopolitan city. It was a rich diversity made

---

[175]The use of small symbolic bits of bread and small sips of wine only began as a practice well after the New Testament era.

up of Jews, Greeks, Romans, slaves, merchants, and rich business types. The problem at their gathering was that the wealthier among them were failing to realize Jesus' /Paul's message: no partiality and no class distinctions! Thus, they were failing to be God's new people and as such, not participating in the "Lord's Supper" at all.

There are three suggestions why this is so:

1. Some believe that there was evidence of "individualism," i.e. many were going ahead with their meal with their own "spiritual gain" in mind.

2. Others think that the rich were eating the food before the poor/slaves arrived to share in the meal. Thus, the rich were gluttons and drunk while the poor went hungry. Broadly speaking, it was "communion without community."

3. The rich were eating a private meal because they enjoyed exclusive seating.

The most likely scenario was the third, with some likelihood of the second as well. There is evidence to suggest that houses at that time had a "dining" area called a *triclinium*. This room could only seat a few people. If the church were bigger than fifteen or twenty, the overflow spilled out into the atrium. One triclinium was located in the area and measured 5.5 by 7.5 meters, while the atrium (hallway) measured 5 by 6 meters. Murphy-O'Connor calculates that the atrium might have held between 30 and 40 persons, with fewer in the triclinium where the couches occupied space.[176] Possibly, the rich made themselves at home in the triclinium while the poor were expected to sit outside in the atrium.

The meal took place in the absence of sharing, love, or unity. Clearly, their inter-personal relationships were in a mess. The rich felt nothing for the poor, which is very different from the church portrayed in Acts 4:32–37.

---

[176]Murphy-O'Connor, *St Paul's Corinth*, p. 156 in Thiselton, A. C. 2000. *The First Epistle*, p. 7.

The Vertical Dimension

Judging by their actions, it seems as if the Corinthians had missed the whole point of Holy Communion – a celebration in honour of the Lord. Their (wealthy) behaviour demonstrated a lack of respect for the magnitude and meaning of the symbols. Thus, the problem in this text was an abuse of the Lord's Table in both a vertical and horizontal sense.

Paul's three-pronged approach

Paul adopted the following approach to deal with the issues at hand:
* Reveal the error of their way (11:17–22)
* Re-educate the Corinthian Church (11:23–26); and
* Emphasize the danger of their ways (11:27–34).

No respect for Christ and the Poor – 1 Corinthians 11:17–22

This section concentrates on some of the specifics of the text.
* What did Paul mean by "and to some extent I believe it" (11:18)? Most likely, he imagined there to be some exaggeration in what he had heard, i.e. that there could have been those patrons who did not act in this manner, but based on other aspects of the report, this abuse was to be expected.

* Secondly, there is uncertainty with regard to what Paul meant by "genuine" (NRSV) or "God's approval" (NIV) (11:19). Horsley suggests that Paul was using irony: "For of course there must be 'discrimination' among you so that it will become clear who amongst you are 'the distinguished ones.'"[177] The irony is that Paul's view of being "distinguished" is contrary to the "well-to-do's" at Corinth.

* His concern is that, by their actions, the rich were demonstrating a lack of understanding regarding the all-encompassing

---

[177]Horsley, R. *1 Corinthians*, p. 159.

nature of the Body of believers and Christ (11:21–22). He says that if the rich want to eat with their own friends enjoying better food than their poor brothers and sisters, they should rather do it at home. At least then, if they indulge in excess, they will not be making a mockery of the Lord's Supper and the poor people in the church. Do they not realise that their actions do not stem from love? Don't they know that God has accepted the poor, just as he has accepted the rich? The poor were ashamed because they could not afford to help provide for the supper. The rich blatantly denied Christian principles and practices.

The Foundations of the Lord Supper – 1 Corinthians 11:23–26

It is interesting to note that the Corinthians were familiar with the Christian tradition established before Paul's writings. It is also reasonable to assume that the Corinthians had not ignored this tradition or doubted its validity. Thus, there is a common foundation to the thrust of his ensuing argument.

There are four separate accounts of the institution in the New Testament. [178]

Mark 14:22–24	Matt 26:26–28	Luke 22:19–20	1 Cor 11:24–25
While they were eating, he took a loaf of bread, and after blessing it he broke it, gave it to them, and said, "Take; this is my body." Then he took a cup, and after giving thanks he gave it to them, and all of them drank from it. He said to them, "This is my blood of the covenant, which is poured out for many."	While they were eating, Jesus took a loaf of bread, and after blessing it he broke it, gave it to the disciples, and said, "Take, eat; this is my body." Then he took a cup, and after giving thanks he gave it to them, saying, "Drink from it, all of you; for this is my blood of the covenant, which is poured out for many for the forgiveness of sins.	Then he took a loaf of bread, and when he had given thanks, he broke it and gave it to them, saying, "This is my body, which is given for you. Do this in remembrance of me." And he did the same with the cup after supper, saying, "This cup that is poured out for you is the new covenant in my blood …	For I received from the Lord what I also handed on to you, that the Lord Jesus on the night when he was betrayed took a loaf of bread, and when he had given thanks, he broke it and said, "This is my body that is for you. Do this in remembrance of me." In the same way he took the cup also, after supper, saying, "This cup is the new covenant in my blood. Do this, as often as you drink it, in remembrance of me." For as often as you eat this bread and drink of the cup, you proclaim the Lord's death until he comes.

---

[178]The NRSV translation is utilized for this comparison.

The process of the institution consisted of a number of steps:

1. He took bread and gave thanks to God.

2. He broke the bread and stated, "this is my body." In saying this, Jesus indicated that he was giving His life in place of theirs. His act would serve to redeem them and establish a new community (body) in which they were all one. As regards the "body," it is crucial to understand that the bread "signified" or was to be "interpreted" as that of Jesus' body sacrificed for us. It does not mean that upon consecration, the bread literally becomes 1) Jesus' body (transubstantiation) which we eat, or 2) once the bread enters the body that we then partake of the real flesh of Jesus (consubstantiation).

3. He took the cup stating that it was "the New Covenant in His blood." Incidentally, this "cup" would have been the third cup of the five utilized in the Passover, viz. "the cup of redemption". The significant word in this verse is "covenant." It is likely that the first covenant in history was the covenant of works between God and Adam (Genesis 2:16–17). Although Genesis does not use the term "covenant" to describe this agreement, Hosea possibly identifies what God and Adam had as a covenant (Hosea 6:7). God made the second covenant with Noah (Genesis 9:8) and the third with Abraham. The latter was an unconditional covenant ratified in (Genesis 15:18) and repeated with Isaac (Genesis 17:19) and Jacob (Genesis 31:44). You might recall that Jacob later became Israel (Genesis 32:28). This leads us to the fourth divine covenant God made, this time with Israel, the nation, on Mt. Sinai (Exodus 19:3–6). This covenant included the Law and the Passover. The fifth covenant was with David (2 Samuel 7:12, 13, 16). Lastly, there is the New Covenant of which Jesus Christ, the second Adam, is Mediator. An important point to remember is that the word "new" does not refer to "new" in terms of chronology, but "new" in terms of "fresh," "unprecedented," "superior" (Hebrews 9). The old covenant fell

away because a better covenant came into being. Two additions to the New Covenant were the Lord's Supper and a change in the human element of the covenant, from Israel to "all" peoples. When Paul uses the word "covenant," he is most likely referring to God's desire and ability to continue in his faithfulness to the initial covenant He established with Israel, albeit in a more all encompassing fashion (Romans 9:4; 11:27).

In the latter part of 11:25–26, Paul adds an additional emphasis: "Do this in remembrance of me" and "you proclaim the Lord's death until he comes."

Why did he use these particular words as none of the other texts refer to them?

- Jesus asked them to remember what he had done, i.e. His teachings, lifestyle, and most of all, His sacrifice.

- In each of the above texts, the theological emphasis is on the fact that the Father "handed Jesus over" to die for our sins (Romans 8:32).

- 11:17–34 centres on those who are weak, the "not so impressive" types of the world: the outcasts, the failures, the slaves; the very people to whom Jesus promised that the Kingdom was now available.

When seen together, it is likely that Paul included the "tradition" along with his own specific emphasis in his rebuke, to drive home a certain argument. At the Lord's Supper, Jesus handed himself over voluntarily, thereby renouncing any self-seeking pleasure and independence. Instead, he placed his life in the hands of God and made no self-defence.

Through this act, he was calling Christians to follow the same lifestyle. Thus, when they "proclaimed" His death, they were emulating this lifestyle. It was not just about adhering to a ritual, saying all the right words, or responding to the needs of the world by calling them to mind. It was about a lifestyle of self-sacrifice, of loving others and bringing glory to God through it.

However, through their actions, the Corinthians reflected selfishness, individualism and "lovelessness" for their brothers and sisters. They were a million miles from proclaiming His death.

"Remembrance of Christ and of Christ's death … constitutes a self-involving proclamation of Christ's death through a life and a lifestyle which derives from understanding our identity as Christians in terms of sharing the identity of Christ who is for the 'other.'" [Furthermore,] "it was precisely because of a self-centred concern for honor, status, or peer group society and because of disregard for 'the weak,' 'the despised', or 'the other,' that the Lord's Supper had come to defeat its very purpose (11:17). For remembrance of Christ and of His death 'for others', it entailed identification with the Christ who denied himself for others (cf. for you)."[179]

Living on Dangerous Ground – 1 Corinthians 11:27–34

The Lord's Supper is a time of fellowship with the Lord and fellow Christians, eaten in memory of what He has done until His Second-Coming.

Paul describes certain consequences that arise when participating in this meal improperly. What lay behind these mysterious occurrences? What did Paul mean by using words like "unworthy," "guilty," "examine," "body," "judge," and "discipline"?

We begin with "unworthy" in an attempt to understand this section: "Whoever, therefore, eats the bread or drinks the cup of the Lord in an unworthy manner" (11:27). The Corinthian Christians were morally out of sorts with the intention or nature of the supper. As a result, they were "guilty" for the body and blood of Jesus. "Guilty" as used here suggests the result of being "held accountable" for claiming to identify with Jesus in sharing what the Lord's Supper proclaims (salvation through Jesus' death, which the bread and cup represent) while at the same time treating the occasion as a casual

---

[179]Thiselton, A. C. *The First Epistle*, p. 879.

party full of sinful behaviour: gluttony, drunkenness, self-gain enhancing their personal status. In so doing, they placed themselves in the same shoes as those who caused Jesus' death in the first place. Therefore, to violate Jesus' body and blood is equivalent to putting Him to death.

They can discover a way out of such guilt if they "examine" themselves (11:28). In this context, "examine" means to test, prove, or scrutinize one's own heart. "Authenticity of heart," means to consider one's beliefs, actions, and attitudes and to establish whether they correspond with the spirit in which Jesus presented himself as a living sacrifice. The question is: does one present oneself in a similar sacrificial and selfless manner, albeit not in the sense of physical death?

The most reliable manuscripts for 11:29 read: "For anyone who eats and drinks without recognizing the body, eats and drinks judgement on himself." Did you notice the absence of the words "of the Lord?" Since this is the correct translation, what does "body" refer to if this is the case? Does it still refer to the physical body of Jesus (11:27), or perhaps the body of believers, i.e. the church?

Some scholars have suggested that it still refers to the "physical body" of Jesus, if you link it with 11:24 and 27. If this is the case, then the judgment came from a vertical sin issue. However, it is much more likely that this time, "body" links with body in 10:17, which referred to the "body of believers." If so, the problem relates to the refusal of the wealthy to be considerate of the poor. "The problem with this section (11:17–34) is to correct an abuse visible at the Lord's Supper. The Corinthians were missing the meaning of the "body" given in death; but Paul was concerned about another "body" too – the church. This interpretation reads the word "discerning/recognizing" as "distinct", that each believer is a part of the body, the "church."

In 11:29, their sin comes to the fore (failure to recognise the Lord and other Christians), whereas 11:30 refers to the consequences thereof. The latter verse cannot refer to enigmatic or parabolic speech; it means what it says. If a person participates in the manner discussed, he/she is in danger of sickness or even death from spiritual causes. Why does not recognizing the "body" at the Supper represent such a serious sin? The "Lord's Supper" is not just another meal. It is an occasion where all Christians come together to proclaim that they have become one body through the death of Jesus and that each one of them makes up a part of this body. Therefore, to fail to recognize one another, and even worse, to abuse or hurt one another in this context, is to cut at the very heart of what Jesus came for and established, His church. This is why their behaviour invites the judgment.

Preventing this frightening occurrence will require action on their part. They are to "judge" themselves. This judging does not only mean critically evaluating oneself and passing verdict on what we are doing that is wrong. We should also consider our position and duties as believers. Are we truly behaving as a Christian should, towards Jesus, and others on a social front?[180]

However, if one does fall under the Lord's judgement, not all is lost because it is the Lord's form of discipline (11:32). Here "discipline" means to "train children, to be instructed or taught or to learn from those who are moulding the character of others." It is a judgement that a father performs with the child's best interests at heart (Hebrews 12:5–6). It does not jeopardise one's salvation. Rather, it is part of the process of being conformed into the image of Jesus.

Paul ends this portion of his letter by giving some practical advice (11:33–34).

---

[180]The judgment on the Corinthian believers was not for sins outside of the context of the Lord's Supper. Many aim to use Paul's admonition in 1 Corinthians 11 to argue that we should not draw near to the Lord's Table with some or other sin still in our life. Certainly unrepentant sin should be dealt with, but if we were to only use the Lord's Supper when we are sinless, none of us would ever partake of it! Indeed one facet of the Lord's Supper is to recall God's forgiveness of us. No, the judgment in this context relates to a specific sin – desecrating the Lord's Supper.

Consider this. Do you suppose that there are other situations where incorrectly discerning the body of believers, and the Lord himself, could incur God's judgement upon us today? I see no reason why not. We are under the same New Covenant and required to observe the Supper in like manner. So let us take heed of these cautions!

As was the case back in Corinth, one significant form of "spiritual elitism" today is characterised by the division of spiritual professionals and the ordinary folk. However, scripture teaches no such division – the body of the Lord is one and all of its members are united and holy. Therefore, Christian ministers ought to take care that they present themselves as ministers and servants to the body, and that they do not subordinate the body of the Lord as their servant. There is a lot of spiritual abuse today. Leaders tend to exploit their communities based on some or other belief that ministers belong to a better class than ordinary Christians. Thus, they feel entitled to special rights and privileges.

Questions and Thoughts for Reflection

1. Is the Lord's Supper a Passover Seder or an event that stands by itself? Before reading ahead, what is your opinion and how would you substantiate your answer? Since the Lord's Supper is extremely important, there is going to be a lot of debate about virtually every topic associated with it, not least this question I have put forward. The long-established position is that it is the Passover Seder. However, there are some who have questioned this view due to various differences between the two events. One major difference has to do with the dates (there is some conflict between John and the Synoptic Gospels here) on which the Supper was held, viz. the Lord's Supper was held a day earlier than the Passover. Because of this, what Jesus and His disciples ate was not the usual Paschal meal. In fact, the usual Paschal lambs were being slaughtered at the very time

Jesus was dying on the cross. There is rich symbolism in this since Jesus was often referred to as a "lamb". In Isaiah 53:7, Isaiah prophesies about one who "was oppressed and afflicted, yet he did not open his mouth; he was led like a lamb to the slaughter". Irrespective of these dating difficulties though, there is no doubt that Jesus had in mind that He was participating in some form of Passover meal. There are direct correlations between the rescue/redemption of the Israelites from Egypt and the reconciling and saving work Jesus was about to embark on.

2. What is your church's attitude towards the poor and destitute? Do they come to your church services, dinners and social events? If they do, how do you treat them? If they do not, why, and how can you become a motivator for change? Consider what Paul said when he was addressing the topic of "love being sincere". "*Contribute to the needs of the saints; extend hospitality to strangers*" (Romans 12:13) and "do not be haughty, but *associate with the lowly*; do not claim to be wiser than you are" (Romans 12:16). Jesus also had much to say about the poor and lowly. One remarkable statement He made was, "For I was hungry, and you fed me. I was thirsty, and you gave Me a drink. I was a stranger, and you invited Me into your home. I was naked, and you gave Me clothing. I was sick, and you cared for Me. I was in prison, and you visited Me" (Matthew 25:35–36 NLT).

3. Explain the dimensions that formed part of the problem at the celebration of the Lord's Supper at Corinth.

4. How must we celebrate the Lord's Supper? What is the process typically followed? Explain!

5. What is the significance of the Lord's Supper for us today? Why should we continue to celebrate it?

6. According to the text, God disciplines us for our good. How exactly does this work (see Hebrews 12:5–13)?

7. How should you examine or judge yourself and at the same time prevent destructive thought patterns from creeping in?

8. What is the link between confessing, repenting and examining?

Chapter Thirteen
Spirituality

Chapters 12–14 fit together with 8:1–10:22. They all deal with issues surrounding worship. Chapter 8 deals with eating in the temples of idols. Chapter 11 covers two other abuses in the church context: women's misbehaviour in church and inappropriately participating in the Lord's Supper. This next section covers the last area of abuse Paul addresses, that of "spirituality".

Each of the above problem's deals with the underlying issue of what it means to be "spiritual." Does freedom imply doing whatever pleases you? Does it give one the right to override the cultural norms of worship at the time? Alternatively, what about gorging/drinking oneself silly to the detriment of the poor?

Taken together, these Chapters suggest that to "be spiritual" means "to edify the community in worship" (12–14), for the perfect has not yet come (13:8–13), and when it does come, it will include the resurrection of the body, albeit as a "spiritual body" (Chapter 15).[181]

The problem in Chapter 12–14 certainly appears to be the abuse of tongues. If you read through Chapters 12–14, you will notice that the word "tongues" is used more often than any other (12:10, 28, 30; 13:1, 8; 14:2, 4, 5, 6, 13, 14, 18, 19, 22, 23, 26, 27, and 39) suggesting its possible importance. Furthermore, the structure

---

[181]Fee, G. D. *First Epistle,* p. 570.

of the argument in Chapters 12–14 suggests that Chapter 12 offers a general word on the problem, and 13 introduces a certain theological issue (love), and Chapter 14 deals with the specific nature of the problem.

Looking at Chapter 14 first (since the other two lead-up to it), Paul's objective in the initial 25 verses is to argue that "intelligibility" in the assembly is of pivotal importance. Then in 14:26–40, he argues for the importance of order within the assembly. Thus, in the former, Paul tackles their faulty belief that tongues is *the gift* of gifts, and in the latter, their specific abuse of tongues in the assembly.

Examining the build up, Paul covers the need for a diversity of gifts within the one body (Chapter 12) and the motive behind the use of every gift should be edification, or love for one another (Chapter 13).

Spirituality? More like Spiritual Indigestion!

Chapter 12 begins with the words "Now about." As mentioned under the section on analysis, these words might be indicative of Paul's response to a letter he had received, and judging by his tact in the return letter, he clearly disapproved of their understanding and practice.

1 Corinthians 14:12, 20 and 37–38 illuminate for us that:

- They were very eager to be spiritual people. (The word for "spiritual gifts" in verse 12 is *pneuma,* or "spirit" – 3:1 and 4:8),

- Paul considered the Corinthians idea of what constituted a "spiritual person," childish; and

- Even though Paul saw their ways as childish, the Corinthian church members did not.

How did speaking in tongues fit in with being a spiritual person? There are at least two explanations:

1. There is an indication in 13:1 that the Corinthians believed

speaking in tongues was speaking in the language of angels. Remember that in Chapter 7, there was evidence suggesting that some of the Corinthians saw themselves as angels, thus abstaining from sexual intercourse. This becomes very significant if you recall one of the Corinthians' problems – over-realised eschatology. The Corinthians believed that they were already living in the fully realised new age of Jesus. Consequently, speaking in tongues of angels would have been a very good way of proving themselves "spiritual."

2. Secondly, in the first century, it was widely accepted that ecstatic speech, trances and other bizarre behaviour, pointed to a person's special closeness to God or the gods (they were thought to be highly "spiritual"). This is probably why epilepsy was called the "divine disease."[182] It is likely that many folk also believed, due to their supposed "amazing spirituality" (closeness with the divine), that they possessed superior spiritual gifts within, which they should manifest (this idea probably dates back to their days of worshiping mute idols).

The above provides us with some idea of what they believed constituted the new life in the spirit. Paul held that their understanding was flawed. For him, life in the "spirit" was an already, not yet mystery. Although he was born of the spirit, he did not make it his goal to separate himself from the world. He did not strive to discard the physical body. He accepted the life of weakness and power. He also believed that life should be lived with an eye on the future; that we must work on building each other up through love and respect and not seek to boost our spirituality and status (the Corinthians false idea of spirituality).

---

[182]Engle. J, Pedley. T. A, Aicardi. J, and Dichter. M. A. *Epilepsy: A Comprehensive Textbook* (3-volume set), p. 42.

Many gifts, but the same Spirit – 1 Corinthians 12:1–11

The first three verses of Chapter 12 are notoriously difficult to interpret.

- The first difficulty concerns the correct meaning of what the NIV translation has coined "spiritual gifts." The term utilized in this verse is *pneumatikos*, which more likely denotes "spiritual things" than "spiritual gifts," the latter more commonly referred to as *charismata* (12:4).

- It is likely that Paul included these comments to contrast their before and after salvation experience in the context of what it means to be "spiritual," which is the topic he tackles in (12:3). Previously, they had worshipped objects as idols. Obviously, these objects could not speak or respond in anyway. However, now that they knew Jesus as their Lord, those old methods of demonstrating spirituality were no longer necessary. Jesus is alive and is not silent. Their varied experiences of the different gifts that God actively apportions (12:4–11) rest upon His choice and initiative, not upon their own self-generated manifestations or attempts.

- One must establish which verses link up with one another. Probably the most sensible way of understanding these verses is to link verses 1 and 2. Thus, the flow is as follows: "I do not want you to be ignorant of spiritual things (12:1). When you were pagans, you were ignorant and being led away to idols who cannot speak (12:2). I am saying this to warn you, because you are in danger of being side-tracked again."[183]

- Our fourth difficulty rests with what Paul meant by "no one speaking by the Spirit of God ever says 'Let Jesus be cursed!' and no one can say 'Jesus is Lord' except by the Holy Spirit" (12:3).

---

[183]Side tracked by what? Self induced spirituality. That is, a self-centred, self-pleasing spirituality, a status spirituality, a "destructive to others" spirituality.

Having considered numerous scenarios on the possible interpretation, I believe Cullmann's view is the most likely. He maintains that this statement was not about tongues, but about confessing Jesus as Lord in the face of persecution. He states,

> There is very probably here a reference to a saying of Jesus in which he promises his disciples the inspiration of the Holy Spirit precisely at the moment when they will stand before their judges in times of persecution and be called upon to confess their faith Matthew 10.17ff. reads: "... for they will hand you over to councils and flog you in their synagogues; and you will be dragged before governors and kings because of me, as a testimony to them and the Gentiles. When they hand you over, do not worry about how you are to speak or what you are to say; for what you are to say will be given to you at that time; for it is not you who speak, but the Spirit of your Father speaking through you."[184]

Cullmann also raises the matter of a letter from the Governor Pliny to Emperor Trajan, which outlines the procedures for dealing with those accused of following Christ. This practice stated that the person thought to be a Christian should confess "Caesar is Lord", make a sacrifice to him and then curse Christ to prove their non-allegiance.

Furthermore, Cullmann demonstrates that confessions like the one found in 12:3 emerged as primitive creedal forms in "the settings of baptism (Acts 8:37; 1 Peter 3:18–22), worship (Philippians 2:6–11; 1 Corinthians 15:3–7), acts of healing or (in the sub-apostolic period) exorcism (Acts 3:13), and persecution settings (1 Timothy 6:12, 13, 16; Romans 10:9; 1 Corinthians 12:3; cf. Matthew 10:17–20)."[185]

Neufeld adds that a vital aspect of their confession was their belief manifesting through the appropriate lifestyle, something the

---

[184]Cullmann, O. *The Christology of the NT,* p. 219.
[185]Thiselton, A. C. *The First Epistle,* p. 918. Thiselton on Cullmann.

Corinthian Christians were sadly lacking.[186] Essentially, one's beliefs were to reflect Christ as Lord. Gifts that did not point to the Lordship of Christ were not from God.[187] Thus, when we relate Cullmann's idea to Paul's caution to stop behaving as they had when they worshipped idols, the argument reads as follows. "In the past, you put on a show to prove your spirituality. Your spirituality was something you conjured up from within yourselves. Your spirituality was for yourselves. Your spirituality was harmful to others. However, let me tell you that proper spirituality is about being able to confess 'Jesus is Lord' and not 'Jesus be cursed' in the face of real danger."

Let us move on to some further errors in their understanding concerning "spiritual gifts." The following phrases in 12:4–11 serve to illustrate the problems with spirituality in Corinth:

- "Varieties of gifts"
- "Who activates all [the gifts]"
- "To each person"
- "For the common good"

This was how the Corinthians conceived of the manifestation of gifts.

- Their focus was singular when it came to gifts; "tongues was the be-all and end all."

- They possibly believed that they were responsible for conjuring up the gift. This is what they were accustomed to doing in pagan festivals.

- Only highly spiritual people, who were in touch with the divine, possessed these gifts.

- These gifts were for their own benefit.

To counteract this, Paul's objective then is to draw their attention

---

[186] *Neufeld.* V. H. *The Earliest Christian Confessions,* p. 144.

[187] Morris, L. *1 Corinthians,* p. 163.

away from these beliefs by emphasizing two themes, "unity" and "diversity." He does this in three distinct fashions.

1. In 12:4–6, he shows them that although there is but one Spirit, Lord and God, there are a wide variety of manifestations and ministries characterising the gifts and that they all originate from God.

2. God demonstrates this diversity through giving different manifestations for the common good (12:7).

3. Paul lists a number of these manifestations as examples (12:8–11).

He uses these two themes numerous times to bring across his point of correction. Fee has highlighted the emphasis on these themes below. The words appearing in bold represent "diversity", while the words in italics represent "unity."

> Now there are **varieties of gifts**, but *the same Spirit*; and there are **varieties of services**, but *the same Lord*; and there are *varieties of activities*, but it is *the same God* who activates **all of them in everyone**. **To each** is given the manifestation of the Spirit *for the common good*. **To one** is given *through the Spirit* the utterance of wisdom, and **to another** the utterance of knowledge according to *the same Spirit*, **to another** faith by *the same Spirit*, **to another** gifts of healing by *the one Spirit*, **to another** the working of miracles, **to another** prophecy, **to another** the discernment of spirits, **to another** various kinds of tongues, **to another** the interpretation of tongues. **All these** are activated by *one and the same Spirit*, who **allots to each one** individually just *as the Spirit chooses* (12:4–11).[188]

God is the source of these diverse manifestations (12:4–6), and these manifestations are for the benefit of the church (12:7–10). Verse 11 serves as a summary of what he has just said.

---

[188]Fee, G. D. *First Epistle*, p. 584.

Two final issues must be investigated in 12:4–6.

1. There is a distinction between "gifts," "services" and "activities."

2. The Trinity plays a part concerning the gifts. Why?

The "gifts" here refer to *charismata,* but the emphasis is upon their bestowal, freely, as expressions of God's favour. Some interpret "services" to mean "ministries," but Paul emphasizes that a "ministry" is a "service." Lastly, the emphasis on "activities" relates to who activates them as well as the effects of their working. Paul's point is that there are numerous ways of identifying the many manifestations of the Spirit. He is not trying to develop a teaching on the difference between them. For instance, apostles and prophets function within a ministry while prophecy is a *charisma.*

As regards the Trinity, Thiselton believes Paul's motive could be the following: "Different types of gifts do not determine "spiritual" ranking amongst believers, because the same Spirit is active in all according to God's own purposes which determines their apportioning. Similarly, different ways of serving, if they are genuine, all honour the same Lord. Finally, whatever activity transpires, it must be seen as work done by one and the same God who brings about everything in everyone."[189]

1 Corinthians 12:7 is a transitional verse. Paul's choice of words changes from "gift" to "manifestation of the Spirit." There are two possible reasons for this:

1. He uses his teachings on gifts, ministries and workings and groups them together under one common class, "spiritual manifestations."

2. Paul wished to draw attention away from the gift and focus on the giver (remember they tended to focus on who had what gift). Thus, as Fee explains, "God gives to each, i.e. to the community at large, different gifts by which the Spirit is visibly evident in their midst … the concern is not with the

---

[189]Thiselton, A. C. *The First Epistle,* p. 933.

gifts, but with the manifestation of the Spirit through the gifts."[190]

This verse also makes two additional points. Every believer should display manifestations of the Spirit; they are not for personal aggrandizement, but "for the common good." Put another way, the gifts of the Holy Spirit are the means whereby the Lord carries out His ministry into the world through His people. Note that the gifts in these verses are the manifestations of the "Spirit." Therefore, it is through the pneumatic *charismata* that the Holy Spirit shows himself. It is the invisible Spirit's visible/audible manifestation. As Williams comments, "Imagine the gifts were thought of as lights that turn on from a hidden electrical current. The current cannot be seen, but when the lights come on, they are vivid evidence and demonstration of its presence and power."[191]

In my paraphrase earlier on, I replaced the words "for the common good" with "a view to profiting" (12:7). I did this because the latter is a more precise translation in that it does not suggest whether the benefit (profit) is for the giver or the receiver. Even though we know that *charismata* come by the Spirit to help others, this particular verse does not imply that. However, in the greater context of this section, (Chapters 12 and 14) it certainly refers to others profiting rather than self.

Verses 8–11 elaborate on 12:7, particularly in the area of the manifestations of the Spirit.

There are several lists of "gifts" presented in the New Testament. There are some points about these lists you should keep in mind.

- None of the lists, or combinations thereof, is exhaustive.

- The order in which the gifts are given varies considerably from list to list. Thus, do not assume that the entries imply an order of importance or particular significance. A possible reason

---

[190]Fee, G. D. *First Epistle*, p. 589.
[191]Williams, J. R. *Renewal Theology. Systematic Theology from a Charismatic perspective*, p. 330.

why tongues and the "interpretation of tongues" appear last in this passage is that Paul's readers were far too prone to exalt these gifts. However, other gifts like wisdom, knowledge, healing and faith also relate to the problems at Corinth.

- Note that "speaking", and specifically "service", are mentioned in 1 Peter 4:11 as well.

New Testament lists of Spiritual Gifts		
Romans 12:6–8	Ephesians 4:11	1 Corinthians 12:1–14
Prophecy	Apostolic	Wisdom
Ministry	Prophetic	Knowledge
Teaching	Evangelical	Discerning of spirits (human, angelic, demonic)
Exhortation	Pastoral	Speaking in tongues
Giving	Teaching	Interpretation of tongues
Leading		Prophecy
Showing mercy (compassion)		Faith
		Working of miracles
		Healing

One must remember that "spiritual gifts" are not exclusive to the New Testament. The Old Testament is also full of examples, some of which we may not have considered as "spiritual gifts" today. For example:

- *The Gift of Artisanship* – "see, I have called him by name, … and I have filled him with divine spirit, with ability, intelligence, and knowledge in every kind of craft, to devise artistic designs, to work in gold, silver, and bronze, in cutting stones for setting, and in carving wood, in every kind of craft" (Exodus 31:2–5).

- *The Gift of Brute Strength* – "The spirit of the LORD rushed on him, and he tore the lion apart barehanded as one might tear apart a kid" (Judges 14:6).

- *The Gift of Literary Skill and Vision and Dream Interpretation* – "To these four young men God gave knowledge and skill in every aspect of literature and wisdom; Daniel also had insight into all visions and dreams" (Daniel 1:17).

When one thinks of the diversity of these gifts, the boundaries of what constitute "Spiritual Gifts" are limitless.

Let us consider the list in Chapter 12 and explore what each means in turn.

- The gift of *wisdom* can mean, "being endowed with a supernatural ability to read into a situation and make divinely intelligent decisions as to what to do." An example would be Solomon's actions regarding the mothers who both claimed a baby was theirs (1 Kings 3:25–26). Although this form of wisdom is certainly available to us through the Spirit, it is unlikely that Paul meant this of "wisdom" contextually. It more likely refers to one's ability to recognise that Christ Crucified[192] is the true wisdom of God, which is only something a person full of the Spirit could know or understand (2:10–13). It therefore relates to the ability to understand salvation and be able to explain and share it.

- The gift of *knowledge* can be the supernatural ability to know of something un-discerned by natural means. "Word of knowledge" commonly refers to "prophetic revelation." However, is that what it meant given the context? Probably not! I tend to agree with Dunn's explanation here. He believes that the "knowledge" Paul mentions in 12:8 and 14:6 is most likely knowledge of a speculative, and not an

---

[192]Many of those caught up in the confusion surrounding "wisdom" would have interpreted Jesus' teachings as wisdom. The idea of him dying would have been viewed in quite a different light. Thus, in that context, to identify what or who you served as God from a fleshly/material stance (so radically different from the day) would indicate the influence of the Spirit of God.

experiential, nature. "'Utterance of knowledge' may therefore quite properly be understood as a word spoken under inspiration giving an insight into cosmic realities and relationships."[193] Dunn suggest that an example of this working itself out in Corinth is seen in 8:4 where the true identity of idols is revealed – "an idol is nothing in the world", i.e. for a Christian at Corinth to realize this would take the gift of knowledge. A modern day example of this would be having somebody entrenched in postmodernism suddenly coming to the realization that "absolute truth" still exists, or to an alcoholic who has become a Christian, suddenly coming to the realization that they are an alcoholic.

- The gift of *tongues* was the centre of attention in the Corinthian context. When one reads Chapter 14, Paul's lesson on the nature of tongues includes the following:

  † The "tongue" was a divine manifestation (12:7, 11, and 14:2)

  † Those who spoke in a tongue could control it (14:27–28)

  † The speech was unintelligible to the speaker and listener (14:14, 16)

  † The tongue is speech directed toward God[194] (14:2, 14–15, 28); and

  † Paul and others probably thought of tongues as an angelic language.[195]

  † One could infer from each of Paul's teachings in this regard that each corrected some misunderstanding or misuse of "gifts" by the Corinthians.

---

[193]Dunn, J. *Jesus and the Spirit*, pp. 217–222.

[194]More will be said about this final point later.

[195]It is unclear whether the tongues were spoken in a human or angelic language; I have little doubt though that tongues can take both forms.

- Regarding the *interpretation of these tongues,* the gift of tongues is unintelligible to a person unless God provides understanding thereof. Hence, the interpretation of a tongue is a gift. Either the original speaker of the tongue or somebody who hears the tongue spoken could receive this gift to unpack its meaning.

- *Prophecy* can be taken as a word or message divinely inspired. The word/message usually declares the purposes of God, whether by reproving and admonishing the wicked, or comforting the afflicted ones or revealing things hidden. Prophecy can also include foretelling future events. Those at Corinth would have also been familiar with certain Old Testament texts like Joel 2:28. Texts like this imply that we can also prophesy because God's spirit is within us. Judging from explanations given in Chapter 14, prophecies would come spontaneously, were understandable, and the speaker could control the process. Therefore, it is unlikely that the prophecies Paul alluded to were prepared sermons.

Some of the other gifts Paul mentions include faith, healing, miracles and the discernment of spirits.

- The person empowered with the gift of *faith* can perform some sort of extraordinary work. Jesus referred to this kind of faith as the faith that moves mountains. It is the supernatural ability to meet adverse circumstances with trust in God's messages and words. Examples of this gift include the behaviour of the centurion who simply asked Jesus to speak the word of healing over His servant lying terribly ill in another location (Matthew 8:5–13), or, Israel's obeying God's command to refrain from utilising the usual methods of attack (in war scenarios) against Jericho (Joshua 6:3–7).

- The gift of *healing* mentioned here would fall within the same category as those performed by Jesus. Powerful supernatural

works of the Spirit. Another definition of healing is supernatural healing without human aid. This brings us to a very
similar gift, that of miracles or power.

- You might have wondered why there is a distinction between
healing, which is a miracle, and *miracles.* Healing is a miracle, but not all miracles are healings. I conclude that miracles include a broader range of power displays, for instance,
nature miracles, like the calming of the sea.

- Lastly, there is the *discernment of spirits.* Consider two possible explanations. Firstly, it could refer to one's ability to
discern between the actions of the Spirit of God and some
demonic force or, secondly, it is the ability to weigh up the
prophecies given by others to establish their authenticity
(14:29). It is most likely that Paul refers here to the latter
form of discernment (14:29).

Paul's aim throughout this section has been to prevent Christians
from exalting one gift above another. He has also emphasised the
unity of the Godhead as the source of spiritual gifts and ministries.

One body, many parts – 1 Corinthians 12:12–26

This section begins with the word "for," indicating that the following verses will further clarify the point made in 12:4–11, viz. the
need for diversity within unity. In order to drive home this point,
he makes use of the metaphor of a body and its parts.

This metaphor would have made a lot of sense to the Corinthians. One of the practices at the temple of Asclepius was to make
replicas of diseased body parts, which is testament to the number
of clay arms, legs, breasts, genitals located at the sight. "It is against
this sort of backdrop that Paul would've seen the dismembered
body parts as representations of everything a Christian should not
be – dead, separated, useless."[196]

---

[196] *Collins,* R. F. *First Corinthians,* p. 462.

I have broken up this portion of text as follows:

- 1 Corinthians 12:12–14 serves as an introduction to the idea that the body is "one," but one consisting of many parts.

- 1 Corinthians 12:15–20 emphasizes the "diversity" aspect for the sake of the lowly at Corinth.

- 1 Corinthians 12:21–26 emphasizes the "unity" with the intention of rebuking the supposedly superior at Corinth.

Thus far, Paul has taught that although there are multitudes of gifts, they all originate from the Trinity. In the next section, beginning with 12:12, Paul introduces another way of explaining the idea of the interaction between the one and the many, "For just as the body is one and has many members, and all the members of the body, though many, are one body, so it is with Christ."

A logical conclusion to the statement in 12:12 might have been: "For just as the body is one and has many members, and all the members of the body, though many, are one body, *so also in the church*" (emphasis mine).

However, how does one make sense of Paul's ending the verse with the words "so it is with Christ"? Later, in Chapter 12:27, the "you" (plural) refers to the church. The same is the case here. Paul says that the church is the body of Christ. Verses 13 and 14 elaborate each in turn, on the idea of unity (12:13 – it is likely that some of the Corinthians were questioning how all Christians could be in unity with one another) and diversity (12:14). His explanation to this possible thought was "For in the one Spirit we were all baptised into one body—Jews or Greeks, slaves or free—and we were all made to drink of the one Spirit" (12:13).

This statement has been the source of much debate, particularly concerning the meaning of "baptized" and "drink of one Spirit." "Baptized" can be interpreted as "water baptism," a "second spiritual baptism" (something like what happened at Pentecost) or actual "spiritual regeneration" (salvation). To arrive at a decision, it is important to look at what Paul emphasizes: not "baptise" but rather "one Spirit" and "one body." Paul is emphasising "unity." The major criterion that distinguished them from non-Christians and did so from the outset is the Spirit's saving action, i.e. their regeneration. This serves as the basis for their unity. If a Christian, through dying and rising with Christ has put on Christ, so have other Christians (Galatians 3:27). Thus, the body of Christ comes into existence in Christ (Romans 12:5) since all Christians have put on Christ and are one in him.

The second part of the verse mentions, "drink of one Spirit." The Roman Catholics relate this to confirmation while Luther and Calvin believed that this referred to the cup drunk at the Lord's Supper. Still others, among them the Pentecostals, believe that this refers to conversion followed by Spirit baptism. The most likely interpretation of these words is that they mean what they meant in the first part of the verse. This is Hebraic parallelism, where the second part of the verse elaborates on the first. Thus, Paul is once again speaking of the Spirit, who saves us into the body. The idea is that "we were immersed in the one Spirit, to become one body," i.e. we have been saved, and our goal is unity in one body.[197]

Now he turns to the other side of the coin. Within that unity, there is room for much "diversity" (12:14). This was probably even more of a problem for the Corinthians than the issue of unity. In their eyes, only tongues proved one's spirituality.

Moving on to the next section (12:15–26), he deals specifically with two different classes of people. One group I will call the "outcasts" (12:15–20) while the other group I will call the "in crowd" (12:21–26).

The intention within the first section (12:15–20) is to explain to those who feel inferior that they should not feel that way because they are as much a part of the body as everyone else.

---

[197]Put simply, a distinction is made between the Pauline use (incorporation into Christ at conversion) and the Lucan use in Luke-Acts (empowerment by the Spirit, modelled more on the Old Testament conception).

The argument progresses as follows: Consider the body parts Paul named. In one case, there was a foot/hand while in the other there was an ear/eye. The following idea is speculative. It seems that in that time a hand and an eye were to be valued above a foot or an ear. It is uncertain whether this was the case, but I do not see it as symbolically important. What is significant is that you realise Paul was speaking to the inferior people who were saying that, because they could not speak in tongues, they were not part of the church and thus had better leave. He intimates that just because they do not do what others do, they do not cease to be part of the body of believers. If every part of the body were the same, the body could not function. What is the point of a body with only an eye or a toenail? No, God planned a body with all kinds of people who together would be able to achieve the purposes of Christ (12:15b, 16b and 17–20).

Next, let us look at the "in crowd"! One can deduce from Paul that some people might have been saying, "I have no need of you," implying that the others were useless. The body metaphor once again addresses this problem beautifully. The body is one unit. It is God's intention to honour what others fail to honour. It is our prerogative to recognise and praise those given little thought or prominence. If someone were to smash a finger, the entire body would react in agony. You cannot isolate a finger, and a finger cannot isolate itself. Likewise, if one part of the body has an exceptional talent, for instance, the fingers of a pianist, one does not say, "My, what amazing fingers you have." No! You would say, "You are an exceptional pianist."

God's ways are above ours, and His wisdom is infinitely superior. Surely, he made the body of believers so diverse within unity because he knew that would be the very best way.

Thus, no Christian should ever think of their Christianity as "private." Judging by the way God established the "body", there seems no place for a one-man-show, self-promotion or unbalanced exaltation of specific gifts. Sound familiar? Clearly, this passage has implications for those who suggest that people cannot be filled with the spirit until they speak in tongues. This sounds like something the Corinthians would say.

Of course, the truth of the matter is that "gifts" do not necessarily make one a spiritual person because they are in actuality the manifestations of the Spirit, not a product of an individual's spirituality. Earlier on, I stated that "spirituality" is to edify the community in worship. Chapters 12–14 argue this point thoroughly. Here is something else to think about: Balaam's donkey had a revelation or vision of an angel of the Lord standing in front of it and then spoke to Balaam. Does this mean that because the donkey displayed a similar gift of prophetic vision to that of a prophet, that it was spiritual?

Christ's Body – 1 Corinthians 12:27–31

The body metaphor has clarified things already, but in this conclusion, Paul repeats it one more time: "Now you are the body of Christ" (12:27). In this context, the church at Corinth is "the body" of Christ, not a local part of it.

Then in 12:28, Paul mentions another list of ministries and gifts. New to the list are apostle, prophet, teacher – forms of assistance and leadership. Many have used this list to determine an order of prominence or importance regarding these functions. In this regard, I tend to agree with Hooker when he says that "Apostles [are] first because unto them was granted the revelation of all truth from Christ immediately. Prophets, he argues, had some knowledge of the same kind, and teachers are necessary to build and to instruct. However, otherwise nothing is meant but sundry graces, gifts and abilities which Christ bestowed, and Paul does not have in general view questions about degrees and offices of ecclesiastical calling."[198]

An apostle is a delegate or messenger, one sent forth with orders. His main concern centres on establishing and maintaining the structure of a church. In a sense, he is the foundational human element of the church. There is a lot of debate about the meaning

---

[198]Hooker, R. *Works,* 5:78:8.

of "prophet" and "teacher." This is particularly so in contemporary society where prophet and teacher tend towards synonymity. Thiselton has offered a very helpful explanation as to the difference between the two.

> ... prophets perform speech-acts of announcement, proclamation, judgment, challenge, comfort, support, or encouragement, whereas teachers perform speech-acts of transmission, communicative explanation, interpretation of texts, establishment of creeds, exposition of meaning and implication, and, more cognitive, less temporally applied communicative acts.[199]

"Form of assistance" is self-explanatory. By "forms of leadership" is meant someone with an ability to see the big picture, someone who can guide a congregation or the like in similar fashion to the way a captain steers His boat through stormy seas.

Chapter 12 reaches a conclusion with the reminder that God has provided a diverse list of gifts. Paul's rhetorical questions now highlight that one category does not classify all. You are not all apostles, as you are not all an eye.

Paul's last statement is somewhat confusing: "But strive for the greater gifts" (12:31). There are several options as to what this means. Firstly, does Paul wish to demote tongues in the face of other gifts in the hope that the Corinthians will begin to focus on other gifts? Secondly, was this a quotation taken from the Corinthian letter? Thirdly, does the original text actually mean, "But you are eagerly desiring the greater gifts"? Finally, is "greater gift" to be understood to mean "greater gift" in terms of intelligibility within the community?

The first sense would be out of place with Paul's previous line of argument emphasizing the diversity of gifts and their need of one another. Ranking gifts would serve to enforce the current problem of some feeling inferior or superior to others. The difficulty with

---

[199]Thiselton, A. C. *The First Epistle*, p. 1017.

the second option is that Paul does not qualify it. In every other instance, he always quotes sayings made by the Corinthians and then qualifies them (6:12, 7:1, and 8:1). In the third instance, this option holds that the true interpretation of this passage is in the indicative "you do eagerly desire" and not the imperative "eagerly desire." The problem with this is that 14:1 repeats this same verb, which certainly means the imperative "eagerly desire." That leaves us with the fourth option that I believe to be correct. You will see as we move ahead that Paul will argue that gifts manifest for encouragement and edification (in the church). Thus, when in church, a gift that is intelligible to others is of higher value than one, which is not (14:5, 12).

Questions and Thoughts for Reflection

1. Before moving on, I would like to raise the issue of gifts in terms of "possession," as in "I have the gift of leadership or prophecy." There are two opposing camps on this matter. One group believes that all Christians receive a gift or gifts by the Spirit that they retain possession of throughout their lifetime, or at least for a lengthy period. Others believe that we do not retain ownership of any gifts, but rather manifest pertinent gifts as and when the need arises. Which of these positions do you hold to? What scriptural backing do you have to support your position? How do you think your use of spiritual gifts might be affected depending on which position you subscribe to? When attempting to answer this, one must remember that there are two different types of gifting. The first often goes by the name "natural talents/abilities"[200] and the second, "spiritual gifts". The former might be giftings such as *administration* and *leadership,* while the latter, *prophecy and healing*, etc. With this in mind, consider my position on this dilemma of "possession" reflected

---

[200]We must guard against having a low estimate of "natural gifts" in light of "supernatural gifts". I say this because all gifts have God as their source.

through the following illustration. You possess two light bulbs connected up to an electricity supply. You have access to the on/ off switch for light bulb A, but only God has access to the on/ off switch for light bulb B. We can deduce from this illustration that you are in "possession" of both bulbs, but that you only have the ability to activate and utilize one of them whenever you want. The other bulb only works when God chooses to switch it on. Applying the four gifts highlighted in italics above to the illustration appears as follows. Think of the first pair of gifts as falling under the category of the light bulb A, and the second pair, light bulb B. Every Christian receives gifts for the benefit of the body and maximum impact for the Kingdom of God. Some of them can be used at anytime. These are the natural talents/abilities I was referring to above[201], viz. leadership, exhorting, helping, giving etc. (light bulb/windmill A). Others, like prophecy, healing, discernment of spirits, and miracles, will only operate through you when the Spirit sovereignly decides to do so (light bulb/windmill B). In summary, my stance is that Christians do possess gifts either permanently or at least semi-permanently, but that the so-called "spiritual gifts" only function as and when God sees fit.[202] There is something further to be said here. God can anoint a person with spiritual gifts completely unfamiliar to them in a given situation. Some scholars and Christian leaders refer to these as "situational anointings".

2. Paul addresses the Trinity in verses 4–7 with respect to spiritual

---

[201]Of course, this does not mean that God cannot supernaturally increase one of your natural talents/abilities to achieve a specific purpose.

[202]Consider Romans 12:6 on "possessing spiritual gifts". Here, "Paul is describing the way in which God, in his grace, has distributed different gifts to his people as a means of building the unity of the body … [and that] believers possess different *charismata* (gifts); but each one is the product of God's *charis* (grace), which all believers have in common." Moo, D. J. 1996. *The Epistle to the Romans*, p. 764. See also 1 Peter 4:10 and 1 Cor. 14.1a on this topic.

gifts. According to him, what role does each of the members of the Trinity play with regard to the apportioning, mediation and origination of spiritual gifts? Once you have considered this, which member of the Trinity is prayer usually addressed to in the New Testament and what is the role of the other members of the Trinity in this regard? In response to the Trinity and gifting, Paul believes that spiritual gifts originate with the Father, are mediated through the Son, and apportioned through the Holy Spirit. In terms of prayer, it is usually addressed to the Father through Jesus Christ and encouraged or even begun by the Holy Spirit.

3. There are many Christians or religious types who believe that their faith is a private matter and or that religion is private. How would you utilise the Epistle to the Corinthians to refute this belief?

Chapter Fourteen
The Most Excellent Way

Have you ever been to a wedding? If so, you will almost certainly have heard some portion of this passage in the sermon or order of service. It is a pity this text does not feature as a reminder in divorce proceedings as well. The portion I am referring to, in particular, is 13:4–7.

Of course, weddings are not in focus here. Rather, its proper context still relates to the matter of "spirituality." We have seen how the Corinthian Christians were a group peppered with all sorts of problems ranging from super spirituality, ballooned egos, self-centeredness and the abuse of the poor and the weak. Then, add to this, a dash of dualism and over-realised eschatology, and it is no wonder they needed lessons on love. They sorely lacked true Christian values and priorities driven by love.

Enter this Chapter. The argument suggests that the gifts they desired and the type of behaviour they typically admired would achieve nothing for them, if they did not act from a heart of love. Following this, Paul outlines the nature of love. Then he draws up a contrast between these gifts and love in terms of their relevant/appropriate timeframes: gifts are temporal, but love is of eternal value. Barth provides the following outline for Chapter 13:

- It is love alone that counts (13:1–3)
- It is love alone that triumphs (13:4–7)

- It is love alone that endures (13:8–13).[203]

Fee makes two additional comments on this section. He suggests that love is not some abstract quality, which would be to miss the meaning of love altogether.

> Love is primary for [Paul] because it has already been given concrete expression in the coming of Jesus Christ to die for the sins of the world. Love is not an idea for Paul, not even a "motivating factor" for behaviour. It is behaviour. To love is to act; anything short of action is not love at all. Secondly, love is not set over against the gifts, precisely because it belongs in a different category altogether. For Paul, it is not "gifts to be sure, but better yet love"; rather, love is the way in which the gifts are to function. To desire earnestly expressions of the Spirit that will build up the community is how love acts in this context.[204]

It is love alone that counts – 1 Corinthians 13:1–3

In just three verses, Paul mentions the word "I" eight times. This is significant because it drives home the point that his main concern is for the person and not just gifts or love, or gifts being motivated by love. Gifts are from God, and God is love, so they are to be admired, but what matters is whether the Christian's life is founded or motivated on/by love, like that of Jesus Christ. If this is not the case, then that person's life is of no value in God's eyes.

Paul touches on two general categories. Both categories were, and still are, keys for many people in characterising the true man or woman of God: spirituality (in their eyes, signs of spirituality included tongues, knowledge, wisdom, prophecy, faith) and charitable deeds (giving one's possessions or life).

---

[203]Barth. K. *Church Dogmatics* 4/2, pp. 824–840.
[204]Fee. G. *The First Epistle*, p. 628.

Paul takes up the issue of tongues first, most likely because that was the main area of dispute. He compares the usefulness of "speaking in a non-interpreted tongue" within the community service with that of resounding gongs/clanging cymbals.[205] Next, he targets prophecy. Once again, no matter how valuable or awesome the revelations may be, they, together with the person proclaiming them, are worthless if that person does not act out of love. The same applies to faith. Giving away all you have, even your own life (surrendering my body to the flames most likely referred to martyrdom) is worthless without love.

Contextually, Paul's word to them might have been: "So you think that you are spiritual because you speak so loudly and frequently in tongues, or because you prophesy often and with great accuracy, or because you give so much? Well, let me tell you that by themselves, spiritual gifts and good deeds equate to nothing; none of them are relevant in showing your spirituality and closeness with God. In fact, brothers and sisters, your so-called gifts and deeds are worth nothing if you do not live a life of love." He might as well have added, "Brothers and sisters, gifts without love are as ludicrous a thought as having a cart without a horse."

So, contemporising this would read: "Christians, you think that you can prove your spirituality through theological genius. Well, amazing knowledge by itself is worthless. Moreover, you who think your style of worship leads to spirituality, it is useless if you do not lead a life of love. And you who think that tongues make you look more in-tune with God, your tongues is of no value to God, if you do not devote yourself to love." Modernizing the "cart" illustration would be tantamount to buying a diesel car in a world without diesel.

This is a good place to stop and check both your church and your attitudes. Be honest with yourself. Is either you or your church

---

[205]This must have been quite disturbing for the Corinthians since clanging gongs and cymbals were closely associated with pagan worship festivals.

claiming a special relationship with God for the wrong reasons. For instance, intellectual knowledge, gifts, size, success, speaking in tongues?

It is love alone that triumphs – 1 Corinthians 13:4–7

In these verses, Paul lists some of the fundamental characteristics of love. That is, evidence of what love looks like in action. This is also not to be taken as an exhaustive list of what love is like. Rather, it is likely that Paul links these character traits with the behavioural problems in Corinth.

Below is a list of problematic behavioural traits contrary to Paul's understanding of the nature of "love."

- Easily angered – 1 Corinthians 3:3
- Boasting – 1 Corinthians 3:6–8
- Proud – 1 Corinthians 3:6–8
- Keeps a record of wrongs – 1 Corinthians 4:3
- Delights in evil – 1 Corinthians 6:12–20
- Impatient – 1 Corinthians 11:21
- Rude – 1 Corinthians 11:21
- Unkind – 1 Corinthians 11:22
- Envy – 1 Corinthians 12:14–16
- Self-seeking – every problem in Corinth

The quality that stands out most for me among all of these is "love is not self-seeking". It is almost impossible to act outside of love if one is acting in the best interests of others. God displayed this kind of love when He gave His only-begotten Son to die for us on the cross (John 3:16). For me, the ultimate expression of love was Jesus' sacrificial act.

It is love alone that endures – 1 Corinthians 13:8–13

One of the "love traits" is that love always perseveres (13:7). To put it another way, love never fails (13:8). Thus, there is a natural connection between these two sections. Verses 8–13 link with 13:1–3 as well. You will remember that Paul contrasted love with gifts and gave love priority. In 13:8–13, he again does this by showing love's permanence in contrast to the temporary nature of gifts. Verse 8 begins with "love never fails," the idea being that love is part of this world and when perfection comes, it will still endure.

Here is an illustration I hope will help jog your memory from time to time.

I like to use the process of metamorphosis to demonstrate the resurrection, but I find it equally appealing to teach on "love's enduring quality." Therefore, let me combine the two. We are all aware of the miraculous event of a caterpillar morphing into a butterfly. However, most do not know that, besides DNA, the only characteristic carried over from caterpillar to butterfly is three sets of legs. A caterpillar has eight sets of legs, the first three of which become the butterfly's legs. Now, let us assume that the process of metamorphosis is symbolic of what happens to us at the resurrection, that love is symbolised by those three pairs of legs, and that all of our other traits are the remaining five pairs of legs. Do you get the idea? Legs pass through metamorphosis as does love through the resurrection.

Before we discuss anything else, we need to establish when this "perfection" will take place and what it means. Welcome to the controversy!

There are numerous theories that attempt to answer these questions. Briefly,

- some believe that "perfection" has something to do with the level of maturity attained by the church or the individual believer, that it relates to the completion of the Canon of Scripture;

- others, that perfection is understood to refer to the time of the coming of the Parousia (2nd coming of Jesus) or when somebody dies and goes to heaven and lastly;

- still others, that "perfection" is the time when the Jews and

Gentiles come together to form one new and "perfect man."

It is my opinion that the second alternative is by far the most acceptable solution to this problem. Can you imagine Paul trying to convince the Corinthians that perfection points to the completion of the cannon of scripture? You must remember that at that stage they did not have one book of the New Testament. It is highly unlikely that either they or Paul would have even had a concept of a New Testament Canon. In answer to the theory of the union of the Jews and Gentiles, one can conclude that this subject was completely irrelevant within this context. The feud within their church was not over Jew versus Gentile. Thus, it would have been illogical for Paul to mean this. That leaves us with the second option. Perfection entails a situation where my knowledge is in some form or another comparable with God's present knowledge of me, "Now I know only in part; then I will know fully, even as I have been fully known (13:12b)". Paul meant here that at the consummation of all things that he expected freedom from the misconception and inability to understand, traits that were currently part of his life. Therefore, "perfection" refers to the eschatological event, i.e. the return of Jesus.[206]

Why does Paul say that the "gifts" are temporal? Well, in the time after "perfection" there will be no need for "gifts" because Christians will be in the presence of God. As Barth once said, "Because the sun rises all lights are extinguished." In 13:9, Paul does not mean that the *charismata* are imperfect,[207] but rather that it is our knowledge and understanding that are incomplete. Thus, we need the "gifts" to work in and through us to assist us with our imperfections. You use crutches when your legs are injured, but you do not keep on using

---

[206]Certain of these theories on "perfection" have significant implications for one's position on the relevance/operation of spiritual gifts today. For instance, if you believe that perfection has come, then you will also believe that gifts died away whenever that perfection was attained.

[207]Please do not read into Paul's comments that he is somehow devaluing the gifts of the Spirit.

them when you are better.

In 13:11, Paul uses the metaphor of children and adults to illustrate two different modes of existence – imperfect (now, a child) and perfect (heaven, adults). The point is that the needs, desires, attitudes, understanding, etc. between an adult and a child are worlds apart. What was appropriate to a child in his existence would no longer be applicable to him as an adult. Similarly, "gifts" are presently appropriate to assist us in our child-like understanding (our seeing but a poor reflection), but later, when perfection has come, they will not be needed because we will see face to face (13:12).

However, "love" is different from "gifts." Paul explains that "love" differs from "gifts" in terms of "appropriateness" both for now and after "perfection" has come. "Love" is the one thing Paul knows will endure forever.

In addition to "spiritual gifts," in 13.13 "love" is listed as being greater than "faith" and "hope" as well. Why is this? Barth suggests that love is "the future eternal light shining in the present. It, therefore, needs no change of form."[208] Faith and hope are traits represented by those discarded caterpillar legs. In Wordsworth's hymn, "Gracious Spirit, Holy Ghost," he addresses faith, hope and love by saying:

Faith will vanish into sight,
Hope be emptied in delight;
Love in heaven will shine more bright.[209]

---

[208] Barth, K. *Church Dogmatics,* 4/2 (sect. 68), p. 840.
[209] Mable, N. *Popular Hymns and Their Writers,* p. 200.

Questions and Thoughts for Reflection

1. Paul provides us with the characteristics of love. These include and exclude the following.

   Love is:
   • patient, kind, rejoices in the truth, bears all things, believes all things, hopes all things, endures all things

   Love is not:
   • envious, boastful, arrogant, rude, irritable or resentful

   Love does not:
   • insist on its own way; rejoice in wrongdoing

   Carefully consider this list in light of your own thoughts and behaviour, then explain in what ways you best express love towards God and others? How can you link other of love's characteristics to your most evidenced ones? Which of Paul's "loveless" characteristics do you practise most often? Consider how you might eliminate these loveless characteristics from your life altogether and then begin a strategy of implementation.

2. In terms of the list in question 1, which of the "loveless" characteristics is most evident in your immediate community? What would happen if you went out of your way to be and do the exact opposite? How about taking the leap of loving in a loveless area of your society?

3. What would you say is the purpose of creation? Carefully consider this and then write half a page reflecting your opinion. Once you are finished, compare your view with mine. I have noticed that the Bible does not give a definitive statement as to the purpose of creation, but all is not lost. It is possible to form an idea by considering scripture as a whole.

   3.1 Firstly, it appears as if God has a desire to mirror His perfection, and He does so most clearly through His masterpiece, human beings. Consider what God says in Genesis 1:26, "Then God said, 'Let us make humankind in our image, according to our likeness; and let them have dominion over ..." This idea of "mirroring" can also be seen by considering the thoroughgoing theme of "glory" in the Bible, i.e. God's motive for all that he does is His own glory (the reflection of Himself). Using human beings as the example again, Isaiah states that God speaks of His sons and daughters as those "... who [are] called by my name, whom I created for my glory, whom I formed and made." (Isaiah 43:7). In terms of God's greater creation, a passage such as Isaiah 6:3 captures this mirroring effect: "Holy, holy, holy is the Lord of hosts; the whole earth is full of his glory." But what has all of this to do with love, which is what we are exploring in this Chapter? Well, this brings me to my second reason for the purpose of creation.

3.2 In the previous Chapter, I briefly touched on the Trinity (God the Father, Son and Holy Spirit). One of the most obvious characteristics of the Trinity is that it/God is a community. When I study this community within scripture, the impression I get is of a community held together by the purest form of love in existence. This love is so remarkable that scripture actually states that, "... <u>God is love</u>." (1 John 4:8) This means that the fullest revelation of what love is, is characterized by who God is and what He does. In terms of purpose, I believe that the second reason for the purpose of creation is God's desire to share this love with his creation. You can observe this powerful theme of love and the importance of it to God by considering what God holds as the two greatest commandments: "You shall love the Lord your God with all your heart, and with all your soul, and with all your mind, and with all your strength ... [and] "You shall love your neighbor as yourself." (Mark 12:30–31). Human beings who do this are mirroring God most closely. Adam and Eve were tested to see if they would love and thereby mirror their creator, but they failed. I say this because love and obedience are virtually synonymous within scripture. Look at what Jesus stated, "If you love me, you will keep my commandments." (John 14.15) Adam did not love because he did not obey God. Bringing this back to 1 Corinthians, Paul knew about God's desire to express and receive love, but he was dealing with a people entrenched in a world virtually absent of it. This is easily seen by the nature of the problems at Corinth. However, God was calling the Corinthian church members out of their worldly existence and into a life of co-regency, and this would mean that they had to learn to love and be loved. That is why Paul placed this Chapter on "love" as the pivotal point within this epistle.

Chapter Fifteen
Gifts of Prophesy and Tongues

We all do like the dramatic, don't we? The first astounding gift of the Spirit that God had given Christians in Acts 2 was the gift of a spiritual language. It served as an outward testimony, but after Acts 2 the gift continued in churches as a language of personal prayer. Colloquially, we, in the 21st century, usually refer to this gift as "tongues" though the term is slightly suggestive of something guttural – very different from a tender prayer language.

The Corinthians placed an unrealistic importance on tongues while belittling other gifts of the spirit. In Chapter 13, the emphasis falls on love being the single goal of their spiritual zeal. The theme of love continues forward in two ways. First, they show love through ensuring intelligibility (understanding) in the congregation (14:1–25). Second, they show love by maintaining order in the congregation (14:26–40). We will come to the latter shortly.

The New Testament does not give us a rigid liturgy of how church has to "happen." Instead, it provides us with a very "organic" feel to the reality of "church." The church is the bride of Christ, a vibrant young woman, not a staid and musty old institution. In keeping with this dynamic reality of what church life is, Paul provides us with governing principles to ensure that this dynamism does in fact occur.

Earlier Paul explained the role of leadership and teamwork in church life. Now he turns to the role of love, order, spirituality and intelligibility. Chances are that you have felt what it is like when a church lacks one of these elements. It is painful to sit in church where the run of the service is a load of sentimental mush, lacking spirituality or understanding. It is also frustrating when the church is just left to "happen" resulting in chaos. The truth is churches can lack any of these elements at any particular point in time.

The argument for intelligibility is broken up into two sections: 14:1–19 addresses the importance of intelligibility for the sake of the believers while 14:20–25 addresses a similar point, except for the unbeliever. To drive home his point, he argues in 14:1–5 and 20–25 that prophecy must take priority over tongues because it is understandable and can thus edify and lead to conversion, while 14:6–19 takes up the same argument from a negative perspective, that tongues is un-intelligible and thus it is unable to edify the community.

It is important from the outset not to think that Paul is devaluing tongues, after all, tongues is one of the Spirit's gifts. His point in this entire section is that believers are to be edified, and this through the motive of love. For this to take place, there must be intelligibility.

The "Preferred" Spiritual Gift – 1 Corinthians 14:1–5

Paul starts out by comparing prophecy with the gift of tongues.

In (14:1), he suggests that they should desire "especially the gift of prophecy," but given the context, it would make more sense to read, "when in the assembly, desire gifts of speech," not because the other gifts are inferior, but because the gift of speech in this context will be more beneficial to all present.

We can deduce the following from Paul's comparison of the speech gifts.

Tongues	Prophecy
The person speaks to God.	The person speaks to people.
No one understands the person (mystery).	People are able to understand (intelligible).
The person edifies self.	The person edifies the church.

With respect to "the person edifies self", it seems strange to think that un-intelligible prayer by the "praying party" could be edifying to them. But, this idea is only strange if one assumes that all forms of edification have to travel through the brains cognitive processes. Think of it like this: There are many medicines on the market today that have a positive impact on people and yet science still cannot explain why. The point; we do not need to understand how the medicine is benefiting us for it to actually benefit us.

I would like to highlight one of the comparisons listed. When a person speaks in a tongue, he or she addresses God. This stands in contrast "to the notion quite common in Pentecostal groups of referring to a message in tongues [from God for the congregation for which] there seems to be no evidence in Paul."[210] "At no point in 1 Corinthians 14 does Paul suggest that tongues equates with speech directed toward people; three times he indicates or implies indirectly that it is speech directed toward God" (14:2, 14–16, 28).

Some may argue that when tongues are "interpreted" that it is different in its content or nature, implying it has now become a message for the congregation, but that would be missing the point here. This form of tongues becomes of equal value[211] to the people because it has become intelligible, not because it becomes a message directed at them. A message spoken in tongues can now be

---

[210]Fee, G. D. *God's Empowering Presence*, p. 218

[211]The notion that prophecy is greater than tongues relates to the context of edifying the community. It has greater potential to exhort and encourage because it is intelligible.

understood and thereby express praise, prayer, joy or longing, which encourages the community.[212]

Some scholars have suggested that the word "interpret" does not convey what transpires when a tongue becomes intelligible language. Essentially, the Spirit enables a person to convert a mystery into comprehendible language. The example of Moses is given. He

---

[212]The only other place where 'tongues' are mentioned in the NT is Acts, and in this case there may be a closer link with prophecy. Consider the most notable case of the use of tongues in Acts 2:11. Bruce states: "… these pilgrims heard the praises of God in all the tongues of the dispersion being uttered by Galileans of all people! The event was nothing less than a reversal of the curse of Babel." Bruce, F. F. *The Book of the Acts*, p. 59. At this point, Bruce is following along the lines of Paul's theology, because he refers to the pilgrims uttering 'praises to God'. However, Keener suggests that "As the Spirit's activity often produced prophetic speech in ancient Israel, so now it produced 'prophetic speech,' but 'of a peculiar kind.' [he believes that] Luke explicitly uses tongues to identify the activity of the Spirit of prophecy (2.17–18), albeit with a particular emphasis on crossing boundaries … [his concluding statement is that] tongues are a sign of prophetic empowerment for the continuing cross-cultural mission." Keener, C. S. *Acts: An Exegetical Commentary*. Volume 1, p. 823–824. Whether the tongues in Acts 2.11 were prophecies aimed at the listeners, or praise to God that simultaneously became a prophecy to the listeners, i.e. the content of the praise was revealing the mysteries of God, is uncertain. I am inclined to believe the latter. My only experience with "the interpretation of tongues" happened in 2005 while in a church service. To set the scene, a few days prior to this church service, I had been studying the events that transpired on the Mount of Olives, following the Lord's Supper in Luke 22:39–46. I remember paying close attention to Jesus' words, "Father, if you are willing, remove this cup from me; yet, not my will but yours be done." (Luke 22:42), in the original language. Coming back to the church service. During worship time, a lady stood up and began to speak in tongues. As I listened, it suddenly became clear to me that this lady was uttering Jesus' prayer, albeit in the original language, which I had studied. This was remarkable since the lady did not know any original biblical languages. I was able to speak out and suggest that the lady was praying to the Lord on behalf of the church, which had been suffering trials in a few areas, using the same words Jesus had used.

felt at a loss for words and requested God provide him with someone who could express in words what he was incapable of expressing
(in his opinion); hence, the arrival of Aaron.[213]

Perhaps we ought to express caution not to undervalue the gift of
tongues either. Certainly, it is somewhat strange to our meticulous,
controlled, modern Western ears, but the giving of such a gift by
God reflects a response by God to some of our very personal struggles. Prayer is difficult. Sometimes we do not know what to say.
Often we feel inadequate before God. On the other hand, we feel
"unspiritual," mundane and dull. Occasionally, we may feel that
cold intellectualism replaces the tenderness of our spirituality. The
tenderness of a spirit language in prayer with God, spirit to Spirit
and Spirit to spirit, should not be thrown out as an anachronism of
a primitive society.

Speak clearly in Church – 1 Corinthians 14:6–12

In this portion, Paul elaborates on the importance of intelligible
manifestations within the congregation.

Considerable debate has arisen regarding Paul's use of the words
revelation/ knowledge/ prophecy and teaching in 14:6. Some scholars suggest that the first two, revelation and knowledge, should be
grouped together because they refer to the content of a message,
while prophecy and teaching refer to the form of content Paul's
speech took. I am not sure that this is relevant. Paul is speaking
about gifts that are helpful to a congregation, and these four words
might have been simple examples of what could be beneficial.

To carry his point further he uses analogies of instruments, battle
trumpets, and foreigners. Musical instruments are not musical if
they do not play an intelligible sequence of notes. Trumpets blew to
command soldiers in battle. If the command sounds of the trumpet were unintelligible, no army would fight a battle successfully. If
someone came to you and spoke to you in a foreign language, you

---

[213]Philo, *Quod Deterius Potiori Insidiari Soleat,* pp. 15–16.

would not be able to understand. Thus, in your understanding, the two of you would remain foreigners.

The point is that if one cannot distinguish, discern, or understand what one hears, it is of no use. If edification is to take place, there must be intelligible content. Tongues without interpretation cannot provide edification for others.

These analogies lead-up to the climax of 14:12. The message he conveys here is that if the Spirit they claim to have in abundance is the Spirit of God, then they should be manifesting His character traits. There should be no evidence of self-seeking and self-promotion among them but rather love and concern for others. "Hence all this burning concern about powers of the Spirit must be redirected into a more Christlike eagerness for the building up of the church community as a corporate whole."[214]

Use your Mind and Spirit in Prayer – 1 Corinthians 14:13–19

This portion begins with "for this reason" (14:3). This paragraph continues to develop the issue of tongues and intelligibility. He does not argue "either/or" on the relationship between spirituality and understanding, but "both/and". For Paul good reasoning and sound understanding should align with mature spirituality, especially in a church context. Indeed, proper understanding even encourages spirituality!

Sometimes we intuitively "feel" that too rigid an order stifles the organic, personal reality of church and worship. It is quite likely that the Corinthians also felt this. Do we just need to "let go" to be spiritual? Not really, but then what is the relationship between freedom and order when worshipping God? In this matter, Paul's address in 1 Corinthians 14 is very useful. He breaks down the word "order" into digestible portions. He gives us two principles: understanding

---

[214]Wolff, C. *Der erste Brief*, pp. 217, 331 in Thiselton, A. C. *The First Epistle*, p. 1107.

and spirituality, and then he gives us a test as to whether these two are keeping together or not.

Firstly, he mentions that he prays with his "spirit." The question is, does this "my spirit" refer to one of the constituent parts of a human being, i.e. body, soul, and spirit, or the Holy Spirit as given to him? The likelihood is the former. His spirit prays as it receives utterance from the Holy Spirit.

The idea Paul conveys here is that when he prays in tongues, his mind remains unfruitful because he does not know what he is saying. "So what should he do?" The answer is that he will pray in both tongues and intelligible language. Both have their appropriate time and are good. Both one's deepest spiritual being and mind requires nourishing.[215] In a congregational setting, he will pray with his mind, intelligible words, in order to edify the church, in order to obtain the AMEN![216] That is, unless his tongues can be interpreted. If not, he will pray in tongues in private. To "sing with my spirit" here would refer to a musical form of tongues. Remember that singing was common to Judaism and practised both corporately and in private.

Then, there is the question of "who is the 'outsider'" (14:16). If you have read Chapter 14, you will also notice that the same word comes up in 14:23. The possibilities in 14:16 are either that the person is a Christian, who has not had tongues interpreted or a non-Christian inquirer.

---

[215]For a fascinating examination of tongues by a Catholic charismatic writer with training in psychology, see Morton Kelsey, *Tongues Speaking: An Experiment in Spiritual Experience,* and *Tongue Speaking: The History and Meaning of Charismatic Experience.*
[216]"AMEN conveys the idea of solemn endorsement or agreement, but it does more in that it is like nailing our own colors to the mast. Jesus, as himself the One who is true, is called the Amen in Rev 3:14. Paul uses the term also in the context of his own commitment in action to what he has spoken in words (2 Corinthians 1:15–22), which in turn reflects God's faithful promise to remain true to what he has spoken (2 Corinthians 1:18, 20)." Ibid.

The word in question here is *idiotes* – "those who don't under-stand." The word in the New Testament means an unlearned, illiter-ate person. However, in later Christian writings this word was also used as a semi-technical term for "catechumens" – a special class of interested inquirer who had not yet been baptised. Therefore, if the latter meaning is what Paul intended in both 14:16 and 23, both references refer to the same class of person. If the former, then it refers to someone who was unskilled in being able to interpret tongues.

Interestingly enough, the test that Paul is presenting in this con-text is a legal one – still used in modern legal systems – that of the "innocent bystander." In South African law, for example, relating to the order of agreements and the existence of tacit provisions the courts ask, "What would an ignorant and impartial bystander con-sider the reasonable belief on the situation?" It is essentially a test for objectivity.

If you consider the context of this section, intelligibility and edification in the meetings, and the inability of the "idiots" to say, "Amen" (it would be unlikely that a non-Christian would say this word) it seems the non-technical word (unlearned person) is cor-rect. We are dealing here with a person who feels out, or embar-rassed that they cannot participate. Considering the context of the Corinthians wishing to be "spiritual," this "outsider" would be an "ordinary Christian" lacking so called "spirituality." We will deal with 14:23 shortly. 1 Corinthians 14:17 is a continuation from 14:16. Its premise is that tongues edify the speaker, while intelligi-ble prophecy edifies its hearers.

What is interesting is that Paul argues that everyone has a role to play in church, even visitors. Indeed, perhaps we can apply this test in a wider context. Visitors can tell us whether our churches func-tion decently and are in order; visitors can tell us whether we are up to our eyeballs in jargon and out of touch with reality. Personally, I feel that this is another manifestation of disorder in our services. Christian jargon easily degenerates into a form of Gobbledy-gook, much like "tongues." Visitors can perhaps even tell us as to whether our churches lack "spirituality" and whether we are just busying ourselves with "cultural" religion.

Following this, Paul's private prayer life is somewhat unveiled. He mentions to the Corinthians that he "spoke in tongues more often than all of [them]." In saying this, he most likely implies three things:

- he too is "spiritual";

- that tongues is a gift from God, which is important and relevant;

- un-interpreted tongues are for use in private prayer.

If anyone is still questioning the use of un-interpreted tongue in the congregation, 14:19 should end all confusion. According to Paul, it is far more edifying to speak five intelligible words than ten thousand unintelligible words in tongues in a public service.

Signs for the Christian and non-Christian – 1 Corinthians 14:20–25

In this section, tongues and prophecy are still set one against the other. However, there are some clues that indicate that this is a separate section. Firstly, unbelievers are now included as a new factor in the argument. Secondly, 14:26–40 assumes that the arguments in favour of congregational edification and intelligibility are accepted. Thus, this section is actually an implementation of those aspects.

From a casual reading, 14:20–25 seems rather confusing. You will recall that from the outset of this book, Paul was in opposition to the Corinthians' pride, their assumed wisdom and maturity. In fact, he revealed to them that he thought them to be so immature that they could not even eat solid foods yet (3:2). In Chapter 14, this immaturity comes out in the form of an over-emphasis on speaking in tongues. As already mentioned, these Corinthians had a mindset of, "the more I can speak in tongues, the greater the chance I have of being super-spiritual." It is possible that some of the Corinthian tongue-speaking fanatics were justifying their fanaticism because they were witnesses, a sign, to non-believers of God's awesome presence in church. We will come back to this shortly.

The confusing portions are between 14:22 and 14:23–25. In the former, Paul says that tongues serve as a sign to the unbeliever, but in the latter, unbelievers respond negatively to tongues.[217] In Judaism, a "sign" indicated God's attitude toward them, be it in the form of judgment or pleasure. Probably, the most significant biblical example of a sign would be the blood sprinkled on the doorposts of the Israelites homes, saving them from death at the hands of the angel, just before the Exodus (Exodus 12:7). In this particular case, Paul is referring to judgment. We see this from his citation of Isaiah 28:9–13 in 14:21.

In this passage, the Israelites had refused to listen to the Lord even though He had spoken clearly. Therefore, because they had done this, he visited them through invading hordes that "spoke" in a language (Assyrian), which they could not understand. Thus, in this case, the "strange tongues" (14:21) of foreigners (Assyrian troops) became a reminder of the Lord's judgement upon His people, and they knew it. Here is a more contemporary example. In fact, this is an actual event. A person arrived at a church, only to be hijacked right outside the front door. Those who perpetrated the hijacking wore a specific type of clothing (blue-collar work) and spoke in a language of a neighbouring country. These people did a lot of harm and, to this day, seven years later, whenever the person sees somebody wearing those clothes or speaking in their language, it serves as a reminder (sign) to him/her of that terrible event.

Returning to the Corinthians, the idea here is that tongues do not make one "spiritual" thereby benefiting the unbeliever. Rather, tongues in this context, serve as a negative sign to the unbeliever in

---

[217]There are at least ten theories explaining these verses. To work through every possible interpretation of this text is beyond the scope of this book. Refer to the likes of Barrett, Blomberg, Carson, Fee and Thiselton for more explanation on this.

the sense that a) unbelievers leave thinking "these church folks are mad" and b) they would not be able to understand, hear the gospel message and come to faith. Conversely, if the unbeliever entered the assembly and heard the moral truth of Christianity under inspired speech, testimonies of saved fornicators, idolaters and the like and prophetic words of God (Hebrews 4:12), they would be convicted of their sin and come to faith (14:24–25). A word of caution though! One error that might arise from 14:22 is that "prophesy" is a positive sign, whereas tongues, is a negative sign. The danger here is for one to think of tongues in an unfavourable light. This would be incorrect. Remember, as I have already said, "tongues" is also a gift from God.

To summarise, the point of 14:20–25 is to add an additional reason for speaking intelligible words within the service – to be more helpful for evangelising unbelievers.

Further confusion may arise in that "tongues" serves as a sign to "unbelievers", whereas prophecy acts as a message to believers. Paul, however, seems to argue the exact opposite: a spiritual language is for personal use and may offend unbelievers, and prophecy has a special ability to draw in unbelievers. We ought, actually, to discern content from delivery. Whereas "tongues" has as their delivery, a context of Christian believers, "prophecy" has the effect of drawing in unbelievers. The gift of spiritual languages came in antithesis to the babbling of Babylon, as a gift of unification of language and speech. Prophecy, on the other hand, is predominantly given as God's speech to His people. (Although the gift does occasionally reach beyond merely His people and can become a profound evangelistic tool.)

We live in a day and age where there is profound stress on church union, reunion and broader themes of ecumenism. The gift of "tongues" may be a special prayer language, but the Spirit does also draw us together in a common speech, that is, common speech that testifies to the union between the Gentiles of different flavours and a dynamic vitality between God's folk. This is not a language brought about by human labour, but by divine grace. This Christian unity and church order is something that flows from Jesus as our head, not from our studious wrestlings to overcome theological differences.

Order in Public worship – 1 Corinthians 14:26–33

Before we look at this section, let us recap on a few things Paul had addressed relating to worship.

1. In Chapter 11, there was the issue of women who had gone against the God ordained "divine order" by speaking out rashly in services and failing to wear their head coverings. The latter was a sign in that culture of this structure (the divine order).

2. In Chapter 12 and 14 the problem was an unhealthy exaltation of the gift of tongues in an effort to prove maturity and spirituality. Gifts were seen as useful for one's self-gratification and development. When confronted by Paul or mature others, these Corinthians would justify their actions by saying that the "tongues" was an evangelistic sign to unbelievers.

3. It is possible that, when asked to stop speaking in tongues or prophesying, these Corinthians indicated that they were unable to because the Spirit was overwhelming them.

Put all these factors together and you have the makings of a very rowdy, confused bunch of people who lacked any form of discipline.

To a greater or lesser degree, Paul has answered these problems in his argument thus far. He has also assumed that his arguments have won favour and now required application. Consequently, he moves on to the next section with a question. Here is my paraphrase: "Okay, now that we have spoken about these issues and are in agreement, what shall we do about them to ensure maximum edification within the congregation?"

Paul begins by re-emphasising two points he made earlier (12:7,

14 and 14:5). The first important aspect about the congregation is its variety. When you come together, everyone has some form of contribution, be it a hymn, a word of instruction, a revelation, a tongue or an interpretation. The list given here is by no means exhaustive. The second is that contributions are for the edification of the church. This idea of doing everything in your life to gratify the self or display the self must stop, especially in the church service.

In 14:27–28, he proposes a way of solving the problems surrounding the issue of speaking in tongues within a service. His proposal includes three suggestions.

1. Only one tongue-speaker may speak at a time. This had obviously not been the case in the past.

2. No more than three should speak in a tongue before evaluating the content. This instruction does not imply a maximum of three speakers in one service though.

3. Each person's tongue must be interpreted for edification purposes.

He wraps up this proposal by indirectly suggesting that anyone who speaks in a tongue has control over himself or herself when they speak. This is so because others who would like to speak in tongues must wait patiently for their turn.

Then, moving on to instruction and correction regarding prophesying (14:29–32), two words are emphasised, "order" and "edification."

As was the case with tongues, Paul places certain limitations upon prophets and prophesying within the church.

• Only one prophet may speak at a time.

• After each prophet has spoken, the entire congregation must carefully distinguish between God-given speech in line with the gospel and speech given from the wrong sources for the incorrect reasons. It is important to realise that all prophets, no matter how accurate they are, will have elements of truth and error in their words because of their human element. No prophet or prophecy is infallible.

- If a revelation comes to another person, the prophet or person speaking must finish up and sit down to give others a chance. I assume that certain people in the services were refusing others a chance to prophesy.

- "The spirits of the prophets are subject to the control of the prophets" implies that the prophet inspired by the Spirit retains control of all their faculties. It is possible that some of the people were saying that they could not stop prophesying when they wanted to because the Spirit had control over them.

These verses also include interchange between "prophet" and "prophesy." The idea here is that the word "prophet" describes a function like that of a translator and simply refers to one who is prophesying. It does not point to some special class of person.

The point of this entire section has been to establish order, thereby ensuring edification of the body of believers.

Paul's last word on this comes in 14:33. He refers to the

ordered nature of God's purposive action in apportioning gifts and in creation and in resurrection, and Paul's larger point is that this order in the nature of the God ... should be reflected in the lifestyle and worship of the people of God. Thus a gift given by the Holy Spirit to benefit everyone (14:28–32) would be undermined in a self-contradictory and chaotic way if the Spirit himself "fell upon" this or that individual in such a way that responsible processes of ministry were disrupted and confused, and some missed out on part of what the Holy Spirit was communicating through responsible human agents.[218]

Let us move on to the problem of women in the church (14:34–35, see also 11:2–16). Here Paul was clarifying that women (I am sure this could have applied to anyone) could not rant and rave in the

---

[218]Thiselton. A. C. *The First Epistle*, p. 1145.

services in the manner they had been doing.

Paul warns the Corinthians – 1 Corinthians 14:34–38

To begin with, the translation and exegesis of 14:34–35 is complicated. According to Thiselton and others, the passage reads: "As in all the churches of the saints, women should be silent in the churches. For they are not permitted to speak, but should be subordinate, as the law also says. If there is anything they desire to know, let them ask their husbands at home. For it is shameful for a woman to speak in church."[219]

These verses have always been difficult to the church, and most exegesis on them concerns what they do not say rather than what they do.

The typical approach to this passage is to see it as either authentic, in which case one has to explain what was taking place at the church to warrant such statements, or, as an interpolation.

Consider the following illustration to explain the meaning of interpolation.

You might have read about or seen on TV how important a crime scene is to an investigator. Often, the scene is scrutinised with a fine-tooth-comb looking for anything that might turn up clues leading to the arrest of the perpetrators. However, one can manipulate a crime scene to strengthen the case against the real criminal or distract detectives off the trail. This usually happens by planting incriminating evidence at the scene of the crime, for instance, drugs, DNA samples like hair or blood, a gun, etc. These "plants" would be similar to an interpolation in a text. Interpolations are additions to a text that might benefit or corrupt the text.

Aside from the possibility of 14:33b–36, another example of an interpolation could be Mark 16.9–18. Just a side note here, even though these portions might be interpolations, you should guard against questioning the authenticity or accuracy of scripture. The

---

[219]Other ancient authorities put verses 34–35 after verse 40.

Bible is by far the best-preserved book from ancient times.

There are many scholars who argue that these verses in 1 Corinthians (possibly 33b included) are in fact an interpolation.[220] James Dunn explains it succinctly by stating that "although these two verses are found in all known manuscripts ... the two text-critical criteria of transcriptional and intrinsic probability combine to cast considerable doubt on their authenticity."[221]

For those scholars who believe that these verses are authentic and correctly placed, the options include:

- that Paul was prohibiting some form of inspired speech adopted by the women. Possibly something relating to tongues or the discernment of prophecy;

- that there were women within the assembly who were disruptive, i.e. they were interjecting when prophecies or the like were being given;

- that these words are not Paul's, but are quotations or a paraphrase of what the Christians at Corinth were saying.

While both the option of interpolation and authenticity are possible, I am of the opinion that the passage is authentic and represents a highly contextualised confrontation of certain disruptive behaviours women were pursuing within the assembly.

Thiselton offers up the best explanation I have read to support this position:

> ... we believe that the "speaking" in question denotes the *activity of* sifting *or weighing the words of prophets, especially by asking probing questions about the prophet's theology or even the prophet's lifestyle in public.* This would become especially

---

[220]Those who argue for the view that either (14:34–35 or 14:33b–36) represent an interpolation include the following scholars, Schmiedel, Weiss, Dautzenberg, Conzelmann, Fitzer, Strobel, Klauck, Fee, Hays, Senft, Schrage, Barrett etc.

[221]Fee, G. D. *First Epistle*, p. 699.

sensitive and problematic *if wives were cross-examining their husbands about the speech and conduct which supported or undermined the authenticity of a claim to utter a prophetic message*, and would readily introduce Paul's allusion to reserving questions of a certain kind for home. The women would in this case (i) be acting as judges over their husbands in public; (ii) risk turning worship into an extended discussion session with perhaps private interests; (iii) militate against the ethics of controlled and restrained speech in the context of which the congregation should be silently listening to God rather than eager to address one another; and (iv) disrupt the sense of respect for the orderliness of God's agency in creation and in the world as against the confusion which preexisted the creative activity of God's Spirit. (Italics his)[222]

Paul has come to the end of a long argument correcting their belief that "speaking in tongues" was a sign of mature spirituality. In his conclusion, Paul sternly opposes the root of their argument. You will recall that all along the Corinthians had regarded themselves as having arrived. They were independent, they were living in the new age, and they were spiritually mature. Why should they listen or follow another's example? Their attitude concerning tongues was just another of the many symptoms of their warped (distorted) beliefs. Ultimately, Paul had to remind them that their attitudes were wrong and that the gospel did not originate with them and neither were they the only possessors of truth (14:36).

There are a number of insights worth mentioning in 14:37–38.

- The words, "what I am writing to you", are a translation from the plural expression for "the matters about which I am writing to you." The latter meaning suggests that what Paul had in mind was all he had written in the epistle and not just this section of the letter in these final verses.

---

[222]Thiselton, A. C. *The First Epistle,* p. 1158.

- The words, "is the Lord's command", reminds the people that everything he had said carries the weight/authority of the risen Christ himself.

- The emphatic positioning of the word "Lord" indicates that Paul writes in submission to the Lord. Therefore, by not submitting to what he writes, the Corinthians were denying the Lordship of Jesus Christ.

- The word "spiritually" – *pneumatikos* is extremely fitting. Turn back to the beginning of Chapter 12. In 12:1, Paul begins with "Now about spirituals, brothers …" At the beginning, the people were interested in what constituted spirituality. At the end, Paul uses this to enforce his words. He says to them, "Anyone who claims to be a prophet, or to have spiritual powers, must acknowledge that what I am writing to you is true."

- Finally, "Anyone who does not recognize this is not to be recognised." This could mean one of three things:
  † whoever ignores Paul's remarks, God will ignore;
  † the greater congregation will ignore whoever ignores Paul's remarks, or
  † whoever ignores Paul's remarks, Paul will also ignore.

In light of the immense claim Paul has just made, that everything he has written is a command from the Lord, the first is the most likely. Paul was not concerned that people were ignorant of what he had written. He was concerned that they would not adhere to what he had written.

Thus to summarise, Paul was issuing a serious warning along these lines, "If you want to pursue your own self-centred ideas of what constitutes spirituality, you are in danger of being totally ignored by God."

Church should be orderly – 1 Corinthians 14:39–40

In 14:39, Paul gives an indication of the relationship between tongues/prophecy and the congregational setting. That is: prophecy is to be heartily encouraged for its edification purposes and tongues not forbidden. His key point – all church proceedings must be orderly.

Questions and Thoughts for Reflection

1. What do you believe about the use of "spiritual gifts" in our times? Sadly, many people's beliefs and use of "spiritual gifts" will depend on the nature of the church movement or denomination they attend. To add to my previous "sadly", I have noticed that many churches which previously pushed the use of the spiritual gifts have all but given up the "walk" and now only do the "talk". If you are in one of these churches, why do you think this has happened. If you are not, try to venture an answer? One could apply this personally as well. I often hear Christians telling stories about their amazing past experiences only to find out that none of that still happens in their lives. Again, why do you think this has happened, and much more importantly, how can the church and the individual return to a faith filled walk of practising the gifts of the spirit?[223] Let me remind you that Paul told the Corinthian Christians on two occasions that they should "eagerly desire gifts of the Spirit." (12:31; 14:1) On another occasion, he also told Timothy "to fan into flame the gift of God, which is in you through the laying on of my hands" (2 Timothy 1:6 NIV). Paul was appealing to Timothy that he should frequently and energetically use his spiritual gifts. This appeal is indirectly applicable to all of us as well!

---

[223]Interestingly, Paul intimated that rekindling gifts involved fervent prayer, strict obedience to the word of God, and expression of active faith. See Paul's discussions with Timothy in 2 Timothy 1.

2. Paul's argument in vv. 21–23 is for a church that does not chase the unbeliever away (At Corinth, unbelievers were possibly being chased away by tongue speaking maniacs.). But, how does this relate to our churches today? Are you perhaps in a church that potentially turns the unbeliever away? Think about aspects such as your church's appearance, decoration, leadership structures, location, preaching and teaching, evangelism, small groups etc. Of course, one can seriously overdo this and head in the direction many "seeker" oriented churches have gone, where topics like sin, hell, repentance, the exclusivity of salvation through Jesus, or generally any doctrine or teaching purporting to the idea of "absolute truth", are never taught or preached. The key is to find a balance. There is a great deal of high quality research on the market in this regard. Doing some research on this would be highly beneficial.[224]

3. Paul mentions in 14:29 (NIV), "Two or three prophets should speak, and the others should weigh carefully what is said." The reality is that there are demonic spirits out there. If you have ever questioned this, just look at the stories of exorcism in the Gospels and Acts.[225] My question is: how would you go about "weighing" a persons apparently inspired message? What would your yardsticks be? In other words, how would you "distinguish between (i) prophetic speech which is God-given and coheres with the gospel of Christ and the pastoral situation and (ii) speech which is merely self-generated rhetoric reflecting the speaker's disguised self-interests, self-deceptions, or errors, albeit under the guise of supposed 'prophecy.'" [226] Do not read

---

[224]One particular book, which I have found invaluable, is "Natural Church Development" by Christian A. Schwarz.

[225]"For our struggle is not against flesh and blood, but against the rulers, against the authorities, against the powers of this dark world and against the spiritual forces of evil in the heavenly realms." (Ephesians 6:12)

[226]Thiselton, A. C. *The First Epistle to the Corinthians: A commentary on the Greek text*, p. 1140.

on until you have given this some considerable thought. It would be a good idea to actually make a list of the yardsticks you would use. John the Apostle also touches on this idea of "weighing prophecy" when he states, "Beloved, do not believe every spirit, but test the spirits to see whether they are from God; for many false prophets have gone out into the world." (1 John 4:1) The background was that a group of John's opponents were claiming that the spirit inspired their teachings. Thankfully, there are quite a few helpful ideas about this. For one, weighing is typically achieved by carefully considering the prophecy in light of the contents of the OT, the gospel of Jesus and all of the churches traditions. If there is any contradiction between the prophecy and these texts, throw it out! In Thessalonians, Paul states, "but test everything; hold fast to what is good" (1 Thessalonians 5:21). In the Didache, it states, "And every prophet teaching the truth, if he doeth not what he teacheth, is a false prophet."[227] Furthermore, in the Hermas manuscript, the following text shows how the Apostolic Fathers weighed prophecy:

> 'How then, Sir,' say I, 'shall a man know who of them is a prophet, and who a false prophet?' 'Hear,' saith he, 'concerning both the prophets; and, as I shall tell thee, so shalt thou test the prophet and the false prophet. By his life test the man that hath the divine Spirit. In the first place, he that hath the [divine] Spirit, which is from above, is gentle and tranquil and humble-minded, and abstaineth from all wickedness and vain desire of this present world, and holdeth himself inferior to all men, and giveth no answer to any man when enquired of, nor speaketh in solitude (for neither doth the Holy Spirit speak when a man wisheth Him to speak); but the man speaketh then when God wisheth

[227]Lightfoot, J. B., & Harmer, J. R. *The Apostolic Fathers, p. 233.*

him to speak.[228]

In summary, weighing prophecy is based on two critical elements: 1) the messages correlation with the revealed Word of God and, 2) the character of the person delivering the prophecy.

4. Answer the following questions about the nature of the problem in Corinth:
    4.1 Explain what the problem in Chapters 12–14 was and suggest reasons why the Corinthians had behaved improperly?
    4.2 How do spiritual gifts relate to ministries?

---

[228]Lightfoot, J. B., & Harmer, J. R. The Apostolic Fathers, p. 435.

Chapter Sixteen
The Resurrection

> The resurrection of Jesus has determined our existence for all time and eternity. We do not merely live out our length of days and then have the hope of resurrection as an addendum. Rather, as Paul makes plain in this passage, Jesus' resurrection has set in motion a chain of inexorable events that absolutely determines our present and our future. Christ is the first fruits of those who are His, who will be raised at His coming. That ought both to reform the way we currently live and to reshape our worship into seasons of unbridled rejoicing.[229]

I consider this Chapter to be one of the most astonishing and encouraging within the Bible. Briefly, it is all about the future we can expect as Christians, and what a future that is going to be! If you fear death, if you are clueless about life hereafter, if you have doubts about the reality of it or your Christian faith, then this Chapter should be very encouraging to you.

1 Corinthians 15 consists of three subsections.

- The issue of Jesus' resurrection and the fact that they all agree to the reality thereof (15:1–11).

- Their two conflicting positions about the resurrection (15:12–34). Note that the argument in this text leads to the

---

[229]Fee, G. D. *First Epistle*, p. 760.

logical conclusions/consequences of their belief.

- The manner in which we rise from the dead (15:35–38). That is, not the method, but rather in what form/type of body it will be.

1 Corinthians 15:12 suggests the general problem giving rise to this Chapter. Some of the Corinthians believed that there was no resurrection of the dead. However, some scholars believe that groups within Corinth could not bring themselves to believe in any form of life after death.[230]

Others, like Chrysostom and Luther, believe one or more groups alleged that the resurrection had taken place a long time ago i.e., that the resurrection had already taken place (2 Timothy 2:18). Thus, they would have thought that the physical body will dissolve and turn back into dust, but the spiritual element within a human will live on no longer trapped in the body.[231]

Still others wrestled with the notion of a "bodily" resurrection. Martins suggests a hypothesis where the lower class of Christians at Corinth might accept a "hierarchy of essences which could make broad sense out of Paul's teaching,"[232] but the intellectual well-to-do-types could not accept the idea. The idea of raising rotten corpses from the grave was primitive and absurd.

Where does this leave us? It is likely that most would have not denied the reality of a resurrection. However, the problem was that "some failed to follow through the eschatological and ethical

---

[230]Note that Paul uses one of the Epicurean maxims "let us eat and drink, for tomorrow we die" (15:32b). Schmithals. W. *Gnosticism in Corinth*, p. 156. Epicureanism was brought about by Epicurus "who subscribed to a hedonistic ethics that considered an imperturbable emotional calm the highest good and whose followers held intellectual pleasures superior to transient sensualism." Available [Online] at http://www.merriam-webster.com/dictionary/epicureanism Note that the Sadducees were linked with Epicurus' way of thought.

[231]Luther, M. *Works*, vol. 28, p. 59.

[232]Martin, D. B. *The Corinthian Body*, pp. 130, 132, 135–36.

entailments of what it meant to share in Christ's resurrection, not least corporately as his body."[233]

With all of this in mind, Paul responds to their problems.

An Astonishing Testimony – 1 Corinthians 15:1–11

Paul knew that their central problem was that some did not believe in the resurrection of the dead. However, he also knew that it would take some clever reasoning to convince them of their error/s. This is how he does it!

Beginning at the "starting blocks," his idea is to again capture the essence of Christianity and the certainty of its inauguration. He does this by highlighting three areas of importance.

1. He reminds them in 15:1–2 and 15:11 that this is what they believed, that is the gospel, which he preached, and they received. Paul's point is that they might have recognised the gospel was important, but it did not seem as if they had understood the contents of the gospel. He suggests that if they profess to believe the gospel, but have not given due consideration to what it implies and demands, then they do not really trust Christ. Their belief is groundless and empty. They lack saving faith – their belief is futile.

2. In 15:3–5, Paul reminds them of what they believed in. Incidentally, these verses are taken to be some form of early creedal formulation common to the ancient church. The technical term for this early creed is *kerygma*. It was a Greek term for preaching and implied, "to cry or proclaim as a herald." At its very heart lie the death, burial and resurrection of Jesus Christ. What is amazing about this kerygma is that it emphasized the resurrection of dead bodies through the words "buried" and "raised on the third day" and not the spiritual revitalization of life after death. Secondly, the

---

[233]Thiselton, A. C. *The First Epistle*, p. 1172.

testimonies of so many sightings gave additional weight to Jesus being visible as a human being this side of the grave.[234]

3. Paul reinforces his apostleship by sharing some of his experience (15:9–11). I would like you to pause for a moment and consider the following. Paul utilized deductive reasoning[235] to prove that believers rise from the dead. The validity of this type of reasoning resides with the accuracy and truth of the general premise. In this case, Christ is resurrected (more on this in the next section). The point I want to make is that the Corinthians accepted his "assertion." This should be tremendously encouraging for us. After all, do you think a group as contentious as they were, would have kept quiet on such a major point in Paul's argument, had Jesus not risen from the dead? Never! The truth is that there were many witnesses they could visit to attest to its validity. As I mentioned at the beginning of this section, this, for me, is astonishing and most encouraging!

No Resurrection – A Terrifying Concept! – 1 Corinthians 15:12–34

Before we begin unravelling Paul's argument in defence of the resurrection, you must understand that "there is no contradiction of logic between 15:12–19 and 20–34, providing that we keep in mind their different methods and aims. The first subsection (15:12–14, 16) sets forth a twofold argument: i) if resurrection in general is impossible, how can it be claimed that Christ was raised? ii) Conversely, if we do proclaim Christ as raised, how can it make sense to deny the resurrection of the dead?"[236]

Remember, the effect of the first Adam was death to all who

---

[234]Fee, G. D. *First Epistle*, pp. 718–719.

[235]Quite simply, this form of reasoning moves from a generally accepted premise to the particular out workings thereof (or from cause to effect).

[236]Thiselton, A. C. *The First Epistle*, p. 1214.

followed. However, in similar fashion, the effect of the second Adam (Jesus) is eternal life, and all who believe shall experience the same.

Utter senselessness – 1 Corinthians 15:12–19

In essence, Paul forces them to admit to the validity of the resurrection of the dead through a progression of logical arguments. He assumes their belief and explains the consequences thereof.

If there is no resurrection of the dead, then:

- Christ has not been raised. The logic here is that if Christ was completely human and died without experiencing resurrection (remember, there were still many living witnesses of his resurrection), then how could any other human being experience the resurrection.

- Both their preaching and faith are futile. The resurrection shows that God is active in Christ. However, if the resurrection did not take place, the gospel is a sham. The Corinthians' faith rested in this gospel. Therefore, if the gospel is a sham, their faith is too. Furthermore, if Christ did not rise from the dead, then a) He is dead and there is therefore, no future life or b) He is physically dead, although spiritually raised, and there is no on-going material existence.

- They are false witnesses about God. In effect, Paul says, "If Christ did not rise we are all liars." We have been testifying against God, not for Him. All along, we have been claiming that God has done something when He never did.

- They are still living in sin. Death has not lost its power and remains the ultimate destructive force. If people are still dead in their sins, what does "Christ died for our sins" in 15:3 mean? If that is the case, Christ's death has accomplished nothing. His death without a resurrection would indicate a condemned Christ, definitely not a justified Christ. How could he justify others if He were dead? In fact, if Christ did not rise, believers would still be living in their sins just like any pagan.

- Those who have died are lost forever. One of the most dramatic changes in the thinking of early Christians was their outlook on death. For pagans, death marked the end of existence. However, for Christians, death was like waking up to a beautiful new day. Jesus had removed death's sting (15:55) through His death and resurrection. However, none of this is possible without the resurrection. In fact, if He did not rise, then we have spent our whole lives hoping, for nothing. We are just a bunch of wishful thinkers. For this reason, pity us above all, for we are seriously deluded people wasting our time instead of having fun.

The noisiness of the empty tomb – 1 Corinthians 15:20–28

After refuting the stark realities of "what if there's no resurrection" through emphasis on the unacceptable logical implications, Paul turns to remind them of the incredible implications and inevitability of the resurrection being a reality. Jesus did rise from the dead. This they agreed on (if not, they would have by this point in the argument), and because he did, the entire situation facing humankind has changed.

Fee suggests that a proper understanding of the resurrection, its affect and Paul's logic, require an understanding of two criteria within Paul's theology.

- His thinking is eschatological. Paul understood that through Jesus' death, resurrection and the impartation of the Spirit, God had set in motion an unstoppable process. Therefore, he believed that Jesus' resurrection guaranteed the resurrection of those in Christ. Imagine a bomb with a very long un-extinguishable fuse. At some point, the fuse ignites (we could say that Jesus' resurrection is the match that lights the fuse) and begins to burn in the direction of the bomb (the general resurrection). We know that the bomb is up ahead, and we can watch the fuse burning next to us. To be "eschatologically" orientated is to allow your every thought and action to be dictated by the burning fuse and preparing for the explosion.

- God raised Jesus. Therefore, Jesus' resurrection has to do with God's authority over all things, including death. Jesus rules, but the enemy is still at large. This means that the resurrection is the ultimate proof that the enemy is defeated, because through it, death has been defeated. This is the point of 15:23–28. Jesus' resurrection must lead to our resurrection, otherwise death has not been defeated, and neither has the enemy.

All of this points to Jesus' work as being crucial: Jesus resurrected; those in Jesus resurrected; the consummation of the saving acts of God; the defeat of all God's enemies so that he can be all in all.

Moving on, Paul begins by drawing on the image that Jesus is the first fruit of those who have fallen asleep (15:20). This image comes from Leviticus where it refers to the first portion of the crop offered to God in thanksgiving. Paul's use of this word emphasises "the pledge of the remainder, and concomitantly, the assurance of a full harvest."[237] As such, Jesus, the first fruit, was waved as an offering consecrating the rest of the harvest. He is the first man saved into a life that knows no death. The metaphor of the first fruits also explains the tension established by the "already-not-yet" nature of the Kingdom of God. Christians must not suppose that their resurrection has taken place. It is still to come. They must remain encouraged because Jesus, whom they follow, did rise. Imagine a vast field of unopened sunflowers. As the farmer sits there on his porch gazing out over his land, he notices one sunflower coming into full

---

[237]De Boer. M. D. *Defeat of Death, Apocalyptic Eschatology in 1 Corinthians 15 and Romans 5,* p. 109.

bloom. He begins to rejoice with his family and workers because he knows with certainty that it is only a matter of time before all the others come into bloom as well.

Paul then draws an analogy between Adam and Christ. Adam stands as representative of the sinful condition of all humans (Romans 1:18–3:20) whereas Christ stands for the justification received by faith (Romans 3:21–5:11). Redemption is the saga of two men. The first disobeyed God and led humanity in the wrong direction.[238] However, the second obeyed God and justifies all who will turn to him in faith.

Of great comfort to us is that no matter how devastating the sin of the first was, the redemptive work of the second reverses the consequences of that sin and places us within a position of favour with God. Only by realising the seriousness of the first, is one able to appreciate the magnanimity of the second.[239]

Two thoughts are worth considering here. The first is: how serious are you about removing sinful behaviour from your life? The second is: are you able to let go of past sins and receive forgiveness? If you are not committed to achieving both, you need to a) pick up

---

[238]"Romans 5.12 states that we were all involved in Adam's sin in some sense. When he sinned, it was us sinning as well. The best way to explain this is through use of 'natural headship'. The entirety of our human nature, physical, spiritual, material and immaterial, has been received from our parents and more distant ancestors by way of descent from the first pair of humans. On that basis, we were actually present within Adam, so that we all sinned in his act. There is no injustice, then, to our condemnation and death as a result of original sin." Erickson, M.J. *Christian Theology*, 2nd Ed, p. 654. On the other hand, an alternative view is "federal headship", which I personally prefer. Human beings receive their physical nature through inheritance, but that God specially creates the soul for each individual and unites it with the body at birth. Thus, we were not present psychologically or spiritually in any of our ancestors, including Adam. Adam, however, was our representative. God ordained that Adam should act not only on his behalf, but also on our behalf. The consequences of his actions passed on to his descendants as well.

[239]Mounce, R. H. *Romans. The New American Commentary*, p. 139.

the plough and start carrying it and, b) realize that you are missing one of the fundamental aspects Jesus came to release you from. There is now no condemnation for those in Christ Jesus (Romans 8:1).

Following this, Paul mentions the words, "But each in his own order" (15:23). This giving of life does not take place all at once. In the first *tagma* (order), there is only Christ, the first fruits. In the second come those who belong to Christ. The second refers to the *Parousia* (Second Coming of Christ). Thus, we can say that at the first coming of Christ, He was raised up alone as the first fruits. However, at the second coming, everyone will rise (the harvest). Those in Christ will rise to join him while those who rejected him will rise to eternal damnation.[240]

Let me summarise what Paul has said. God the Father has entrusted God the Son with a mission. Evil forces usurped some of God's authority. It was Christ's task to reclaim this sovereignty by overcoming the powers, and recovering the submission of creation as a whole. In due course, He will complete this mission, death itself being the last of these forces to hold out. As Christians, we would do well to apply these truths in our lives.

Take a look in the mirror – 1 Corinthians 15:29–34

Paul has already stated his main point in the previous section; that Christ's resurrection is the beginning of God's eschatological act that will end in the resurrection of believers (and nothing can stop it!). THE FUSE IS LIT!

In this section, Paul appeals to their experiences, actions and feelings in an effort to convince them of the resurrection of believers.

He begins with a rhetorical question "that if there is no

---

[240]Although those "not in Christ" are excluded in regard to being raised up, it does not mean that Paul denied their future resurrection. This would be contradictory to Acts 24:15. Their omittance is most likely due to Paul's not focusing on them in this section.

resurrection, why then are they baptising people in proxy for those who have died?" (15:29) To him, this was a contradiction in terms and hardly the type of argument we would expect Paul to use to verify the resurrection. The problem is that there is no historical or biblical precedent for this type of behaviour, particularly in the New Testament, early church or any orthodox community shortly thereafter. Outside of orthodoxy, there is some evidence of this practice within Marcionism.[241] Marcionites would baptise each other on behalf of those in their sect or group who had died without being baptised.[242]

This practice goes against the theology of salvation. I say this because salvation comes by grace through OUR decision to follow Christ. Therefore, those who did not make a decision for Christ before death cannot now have that decision made for them by another still alive (Romans 10:8–11; Ephesians 2:8–9). Therefore, why would Paul appeal to this strange practice of theirs without any apparent disapproval, knowing that they were in theological error? Unfortunately, we do not know. However, we are not totally in the dark.

---

[241]Marcionites "rejected the writings of the <u>Old Testament</u> and taught that Jesus was not the <u>Son</u> of the <u>God of the Jews</u>, but the Son of the good God, who was different from the God of the Ancient Covenant. They anticipated the more consistent <u>dualism</u> of <u>Manichaeism</u> and were finally absorbed by it. As they arose in the very infancy of <u>Christianity</u> and adopted from the beginning a strong <u>ecclesiastical</u> organization, parallel to that of the <u>Catholic Church</u>, they were perhaps the most dangerous foe <u>Christianity</u> has ever known."
Available [Online] at <u>http://www.newadvent.org/cathen/09645c.htm</u>

[242]The Mormons also baptize for the dead because they believe that the family unit will endure unto the eternal ages. Therefore, if some one in their family did not get baptized or did not receive the baptism of the Holy Spirit, they do it in proxy for that person to ensure that they will be together in eternity. They defend the authenticity of this practice by using (15:29). The problem is that there is no evidence of this practice and no clarity about what they were actually doing, let alone Paul's potential disapproval thereof.

Firstly, based on the language usage, not everyone in the community was practising this, but it seems as if pretty much everybody was aware that baptisms were taking place. We must also assume Paul's lack of disapproval might imply they were doing something far less heretical than supposed.[243] It could furthermore be that Paul was not trying to deal with their error, but thought to use it to demonstrate any form of spiritual existence beyond the grave was non-existent without there first being the resurrection of Christ.

Secondly, he asks the Corinthians to think of the danger he was exposing himself to. Mention is made of "wild beasts." It is likely that this was a metaphor referring to his struggle with opponents in Ephesus.[244] The point is that he would have to be crazy to suffer these struggles and live at purely a human level like all the others who die without any hope.

His last argument refers back to Isaiah 22:13, "but instead there was joy and festivity, killing oxen and slaughtering sheep, eating meat and drinking wine. 'Let us eat and drink, for tomorrow we die.'" This verse reflects back on the occasion where the citizens/

[243]It is highly likely that this practice was not a form of vicarious baptism, i.e. not the type of baptism where one substitutes or suffers on behalf of another. It could have been a form of baptism for (for the sake of) the dead, i.e. it is "not in order to remedy some deficiency on the part of the dead, but in order to be reunited with them at the resurrection." *Howard, J. K. Baptism for the Dead; A Study of 1 Corinthians 15:29*, p. 140. "Paul could well be referring to a much commoner, indeed a normal experience, that the death of Christians leads to the conversion of survivors, who in the first instance 'for the sake of the dead' (their beloved dead) and in the hope of re-union, turn to Christ – e.g., when a dying mother wins her son by the appeal 'Meet me in heaven!' Such appeals, and their frequent salutary effect, give strong and touching evidence of faith in the resurrection". *Findlay, G. G. St. Paul's First Epistle to the Corinthians.* Expositors Greek Testament, 2, p. 931.

[244]The term "wild beasts" was a common metaphor in moralistic Hellenism. Furthermore, Paul was a Roman citizen, which would have excluded him from fighting beasts in an arena. Those who fought wild beast in the arena faced certain death. Fee, G. D. *First Epistle*, pp. 770–771.

Israelites in Jerusalem were facing siege and annihilation by the Assyrians. Instead of repenting, they were "partying it up". Essentially, what Paul was saying is that if there is no resurrection, those at Corinth may as well live an immoral lifestyle if it gets them what they want. "Have fun; after all, you only live once and life is short." It seems as if some people were living in this manner based on the statements made in 15:33–34.

Jars of Gold – 1 Corinthians 15:35–58

Paul has argued in favour of a resurrection for believers. However, how does a dead and decaying body rise to life? It is impossible!

This section splits in two
- The old manhood and the new (15:35–49); and
- The Christian Apocalypse (15:50–58).

Firstly, the logical unintelligibility and inconceivability of the bodily resurrection comes to the fore (15:35–49). Paul reflects on two important themes: 1) there are differences between bodies, and 2) Christians must realize that God's infinite capabilities are already visible through creation.

Secondly, he reflects on the gospel principle of transformation in terms of the future (from weakness to glory – 15:50–57).[245] Paul could have taken this direction because a group within the church believed that their resurrection had already taken place, hence their libertine reckless behaviour.

This dramatic portion of scripture concludes with a reminder of what God has accomplished through his grace, namely victory over sin and death.

The Worm and the Butterfly – 1 Corinthians 15:35–49

"How are the dead raised? With what kind of body will they come?" Everybody knows that when a person dies, his or her body decom-

---

[245]Thiselton, A. C. *The First Epistle*, p. 1259.

poses and eventually returns to dust. These days the popular word is "cosmic dust." Therefore, to suggest that this same body can resurrect is bordering on insanity. "What kind of body would arise from a heap of decomposed rubbish"? Paul deals sharply with these statements, "how foolish!" He continues along the following lines, "Do you not see all the miracles around you? Consider a grain of wheat, a mere pod, and then what it produces. Have you forgotten whom you are dealing with? This is the sovereign Lord who can create from nothing."

"Paul uses the model of sowing in the ground to underline the universal connection between being brought to life as the crop or fruit and transformation of form or different mode of existence in continuity of identity."[246] The same point is made in John 12.24 (unless a grain of wheat falls into the ground and dies).[247] Paul is not using the figure to bring out the necessity of death here, but rather the fact of transformation through death and revivification.[248]

Another good metaphor from nature would be that of the caterpillar/butterfly metamorphosis. There is no way that the caterpillar could change itself or even envisage changing itself into a butterfly. Nevertheless, it happens all the same. Would you believe that this could happen if you had not seen it with your own eyes? Well, the same applies to our bodies. We have to accept that this miraculous event lies in the hands of God, that he has said it will happen, and he knows how to make it happen!

Paul makes a second point in these first five verses about the "body." He shows them that there are many bodies different in form

---

[246]Ibid., p. 1263.

[247]The original cells that divided and multiplied in the formation of a baby died and were replaced. This is also the case with wheat. The original cells, constituting the seed, die as cell-multiplication progresses and the plant begins to grow. Eventually, the original seed dies off completely. What is also amazing is how prolific one grain of wheat can be – it can produce substantially from itself.

[248]Barrett, C. K. *The First Epistle To The Corinthians,* p. 300.

(man, animals, fish, birds, sun, moon, stars, heavenly and earthly bodies) because they all serve distinctive purposes suited to certain types of existence. Then he reminds them that God created all of these bodies.

In 15:42–44, Paul clarifies what he has already said earlier (15:36–37) about the metaphor of a seed, by changing from the metaphor (seed) to reality (body). Just as the seed dies, (ceases to exist in that form) so does the body (it continues to exist in another form). The "old" is sown perishable, natural, in weakness and dishonour. The "new" is raised imperishable, spiritual, in honour and power. When Paul states, "It is sown a physical body, it is raised a spiritual body (15:44)," you need to be aware that by "spiritual" he does not imply an "immaterial" body, but rather a supernatural, tangible body, which is beyond nature as we know it. It will be a body adapted to life in God's New Heaven and Earth.[249]

Finally, in 15:45–49 Paul takes what he has just written about the existence of two different kinds of bodies for people (natural and spiritual) and applies it to the earlier metaphor of Adam and Christ. The believers all shared the body of the first Adam (natural man. Therfore, they will also share the body of the second Adam, (spiritual) Christ.

In the blink of an eye – 1 Corinthians 15:50–58

This section draws Paul's argument to a close. He defended the truth that there will be a resurrection of the body, which will take place through a transformation process. Through his arguments, he has also shown them that it is actually absurd to have any religion

---

[249]Paul's argument is that "if there is a soma psychikon [soulish body], he declares – to which the answer is, of course there is: that is the normal sort of human soma, a body animated by the ordinary breath of life – then there is also a soma pneumatikon [spirit body], a body animated by the Spirit of the living God, even though only one example of such a body has so far appeared." Wright, N.T. *The Resurrection of the Son of God,* p. 354.

(faith) if they do not believe in the resurrection. After all, what is the point of religion (faith) based on something dead? He also alludes to the credibility of the resurrection by using Christ' resurrection as proof.

He answers their question in 15:35 by stating that no person in this present existence (flesh and blood) can enter the Kingdom of God.[250] This includes two classes: those who are still alive (flesh and blood) at Christ's Second Coming, and those who have already died (perished). Therefore, we will all have to undergo change in order to fit in with the new environment (Heaven). When that time of change comes,[251] it will occur in the blink of an eye. Paul calls it a "mystery" because it is a previously unfathomable event.

As regards "sting," "death," "sin" and "law," Fee comments:

> The relationship of the law to sin is that the former is what gives the latter its power. In Romans 5:13, Paul explains: Sin is not taken into account where there is no law. That is, the law not only makes sin observable as sin, but also, and more significantly, demonstrates that one's actions are finally over against God, and thus leads to condemnation (cf. 2 Corinthians 3:6). The law, which is good, functions as the agent of sin because it either leads to pride of achievement, on the one hand, or reveals the depth of one's depravity and rebellion against God, on the other. In either case, it becomes death-dealing instead of life-giving.[252]

Finally, Paul ends with words exhorting the Corinthians to stand firmly on that which they first believed.

---

[250]The "kingdom of God" refers to the rule and reign of God and not a physical realm. If one were to think of the kingdom of God as a realm, it would be the realm of those who are saved.

[251]"At the last trumpet" is indicative of the Second Coming of Christ.

[252]Fee, G. D. *First Epistle*, p. 806.

An empty tomb – What's that to me?

Paul has delivered a discourse refuting their lack of belief in the resurrection, and particularly, the "bodily" nature of it. This has meant he had to use arguments emphasising the implications of Christ not having risen from the dead. Even so, if one were to turn this situation around, what could we deduce from Christ's having risen from the dead?

- We can be confident that his death has satisfied the penalty required of man for his sin, and that we are free from blame or guilt (Romans 4:25).

- Jesus is alive and we can talk to him NOW!

- Our resurrection is certain because we know and follow him.

- We should no longer fear death and the afterlife.

- Jesus' resurrection gives us victory over sin if we trust him. The Holy Spirit raised Him up and sanctifies us.

- Jesus' resurrection body is the model for our future resurrected bodies (15:35–38; 42–43; 49). It is immortal, tangible and recognizable, but how, we do not know.

- Jesus' resurrection is a guarantee of his return (15:51; Acts 17:31). He spoke of His resurrection after three days, and it came true. He also said that He would return, and He will.

- His resurrection should spur us on because we know He has infinite power and speaks the truth. If ever there was an answer to "the search for the meaning of life," this is it.

Questions and Thoughts for Reflection

1. Paul provides the Corinthians with a summary of the Gospel message prior to arguing for the resurrection, "Christ <u>died</u> for our sins in accordance with the scriptures, and that he was

buried, and that he was <u>raised</u> on the third day *in accordance with the scriptures*" (15:3–4). Firstly, what was Paul's motive for alluding to the contents of the gospel he preached and they believed? Secondly, can you capture the theological meaning of the crucifixion and resurrection within the purpose of God for creation, in one paragraph? It is critical for you to know this for yours and others benefit. Remember what Peter said, "Always be prepared to give an answer to everyone who asks you to give the reason for the hope that you have." (1 Peter 3:15, see Romans 5:10 for a big clue). Thirdly, did you notice how Paul ends off his brief summary of the criteria constituting the gospel message, "in accordance with the scriptures?" He is pointing out that all that happened to Jesus was in fact prophesied in the OT before it happened. In light of this, reflect back on Jesus' life, that is the abuse from religious leaders and their efforts to do anything to stop Him, the general confusion and shock over what He said and did, the fear and pain experienced by His disciples at His death. What does this tell you about those ancient people? Cast your reflections forwards. How does Western society respond to the crucifixion and resurrection today? Again, what does this tell you about people today? Think before reading on! Firstly, the ancient religious leaders and the people who went to the synagogues heard all of these prophecies read allowed day after day, and yet most of them missed the outworking of these prophecies right before their eyes. Why? For one, their hearts were hardened. They were more interested in their own agendas than pursuing the truth. Would Jesus have rebuked them if they had no option to pursue the truth He was offering? Of course not! The same applies today. People hear or read of these gospel message events and think them bizarre, barbaric, mythological, pitiful etc. Part of the reason is that they do not investigate the scriptures, and thus they do not see the genius of God. Secondly, their hearts are hard. Their own agendas have overwhelmed them to the point where they cannot see and understand (See Isaiah 6:14–15, also stated in Matthew 13:13–15).

2. Paul has gone to great lengths to prove various aspects about the resurrection. But, what do you believe will happen when you die? Where will you go? If your answer is heaven? What is heaven for you? What will it be like – will you have a body, will you be recognised? Will heaven be where you spend eternity (I am not here suggesting the alternative as hell, but rather, is there something else in store for the Christian besides heaven)? As I have said before, do not read ahead until you have given this some deep thought. It is important for you to work out what you actually believe presently? As I see it, most Christians believe that when they die, they will go to a form of spiritual heaven. There, they will join with other Christians and myriads of angels and sing praises to God for eternity. But, part of this belief is not actually scriptural. There is no doubt a heaven, and that Christians will go there, see their Christian family members, relatives and friends, and encounter myriads of angels. However, scripture is clear that heaven is not a Christian's final destiny. Heaven is more like a temporary abode, where people reside in a bodiless state, in the presence of God. Scholars often call this period "the Intermediate State." This experience of dying and going to heaven is called "life after death." However, there is something much more important that will happen to us after death, and Paul has been pointing this out in Chapter 15 – our resurrection! Paul has stated that this event will occur at the end of time, the Parousia. It is then when God will literally remake our physical bodies like Jesus' and return us to a newly created world represented by heaven (the abode of God) and earth coming together to form a new reality. (See Isaiah 65:17, 66:22; 2 Peter 3:13 and Revelations 21). N.T. Wright calls this post heavenly existence "life after life after death."

3. How does it make you feel to know that even a bunch of ar-

gumentative cynics in the church at Corinth did not challenge Paul on the validity of Jesus' resurrection? What was a major part of the reason why they did not challenge Paul on this issue?

4. What are the implications of Christ's bodily resurrection having never happened? Were you aware of these implications before? What would the implications be for us if Christ did not experience the crucifixion, i.e. He only experienced the resurrection or metamorphosing of His body?

5. Is it possible to have a different view than that stated by Paul on the bodily resurrection and still be Christian? Explain your answer.

6. Explain the nature of our physical resurrection and future appearance. Read John 20–21 while carefully constructing for yourself an idea of what Jesus resurrected body is like.

7. In 1 Corinthians 15, Paul interprets the resurrection through his Jewish lenses. However, in 2 Corinthians 4:7–5:10, he considers the resurrection more specifically from a Hellenistic/Platonic perspective. Discuss what additional aspects we may learn about the resurrection from this second epistle, and also what clues you can pick up hinting at a more Hellenistic/Platonic lens.

Chapter Seventeen
Adio!

The first epistle to the Corinthians is the result of a report and letter Paul received while in Ephesus. Throughout, we have been systematically working through each of the issues raised through those sources. The last issue that the Corinthians were likely enquiring about related to the collection. Paul's instructions in this regard appear in 16:1–4. He concludes with some of his requests in 16:5–18, and a final greeting in 16:19–24.

Money, money, money! – 1 Corinthians 16:1–4

One of the difficulties with this section is that Paul's comments are very brief. It seems as though the collection Paul referred to in 16:1 was a major part of his third missionary journey (see also Acts 24:17, Romans. 15:25–27, 2 Corinthians 8:1 and 9:1).

Apparently, this collection was headed for Jerusalem (16:3). Paul was intending to take it to Jerusalem where it would be utilised to help the Christians living in that area.

The second part of 16:1b is puzzling. The problem in this section is that Galatians never mentions what Paul refers to here. The closest one comes to raising issues about persons in need is when Peter, James, John and Paul agreed to remember the poor (Galatians 2:10).

There are a few certainties about this collection. Firstly, it was a special effort. It was not alluding to the customary half shekel that all male Jews throughout the world sent annually to Jerusalem as temple tax (Exodus 30:3). Secondly, there was no obligation to give towards this collection. This is another reason why it could not have been temple tax. Thirdly, the collection was not to support a kind of "Christian equivalent" of the temple.

However, why take up an offering for the Jerusalem church? Well, it could be because Jerusalem was generally a poor city. There were many older widows living there and they were dependent upon Jews outside of Palestine for their support. When that support did finally arrive, the Christians, subject to hostility and persecution (1 Thessalonians 2:14), never received any of it. Thus, they might have been in a crisis. There is also evidence to suggest that famines occurred from time to time (Acts 11:28–30). They may have suffered from the practice of having all things in common accompanied by poor resource management in the church's earlier days (Acts 4:34). In any event, whatever the ultimate cause might have been, we know that Paul felt that this collection was a high priority.

Besides "impoverishment," Paul could well have been motivated by the idea of building unity within the church. The fact is that many in the Jerusalem church were suspicious of Paul and the Gentile church community. A generous hand from the Gentile churches would have gone a long way to allaying those suspicions.

Accordingly, how were they to collect money for those in Jerusalem?

- They were to conduct this collection on the "first day" of every week (16:2). The Sabbath took place on the seventh day of the week, which was a Saturday. The fact that this collection was taken up and stored on each first day is a strong indication that Christians were observing that day as a commemoration of the resurrection (see John 20:19, 26, Acts 20:7 and Revelation 1:10).

- Paul also mentioned that their giving was to be in proportion to what they earned.[253]

- They were to take up this collection over a lengthy period of time and not just as one big collection when he arrived. Possible reasons for this include: Paul might have been concerned that the Corinthians would let him down by not preparing the collection in time for his coming, thus forcing an uncoordinated, rushed effort. This in turn could lead to a collection taken under emotional pressure, forcing certain people to give with wrong motives. This process would also rob Paul of the time he could devote to important issues. There was also a good chance that if people did not put away a small amount every month that they would not have been able to give as much at one go (2 Corinthians 9:4–5).

- The church was to select men of good standing from among themselves, either to take the collection alone or to travel in tandem with Paul to Jerusalem. Paul most likely suggested this to prevent trouble with the Corinthians in the future; accusations about taking or losing all of that money did not sit well with him.

- Finally, Paul speaks about himself. He would go along with them only "If it seems advisable that I should go" (16:4) i.e., if there were no objections from the church about the idea.

Paul's Aegean Ministry[254] – 1 Corinthians 16:5–18

There are a few areas of interest here.

Paul suggested that a door of opportunity had become available, but with much adversity attached (16:9). We can learn from this. Where there is a great opportunity for extending the Kingdom,

---

[253]"Giving" is discussed in detail in 2 Corinthians 8–9.
[254]Bimson, J. J., & Kane, J. *New Bible Atlas*, p. 81.

there will also be a total onslaught by the enemy.

Then, Paul encouraged the Corinthians to remain strong in their faith (16:13–14). This might have been alluding to being alert to the nearness of the eschatological events of the future, the Second Coming of Christ (see also Mark 13:35–37; Revelation 3:3),[255] and to refrain from living an immature, self-centred, loveless Christian lifestyle.

The church is served with a practical example of the people they should emulate (16:15–18). Stephanas and his family had dedicated themselves to serving God's people. They were shining examples of mature Christian believers; remember that they were part of the group who brought word to Paul of all the struggles within the church.

Final Greetings – 1 Corinthians 16:19–24

"Saying goodbye" in the Greco-Roman period did not follow the rigid structures commonly associated with their greetings.[256]

Of interest in this conclusion are Paul's strong words concerning those who do not love the Lord, and here, by love, he means covenant loyalty (16:22). "The commandment to love God is the focal point in the Shema ... The consequence of breaking the covenant is curses, and for keeping the covenant, blessings."[257] Therefore, the warning is addressed to those who reject the Lord.

Paul has preached the kerygma of the cross and the content of the gospel through an array of pastoral, ethical, and theological issues that bubble away at Corinth: "Come on," he concludes; "are you in

---

[255]There is evidence suggesting that Paul believed that Jesus' return was imminent, i.e. within his lifetime (see 7:29 and 15:52). The fact is, whether He comes during our lifetime or not, life is short and we will soon fall asleep and meet Him face to face.

[256]Please refer back to the beginning of this book for my comments on greeting formats.

[257]Erikson. A. *Traditions as Rhetorical Proof – Pauline Argumentation in Corinthians*, p. 292.

or out?"[258]

Last Questions and Thoughts for Reflection

1. There is still a lot of confusion today on the matter of "tithing". Most of the confusion focuses on what it is, whether it is still relevant for today, and how much should be given (percentage wise). Then there is "giving", which apparently relates to the New Testament. What is that all about? How much should be given (percentage wise)? Does it take the place of the tithe or is it in addition? Before reading further, what are your responses to these matters on tithing and giving and more importantly, what do you practice? Let me begin with tithing. The practice was based on the idea of giving, as holy to the Lord, a tenth of one's harvest or livestock, i.e. anything that could be converted to income possibly. It originated before the law was established in the Old Testament (Genesis 14:18–20; 28:22; Hebrews 7:1–13). When the law was established through Moses, the tithe was established to care for the Levites who worked for God (Numbers 18:21–24; Nehemiah 10:37–38; Hebrews 7:5), and as a three yearly gift to the poor (Deuteronomy 14:28–29). Tithes were paid in Jerusalem and in towns every three years when the tithe feast was eaten (Deuteronomy 12:5–6; 14:22–29 and 26:2). Even the Levites gave a tenth of what they received to the Lord (Numbers 18:25–29; Nehemiah 10:39). In addition to the tithe, one could also make freewill offerings (Exodus 36:3; Leviticus 7:12–18; Numbers 15:3; Ezra 1:4). They were usually given according to one's ability (Deuteronomy 16:10) and finally, there was blessing promised for those who tithed (Malachi 3:10). But, what happened with respect to the tithe when Jesus initiated the New Covenant? To be sure, there is no command or law instituted that suggests that the tithe be continued. However, there are many statements associated with the

---

[258]Thiselton, A. C. *The First Epistle*, p. 1351.

idea of tithing. For example:

> those who minister are entitled to receive support (1
> Corinthians 9:14); the poor and needy should be cared
> for (1 Corinthians 16:1; Galatians 2:10); those who give
> can trust God, as the source of all that is given (2 Cor-
> inthians 9:10), to supply their needs (2 Corinthians 9:8;
> Philippians 4:19); and giving should be done joyously (2
> Corinthians 9:7). The New Testament directs that taxes
> be paid to the state (Romans 13:6–7), which replaced
> Israel's theocracy. Paul's vocabulary and teaching suggest
> that giving is voluntary and that there is no set percent-
> age. Following the example of Christ, who gave even
> his life (2 Corinthians 8:9), we should cheerfully give
> as much as we have decided (2 Corinthians 9:7) based
> on how much the Lord has prospered us (1 Corinthians
> 16:2), knowing that we reap in proportion to what we
> sow (2 Corinthians 9:6) and that we will ultimately give
> account for our deeds (Romans 14:12).[259]

2. Paul makes an interesting comment about an "open door" for
    effective ministry being made available for him (16.9, see 2
    Corinthians 2:12 and Colossians 4:3, where Paul uses the same
    metaphor). In effect, this door is a metaphor for opportunity.
    Paul also mentioned that this great opportunity was accompa-
    nied by much adversity. What, if anything, do these two aspects
    teach you about how Paul viewed work?

3. What is the paradox within 16:15–18 that Paul alludes to so
    many times, and what does this teach us about how we should
    conduct our lives?

---

[259]Elwell, W. A., & Elwell, W. A. 1996. *Evangelical Dictionary of Biblical Theology.*

Bibliography

Allo, *Première Épitre,* Paris, Librairie Lecoffre, J. Gabalda, 1934.

Bailey, K. E. *Paul's Theological Foundation for Human Sexuality: The Theological Review* (Near East) 3. 1980.

Barrett, C. K. *Black's NT Commentary: The First Epistle To The Corinthians.* Hendrickson Publishers. 1968.

Barth, K. *Church Dogmatics*, 4/2. T&T Clark. 1970.

Barth, K. *The Resurrection of the Dead.* tr. H. L. Stenning. Hodder & Stoughton. 1933.

BDBG, *Hebrew Aramaic English Lexicon.* 1980.

Bimson, J. J., & Kane, J. *New Bible Atlas.* Wheaton, IL: InterVarsity Press. 2000, c1985.

Blomberg, C. *The NIV Application Commentary.* Zondervan. 1995.

Borthwick, P. *Leading the Way.* Navpress. 1989.

Bound, J. F. "Who Are the 'Virgins' discussed in 1 Corinthians 7:25–38?" *Evangelical Journal 2.* 1984.

Bruce, F. F. *1 and 2 Corinthians.* Wm. B. Eerdmans Publishing Company. 1980.

Bruce, F. F. *The Book of the Acts.* The New International Commentary on the New Testament. Wm. B. Eerdmans Publishing Co.: Grand Rapids, MI. 1988

Caird, G. B, *Language and Imagery.* Gerald Duckworth & Co. Ltd. 1980.

Collins, R. F, *First Corinthians.* The Liturgical Press. 1999.

Conzelmann, H. *1 Corinthians.* Fortress Press. 1988.

Chrysostom, J. *Hom. in 1 Corinthians. 8:5.*

Cullmann, O. *Christ and Time.* The Westminster Press. 1950.

Cullmann, O. *The Christology of the NT.* SCM Press Ltd. 1959.

De Boer, M. D. *Defeat of Death, Apocalyptic Eschatology in 1 Corinthians 15 and Romans 5.* (Man and the Biosphere Series). JSOT Press. 1988.

Deissmann, A. D. *Light from the Ancient East.* Hendrickson Publishers. 1995.

Duby, G. and Perot, M. (eds.) *A History of Women in the West, I: From Ancient Goddesses to Christian Saints.* Cambridge, Mass.: Harvard University Press. 1992.

Dunn, J. D. G. *Jesus and the Spirit. A Study of the Religious and Charismatic Experience of Jesus and the First Christians as Reflected in the NT.* Wm. B. Eerdmans Publishing Company. 1997.

Dunn. J. D. G. *The Theology of Paul the Apostle.* Wm. B. Eerdmans Publishing Company. 1998.

Edwards, T. C. *A Commentary on The First Epistle to the Corinthians.* Kessinger Publishing. 1885.

Engle, J, Pedley. T. A, Aicardi. J, and Dichter. M. A. *Epilepsy: A Comprehensive Textbook* (3-volume set). Lippincott Williams & Wilkins; 2 edition. 2007.

Elliott, J. K., *Paul's Teaching on Marriage in 1 Corinthians: Some Problems Considered.* NTS 19. 1973.

Elwell, W. A., & Elwell, W. A. *Evangelical Dictionary of Biblical Theology.* Baker Book House: Grand Rapids.1996.

Erickson, M.J. *Christian Theology*, 2nd Ed. Baker Book House. 2003.

Eriksson, A. *Traditions as Rhetorical Proof – Pauline Argumentation in Corinthians.* Almqvist & Wiksell. 1998.

Fee, G. D. *Corinthians – A Study Guide*, 2nd Ed. ICI University Press. 1985.

Fee, G. D. *God's Empowering Presence.* Hendrickson. 1996.

Fee, G. D. *Paul, the Spirit and the People of God.* Hendrickson. 1996.

Fee, G. D. *The First Epistle to the Corinthians.* NICNT. Wm. B. Eerdmans Publishing Company. 1987.

Findlay, G. G. *St. Paul's First Epistle to the Corinthians.* Expositors Greek Testament. Wm. B. Eerdmans Publishing Company. 1900.

Ford, J. M. "Levirate Marriage in St Paul (1 Corinthians. vii)". *NT Studies 10.* 1964.

Hamilton, V.P. *The New International Commentary on the OT: The Book of Genesis Chapters 1–17*. Wm. B. Eerdmans Publishing Company. 1990.

Hooker, R. *Works*. Oxford: Clarendon Press. 1878.

Horsley, R. *1 Corinthians*. Abingdon NT Commentaries. Abingdon Press. 1998.

Howard, J. K. "Baptism for the Dead; A Study of 1 Corinthians 15:29." *Evangelical Quarterly 37* (July-September 1965).

Howitt, Q.J. *1 Corinthians*. Unpublished Textbook for the South African Theological Seminar. 1996.

Hurd, J. C. *The Origin of 1 Corinthians*. Mercer University Press. 1983.

Kaiser, W. C. *Hard Sayings of the Bible*. InterVarsity. 1997.

Keener, C. S. *Acts: An Exegetical Commentary*. Volume 1. Baker Book House. 2012.

Keener, C.S. *1 and 2 Corinthians*. The New Cambridge Bible Commentary. Cambridge University Press. 2005.

Kittel, G. Friedrich, G. Bromansiley, G. W. *Theological dictionary of the NT*. Translation of: *Theologisches Worterbuch zum Neuen Testament*. Wm. B. Eerdmans Publishing Company. 1995.

Lampe, P. "*Theological Wisdom* and the 'Word about the Cross': The Rhetorical Scheme in 1 Corinthians 1–4," *Int* 44. 1990.

Levy, R. *Confident Living*, November 1987.

Lightfoot, J. B., & Harmer, J. R. *The Apostolic Fathers*. Macmillan and Co.: London. 1891

Luther, M. *Works*. Fortress Press. 1971.

MacArthur, J. *First Corinthians: NT Commentary*. Macarthur NT Commentary Series. Moody Publishers. 1984.

Mable, N. *Popular Hymns and Their Writers*. Howard Press. 2007.

Martin, D. B. *Slavery as Salvation*: The Metaphor of Slavery in Pauline Christianity. Yale University Press. 1990.

Martin, D. B. *The Corinthian Body*. Yale University Press. 1999.

Meyer, H. A. W. *Critical and Exegetical Handbook to the Epistles to the Corinthians* Eng. trans. 2 vols. T. & T. Clark. 1892.

Mishnah Yebamoth 6.6

Mitton, C. L. *The Gospel according to St. Mark*. Epworth. 1957.

Moffatt, J. *The First Epistle of Paul to the Corinthians*. London:

Hodder and Stoughton; First Edition. 1938.

Moo, D. J. *The Epistle to the Romans*. The New International Commentary on the New Testament. Wm. B. Eerdmans Publishing Co.: Grand Rapids, MI. 1996.

Morphew, D. J. *The Spiritual Spider Web, a Study of Ancient and Contemporary Gnosticism*. Vineyard International Publishing. 2000.

Morris, L. *1 Corinthians*. The Tyndale NT Commentary. Wm. B. Eerdmans Publishing Company. 1985.

Moule, C. F. D. *An Idiom Book of NT Greek*. Cambridge University Press; 2 edition. 1959.

Mounce, R. H. Vol. 27: *Romans. The New American Commentary*. Broadman & Holman Publishers. 2001.

Muirhead, J. *The Institutes of Gaius and Rules of Ulpian*. T. & T. Clark. 1880.

Neufeld, V. H. *The Earliest Christian Confessions.* Wm. B. Eerdmans Publishing Company. 1963.

Louw, J. P., & Nida, E. A. *Greek-English lexicon of the New Testament: Based on semantic domains* (electronic ed. of the 2nd edition.). Vol. 1. United Bible Societies: New York. 1996.

Nolland, J. *The Gospel of Matthew*. NIGTC. Wm. B. Eerdmans Publishing Company. 2005.

Quintilian. *Institutio Oratoria*. Vol. IV of the Loeb Classical Library edition. 1920.

Pannenberg, W. *Systematic Theology*, Vol. 2. Wm. B. Eerdmans Publishing Company. 1994.

Papyrus Oxyrhynchus. Greco-Roman Memoirs; London: British Academy for the Egypt Exploration Society. 1898– (67 vols. to date).

Pantel, P. S. *A History of Women in the West*. Harvard. 1992.

Peterson, E. H. *The Message: The Bible in contemporary language*. NavPress. 2002.

Phillips, R. D. Phillips. S. L. *Holding Hands, Holding Hearts: Recovering a Biblical View of Christian Dating*. P & R Publishing. 2006.

Philo, *Quod Deterius Potiori Insidiari Soleat*. Translated by F. H.

Colson and G. H. Whitaker. Vol. 2. 12 vols. Philo: In Ten Volumes (and Two Supplementary Volumes). Edited by Capps. E. Page. T. E. Rouse. W. H. D. Harvard University Press. 1929.

Pogoloff, S. *"Logos and Sophia: The Rhetorical Situation of 1 Corinthians." Society of Biblical Literature*. 1992.

Schmiedel, P. W. *Die Briefe an die Thessalonischer und an die Korinther. Mohr.* 1892.

Schmithals, W. *Gnosticism in Corinth.* Abingdon Press. 1971.

Schnackenburg, R. *Baptism in the Thought of Paul.* Herder. 1964.

Schrage, W. *Der erste Brief an die Korinther.* Benziger/ Neukirchener Verlag. 1995.

Seneca the Elder: *Declamations, Volume II, Controversiae*, Books 7–10. Suasoriae. Fragments. Loeb Classical Library. 1974.

Swete, H. B. *The Holy Spirit in the NT*. Macmillan. 1909.

Trible, P. *God and the Rhetoric of Sexuality.* Fortress Press. 1978.

Thiselton, A. *Realized Eschatology at Corinth.* New Testament Studies. Vol. 24 / Issue 04. Cambridge University Press. 1978.

Thiselton, A. C. *The First Epistle to the Corinthians*: A commentary on the Greek text. Wm. B. Eerdmans Publishing Company. 2000.

Thiselton, A.C. *1 Corinthians: A Shorter Exegetical Commentary & Pastoral Commentary,* Wm. B. Eerdmans Publishing Company. 2006

Venter, A. *Doing Healing.* Vineyard International Publishing. CT. 2009.

Williams, J. R. *Renewal Theology. Systematic Theology from a Charismatic perspective.* Zondervan. 1996.

Wendland, D. *Die Briefe an Die Korinther.* Vandenhoeck & Ruprecht; Reprint edition. 1980.

Wiseman, J. *"Corinth and Rome*, I: 228 B.C. to A.D. 267." ANRW II. 1979.

Witherington, B. *Conflict and Community in Corinth*: A Socio-Rhetorical Commentary on 1 and 2 Corinthians. Wm. B. Eerdmans Publishing Company. 1995.

Wolff, C. Der erste Brief des Paulus an die Korinther. Evangelische

Verlagsanstalt. 1996.

Wolfgang, S. *Der erste Brief an die Korinther,* EKKNT. 3 vols. Zürich: Benziger and Neukirchen-Vluyn: Neukirchener. 1991, 1995, 1999.

Wright, N.T. *Paul for Everyone: 1 Corinthians.* Westminster John Knox Press. 2004.

Wright, N. T. *The New Testament and the People of God.* Christian Origins and the Question of God. Society for Promoting Christian Knowledge: Vol. 1. London. 1992.

Wright, N.T. *The Resurrection of the Son of God.* Christian Origins and the Question of God. Society for Promoting Christian Knowledge: Vol. 3. London. 2003

Zodhiates, S. *The Complete Word Study Dictionary: New Testament* (electronic ed.). AMG Publishers: Chattanooga, TN. 2000.

Internet

Epicureanism. Merriam-Webster Dictionary http://www.merriam-webster.com/dictionary/epicureanism

Gagnon, R.A.J. The Bible and Homosexual Practice: An Overview of Some Issues. http://www.robgagnon.net/ZenitInterview.htm

Halal: About.Com Islam http://islam.about.com/od/dietarylaw/a/diet_law.htm

Holy Land Photos www.HolyLandPhotos.org

Kosher Food. KIR Certification. http://www.koshercertification.org.uk/whatdoe.html

Leaven. Hag HaMatzot: Feast of Unleavened Bread http://www.therefinersfire.org/yeast_or_leaven.htm

Man as Body and Soul. Volume Thirty-Eight – Article 3. http://www.presenttruthmag.com/archive/XXXVIII/38-3.htm

Marcionism. Catholic Encyclopaedia. http://www.newadvent.org/cathen/09645c.htm

Plato. Stanford Encyclopedia of Philosophy http://plato.stanford.edu/entries/stoicism/

Smith, G. Maps. Christian Classics Ethereal Library: http://www.ccel.org/bible/phillips/CN092MAPS1.htm

Purgatory. Catholic Encyclopedia http://www.newadvent.org/cathen/12575a.htm

News Papers

The Citizen News Paper

49603615R00162

Made in the USA
Lexington, KY
12 February 2016